ROUTLEDGE LIBRARY EDITIONS: TRANSPORT ECONOMICS

Volume 15

MARINE TRANSPORTATION MANAGEMENT

MARINE TRANSPORTATION MANAGEMENT

HENRY S. MARCUS

Routledge
Taylor & Francis Group

LONDON AND NEW YORK

First published in 1987 by Croom Helm Ltd

This edition first published in 2017
by Routledge
2 Park Square, Milton Park, Abingdon, Oxon OX14 4RN

and by Routledge
711 Third Avenue, New York, NY 10017

Routledge is an imprint of the Taylor & Francis Group, an informa business

British Library Cataloguing in Publication Data
A catalogue record for this book is available from the British Library

ISBN: 978-0-415-78484-9 (Set)
ISBN: 978-1-315-20175-7 (Set) (ebk)
ISBN: 978-1-138-63234-9 (Volume 15) (hbk)
ISBN: 978-1-138-63237-0 (Volume 15) (pbk)
ISBN: 978-1-315-20831-2 (Volume 15) (ebk)

Publisher's Note
The publisher has gone to great lengths to ensure the quality of this reprint but
points out that some imperfections in the original copies may be apparent.

Disclaimer
The publisher has made every effort to trace copyright holders and would welcome
correspondence from those they have been unable to trace.

MARINE TRANSPORTATION MANAGEMENT

HENRY S. MARCUS

CROOM HELM
London & Sydney

AUBURN HOUSE PUBLISHING COMPANY
Dover, Massachusetts

© 1987 Henry S. Marcus
Croom Helm Ltd, Provident House, Burrell Row,
Beckenham, Kent, BR3 1AT

Croom Helm Australia, 44-50 Waterloo Road,
North Ryde, 2113, New South Wales

British Library Cataloguing in Publication Data

Marcus, Henry S.
  Marine transportation management.
  1. Merchant marine — Management
  I. Title
  387.5'068   HE735

  ISBN 0-7099-4641-4

Auburn House Publishing Company,
14 Dedham Street, Dover Massachusetts 02030

Library of Congress Cataloging-in-Publication Data

Marcus, Henry S.
  Marine transport management.

  Includes index.
  1. Merchant marine. 2. Shipping. 3. Merchant ships.
4. Steamboat lines. I. Title.
HE735.M37   1987   387.5'44'068   86-22188
ISBN 0-86569-158-4

Printed and bound in Great Britain by
Biddles Ltd, Guildford and King's Lynn

CONTENTS

To Glenn and Daniel

ACKNOWLEDGEMENTS

A great number of people aided in the development of this book. Dean James Heskett of the Harvard Business School (HBS) helped to arrange a year's sabbatical at HBS, where I was provided with the resources I needed to write several of the case studies in this book. Professor Daryl Wyckoff of HBS had been successful in writing case study books in other modes of transportation. I discussed the feasibility of this book with him and borrowed the format to a large extent from his books.

Although I either authored, co-authored, or supervised each chapter of the book, I had help from the following people: Charles "Chuck" Richards and Alvin Cheng (assistance with exhibits in Chapter 1 and some editorial work on Chapter 11), Kevin Fox (primary author of the original draft of Chapter 5), Richard du Moulin (primary author of the original draft of Chapter 7 and considerable aid in Chapter 8), Raphael Vermeir (background data for Chapters 9, 10, 13,and 14, and invaluable help with Chapters 10 and 14), Olivier Cauro (primary author of the original draft of Chapter 11), Jean-Marc Cangardel (primary author of the original draft of Chapter 12), and Craig McKay (primary author of Chapters 13 and 14).

I also would like to express my sincere appreciation to the many people in the industry who allowed us into their companies. They were most generous in giving their time and information.

These case studies were written over a period of several years, with typing performed by secretaries at MIT, HBS, and in industry. I appreciate all their efforts. Denice Brouillette and P.J. Gardner deserve special mention for their typing. P.J. Gardner also performed the valuable task of developing and implementing a consistent format for this book. I

Acknowledgements

would also like to thank Christoph Goeltner and Dhanesh Samarasan for their meticulous proofreading.

Finally, several classes at MIT and HBS have provided "constructive criticism" to earlier drafts of these case studies. The book is substantially improved by the revisions that these case studies have undergone. Professor Marvin Manheim reviewed earlier drafts of this manuscript and suggested the addition of further material, which has also improved the quality of the final product.

While I thank all the people that have generously aided me, I, of course, take sole responsibility for any errors of commission or omission.

Henry S. Marcus
Acton, Massachusetts

Chapter 1

INTRODUCTION

The past two decades have seen dramatic changes in
vessel technology. The first tanker of 150,000
deadweight tons (DWT) was launched in 1966. The same
year, the first fully cellular containership service
started in international trade using converted World
War II vessels. Now ultra-large crude carriers
(ULCC) over 550,000 DWT exist. Huge containerships,
roll-on/roll-off vessels, and barge-carrying vessels
are now commonplace.

Changing vessel technology presents a major
challenge to shipping management. Vessels cost tens
of millions of dollars and have a physical life of
more than 20 years. A change in vessel design for a
company may also require a change in port facilities,
information systems, and marketing techniques.

Shipping managers must carefully evaluate new
technologies. They must be ready to adapt to change
in order to be competitive, but they must be careful
not to choose a technology that cannot be
successfully implemented in their market environment.

The next 14 chapters deal with many of the
vessel technology issues that shipping companies have
confronted in recent years. Specific technologies
are described along with their economic, regulatory,
and political aspects. The rest of this chapter is
devoted to providing the reader with an overview of
the shipping industry, as well as the format of the
book.

INDUSTRY BACKGROUND

The desire for maritime transportation services is a
derived demand. That is, shipping results from a
requirement to move goods, whether computers or crude
oil. Consequently, demand for shipping is affected

1

Introduction

by all the factors that influence international trade, such as: economic booms or busts, wars, droughts, canal closures (e.g., Suez), and embargoes. The cyclicality of the shipping market is reflected in Exhibit 1.1, which shows nine major world shipbuilding market cycles over the last century. As can be seen, the length of a cycle is typically much shorter than the life of a vessel; however, the timing and length of the next cycle is always impossible to predict.

Exhibit 1.2 describes the size of the principal merchant fleets of the world. Vessels in the world merchant fleet generally operate in either the liner or the bulk trade. The liner trade is characterized by small customer shipments of manufactured or semi-manufactured goods. The carriers typically form conferences that set freight rates. Within an effective conference, the shipping lines compete on the basis of service quality (e.g., speed, reliability, schedule) rather than price. Vessels stop at several ports on a round-trip voyage in order to try to obtain a reasonable amount of cargo in both directions. Liner firms are common carriers that publish their schedules and their tariffs.

In contrast, the bulk trades are characterized by private or contract carriers. Prices are set by supply/demand considerations and fluctuate considerably. The tanker market is often cited as a textbook example of perfect competition. Bulk carriers typically operate full between an origin and destination port, then run empty until they reach the next loading port. In order to understand the composition of each segment of the world fleet, each major vessel type is discussed separately.

BULK CARRIERS (LIQUID AND DRY)

Oil tankers are by far the largest single vessel type in the world fleet. The tanker fleet is still in the process of recovering from the oil embargo of October 1973 that occurred in the middle of a shipping boom. Exhibits 1.3 and 1.4 provide an interesting comparison by showing tonnage statistics for the existing tanker fleet and those on order in 1973 and 1985, respectively. Note that during the tanker boom of 1973, the scheduled deliveries as a percent of the existing fleet were 94.7%, with 74% of the tonnage on order over 225,000 DWT. During the depressed shipping market of 1985, tankers on order equal only 5.4% of the existing fleet, while 72% of the tonnage on order consists of tankers less than 90,000 DWT. As would be expected, the amount of inactive tankers has also varied dramatically between these two years. In 1973, only a negligible percentage of the tanker fleet was laid up; in June 1985, about 27% of the tonnage was inactive.

After the tankers, the next largest segment of the world fleet is dry bulk carriers. Exhibit 1.5 shows the existing fleet and the vessels on order. At the end of June 1985, approximately 5% of the tonnage was inactive and the orderbook equalled 12.3% of the existing tonnage.

Combined carriers have the ability to carry either liquid or dry bulk on a given voyage. Therefore, when the tanker or dry bulk carrier market booms, the combined carriers aim for that segment of the market. In June 1985, with both markets depressed, 23% of the combined carrier fleet was in the oil trade, 72% was in the dry cargo trade, and 5% was inactive. Exhibit 1.6 presents data on the existing combined fleet and orderbook.

LINER VESSELS

Unitized cargo vessels (e.g., containerships, roll-on/roll-off vessels, barge-carrying vessels) play a dominant role on all trade routes between industrialized nations. Exhibit 1.7 shows the world containership fleet, existing and on order. Capacity is expressed in twenty-foot equivalent units (TEU).

Many less developed countries (LDC's) have not yet built container terminals. Consequently, much of their general cargo trade is still carried in conventional break-bulk vessels. The future merchant marine policies of LDC's may be affected by activities of the United Nations Conference on Trade and Development (UNCTAD).

UNCTAD LINER CODE

The first UNCTAD meeting was held in 1964 and was attended by 120 nations. LDC's in Latin America, Africa, and Asia then totalled 77. This "Group of 77" coalition held a numerical majority at the first UNCTAD meeting and created at it a forum for the analysis of world trade.

After a decade of work by the LDC's, UNCTAD in 1974 adopted (as differentiated from ratified) the Code of Conduct for Liner Conferences, also called the UNCTAD Liner Code. This code declares that each trading nation has the right to reserve a significant portion of its trade, such as 40%, for its national-flag carriers. The residual 20% will typically be handled by third-flag carriers, also referred to as cross-traders.

The UNCTAD Liner Code has now been ratified and theoretically went into effect in October 1983. The United States opposes the Code and will not be a party to its implementation. It is not clear to what extent the Code is being implemented in other parts of the world and what impact it will have on liner firms. The majority of LDC's that have ratified the Code also have begun attempts to extend the principle of national-flag preference to the bulk trades.

FLAGS OF CONVENIENCE

Most LDC's would like to phase out "Flags of Convenience" or "Flags of Necessity" or flags of "Open Registry" nations. Most LDC's feel there is no "genuine link" between the nations of registry and any ownership or control of the vessels in these countries. However, there is no clear definition of "genuine link" or "flag of convenience." Countries generally considered to be in this category are: Liberia, Panama, Singapore, Cyprus, Bermuda, and the Bahamas.

A study by the UNCTAD Secretariat has reported the true management of open-registry fleets as shown in Exhibit 1.8. The "true manager" is the person, company, or organization responsible for the day-to-day husbandry of the vessel involved; the country of management is the country of domicile of the true manager.

Initial attempts of the LDC's to expand the national-flag preferences to the bulk trades have not been successful. However, owners of bulk carriers would not be wise to ignore these activities in the future.

FORMAT OF THE BOOK

The next 14 chapters describe a range of case studies and technical notes where management must deal with certain aspects of changing vessel technology. Each case study is based on an actual management situation. However, in some cases the names and/or the data have been disguised.

The book is divided into three parts. Part I (Chapters 2 through 6) describes liner shipping. Part II (Chapters 7 through 13) deals with liquid and dry bulk shipping. The final section, Part III (Chapters 14 and 15), focuses on the ship-port interface.

Introduction

Exhibit 1.1

NINE MAJOR WORLD SHIPBUILDING
MARKET CYCLES
1893-1984

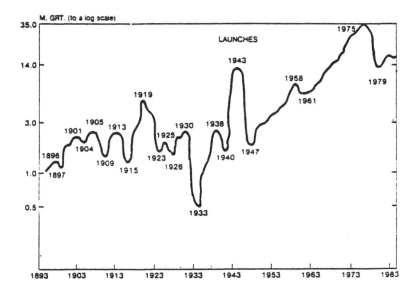

Note: Throughout the exhibits in this book, M. represents measurements in thousands, and MM. measurements in millions.

Source: "Lloyd's Register of Shipping." Reprinted with permission.

Exhibit 1.2

PRINCIPLE MERCHANT FLEETS OF THE WORLD
IN 1984

Country	thousand tons gross	Country	thousand tons gross
Liberia	62,025	Sweden	3,520
Japan	40,358	Canada	3,449
Panama	37,244	Philippines	3,441
Greece	35,059	Poland	3,267
U.S.S.R.	24,492	Bahamas	3,192
U.S.A.*	19,292	Turkey	3,125
Norway	17,663	Yugoslavia	2,682
United Kingdom	15,874	Romania	2,667
China+, People's		Kuwait	2,551
Republic of	13,259	Argentina	2,422
Italy	9,158	Belgium	2,407
France	8,945	Australia	2,173
Spain	7,005	Finland	2,168
Korea (South)	6,771	Iran	2,106
Cyprus	6,728	Indonesia	1,857
Singapore	6,512	Malaysia	1,664
India	6,415	Portugal	1,571
Germany, Federal		Mexico	1,489
Republic of	6,242	German Dem. Rep.	1,422
Hong Kong	5,784	Algeria	1,372
Brazil	5,722	Malta	1,366
Denmark	5,211	Bulgaria	1,283
Netherlands	4,586	Iraq	1,074
Saudi Arabia	3,863	Venezuela	1,003

Notes: At the end of 1983 the world fleet stood at 418.7 million gross tons.

*Including U.S. National Defense Reserve Fleet estimated at 2.2 million gross tons.

+The total tonnage for the People's Republic of China includes 3,958,418 gross tons for Taiwan.

Source: "Lloyd's Register of Shipping, Statistical Tables, 1984." Reprinted with permission.

Introduction

Exhibit 1.3

TANKER TONNAGE STATISTICS
NUMBER AND TOTAL DWT
OCTOBER 31, 1973

SHIP SIZES	EXISTING FLEET		TOTAL FUTURE SCHEDULED DELIVERIES		SCHEDULED DELIVERIES EXPRESSED AS A % OF EXISTING FLEET DWT CAPACITY
	NR	DWT	NR	DWT	
10/ 19,999	746	12,310.5	41	618.0	5.0%
20/ 29,999	614	14,682.1	71	1,741.9	11.9%
30/ 49,999	709	27,250.4	143	4,849.0	17.8%
50/ 69,999	347	19,948.9	19	1,142.1	5.7%
70/124,999	423	37,948.9	195	19,014.4	50.1%
125/174,999	63	8,999.8	139	19,474.7	216.4%
175/224,999	162	34,584.8	15	3,059.7	8.8%
225/299,999	188	46,750.0	327	83,967.0	179.6%
300,000+	11	3,778.6	169	61,417.1	1,625.4%

```
TOTAL          3,263  206,254.0  1,119  195,283.9      94.7%
AVE. SIZE         63.2                   174.5


RUNNING TOTAL
NUMBERS        3,263                 1,119
000 DWT     206,254.0             195,283.9             94.7%


100% COMBINED
CARRIER FLEET    341   34,200.9    115   16,546.5      48.4%


RUNNING TOTAL, TANKERS
& 100 % COMBINED
CARRIERS

NUMBERS        3,604                 1,234
000 DWT     240,454.9             211,830.4             88.1%
```

Source: "Shipping Statistics and Economics," published by H.P. Drewry Ltd., London, November 1973. Reprinted with permission.

Exhibit 1.4

TANKER FLEET AND ORDERBOOK
JUNE 30, 1985
(MM. OF DWT)

SIZE (M. DWT)	30/6/85 FLEET			IDLE %	30/6/85 ORDERBOOK		% OF PRESENT FLEET
	TOTAL	ACTIVE	IDLE		NO.	MM. DWT	
10- 25	9.4	8.8	0.6	6.4	31	0.5	5.3
25- 30	5.3	5.0	0.3	5.7	21	0.6	11.3
30- 35	6.8	6.5	0.3	4.4	15	0.5	7.4
35- 45	10.0	9.4	0.6	6.0	37	1.4	14.0
45- 55	6.2	5.1	1.1	17.7	22	1.0	16.1
55- 65	8.8	8.3	0.5	5.7	15	0.9	10.2
65- 80	9.7	8.7	1.0	10.3	19	1.4	14.4
80- 90	16.7	16.2	0.5	3.0	43	3.6	21.6
90-100	8.3	7.9	0.4	4.8	5	0.5	6.0
100-125	11.2	10.1	1.1	9.8	10	1.1	9.8
125-150	18.3	17.1	1.2	6.6			
150-175	9.5	7.7	1.8	18.9			
175-200	2.6	2.6			1	0.2	7.7
200-225	5.2	3.9	1.3	25.0	2	0.4	7.7
225-300	88.6	53.0	35.6	40.2	7	1.7	1.9
300+	37.6	14.5	23.1	61.4			
Total	254.2	184.8	69.4	27.3	228	13.8	5.4

Source: "Shipping Statistics and Economics," published by H.P. Drewry Ltd., London, July, 1985. Reprinted with permission.

9

Introduction

Exhibit 1.5

WORLD BULK CARRIER FLEET
AND FUTURE DELIVERIES*
JUNE 1985
(M. DWT AND NUMBER OF VESSELS)

Size (M. DWT)	Current Fleet		Idle Ships		Total on Order	
	NO.	DWT	NO.	DWT	NO.	DWT
10 - 30	2,602	56,822	207	4,524	156	3,726
30 - 50	1,416	53,018	62	2,383	211	8,111
50 - 80	750	46,903	36	2,310	78	4,919
80 - 100	48	4,112	1	99	2	164
100 +	227	30,763	4	580	41	6,589
TOTAL:	5,043	191,618	310	9,896	488	23,509

----

* Excludes vessels confined to Great Lakes trading.

Source: "Shipping Statistics and Economics," published by H.P. Drewry Ltd., London, July 1985.

Exhibit 1.6

COMBINED CARRIER FLEET AND ORDERBOOK
JUNE 1985

Ship Size (M. DWT)	Current Fleet		Total on Order	
	NO.	M. DWT	NO.	M. DWT
10 - 50	12	455	10	370
50 - 80	86	6,057	5	318
80 - 100	40	3,611	2	196
100 - 125	79	8,793	3	340
125 - 150	44	5,956	-	-
150 - 175	64	10,323	5	783
175 - 300	31	7,410	3	824
300 +	-	-	3	910
TOTAL:	356	42,605	31	3,741

Source: "Shipping Statistics and Economics," published by H.P. Drewry Ltd., London, July 1985. Reprinted with permission.

Exhibit 1.7

WORLD CONTAINER SHIP FLEET JUNE 1985 (M. TEU)

Fleet End May 85

TYPE/TEU	ACTIVE		IDLE		TOTAL		ORDERBOOK		ORDERBOOK OF CURRENT FLEET
	NO.	TEU	NO.	TEU	NO.	TEU	NO.	TEU	
Full Container(b)									
400 - 700	172	91.8	5	1.1	177	92.9	26	12.1	13.0
700 - 1,000	126	105.7	9	8.6	135	114.3	13	10.0	8.7
1,000 - 1,500	199	249.9	17	18.6	216	268.5	25	30.8	11.5
1,500 - 2,000	135	245.2	3	4.9	138	250.1	17	30.1	12.0
2,000+	104	307.0			104	307.0	54	146.1	47.6
TOTAL F/C	736	999.6	34	33.2	770	1,032.8	135	229.1	22.2
Cont - Ro/Ro(a)									
400 - 700	130	62.9	20	11.5	150	74.4	33	16.1	21.6
700 - 1,000	40	32.4	3	2.4	43	34.8	4	3.4	9.8
1,000 - 1,500	70	88.9	6	6.8	76	95.7	5	5.5	5.7
1,500+	28	55.2			28	55.2	1	1.9	3.4
TOTAL C-Ro/Ro	268	239.4	29	20.7	297	260.1	43	26.9	10.3
TOTAL FLEET	1,004	1,239.0	63	53.9	1,067	1,292.9	178	25.6	19.8

(a) Excludes vessels less than 400 TEU.
(b) Includes barge carriers.
(c) Includes pure Ro/Ro and Ro/Ro containerships of 400 TEU+.

Source: "Shipping Statistics and Economics," published by H.P. Drewry Ltd., London, July, 1985. Reprinted with permission.

Exhibit 1.8

TRUE MANAGEMENT OF OPEN-REGISTRY FLEETS AS OF JULY 1ST, 1980

Country or territory of registration

Country or territory of true managers	Liberia No.	Liberia 1000 DWT	Panama No.	Panama 1000 DWT	Singapore No.	Singapore 1000 DWT	Cyprus No.	Cyprus 1000 DWT	Bermuda No.	Bermuda 1000 DWT	Bahamas No.	Bahamas 1000 DWT	TOTAL No.	TOTAL 1000 DWT
US	515	50 734	227	3 608	3	30	1	3	17	172	6	30	769	54 577
Hong Kong	584	36 063	581	10 318	32	388	3	18	9	63			215	46 850
Japan	280	19 215	579	7 001	58	861		30	51	2 482	1	16	380	21 837
UK	180	13 611	72	685	52	829	25	135					637	17 820
Greece	125	11 902	185	158	57	55	319	1 694					112	15 825
Monaco	76	7 185	3	101				5					112	10 291
UK-based Greek	85	6 731	36	872	4	70	22	207	1	31			188	7 341
FR of Germany	53	2 641	127	576	155	2 162	46	223	3	21			384	6 529
Singapore	59	2 078	97	596	373	133	1	12					489	5 385
Unspecified	3	116	167	136	4	28	1	13					251	
Switzerland	55	2 584	63	881		129	1	9	3	52	1	25	126	4 095
Norway	81	1 650	14	190	7	250	5	88	2	6			118	3 053
Italy	23	1 616	60	603	1	3		83					92	2 000
Netherlands	22	1 016	7	283	12	37	6	19					29	909
France	24	1 013	84	980	3	61							124	812
Republic of Korea	10	729	20	106					4	81	2	2	50	1 428
Canada	11	957	114	695	4	307	1	10					128	1 000
Indonesia					1	2	1	1					28	1 111
US-based Greek	28	507	43	23									70	1 074
	28	994	10	79									35	
60 countries, entities or (o) territories	89	2 675	846	2 077	30	318	90	843	25	248	8	17	691	6 070
Unidentified	10	360	184	789	12	169	43	187	6	21	3	2	258	1 488
TOTAL	2,318	158 185	3,183	40 159	778	12 801	574	3 096	121	3 100	21	92	6,991	217 496

(o) Each managing less than 1 million DWT.

---

o Each managing less than 1 million DWT.

Source: "Beneficial ownership of open-registry fleets 1980," report by the UNCTAD Secretariat, TD/B/C.4/218, November 6, 1980; based on a report prepared for the UNCTAD Secretariat by A.P. Appledore Ltd.

Part I

LINER SHIPPING

The liner shipping industry has undergone
revolutionary changes in technology in the past
20 years. In turn, these changes must be accompanied
by modifications in marketing and management.
   For a liner company considering new vessels with
a different technology (e.g., containership, roll-
on/roll-off carrier), the firm must evaluate the
potential of the new technology. Will it really be
more profitable? What are the obstacles to
implementation? Will adopting this new technology
require that the firm turn away existing customers
with cargo not suitable for the new ships? Does the
company possess the management skills and financial
strength to upgrade its fleet to this new technology?
   Even when a company has decided to adopt a new
technology, its decisions are not over. A key trade-
off to be made is the one between a specialized
vessel and a general-purpose vessel. A ship that
specializes in only one type of cargo (e.g.,
containers, wheeled vehicles) is the most economical
for that type of cargo. However, the liner firm, as
a common carrier in the marketplace, has no guarantee
that its ships will be filled with the type of cargo
it wants. In contrast, a liner company can build a
new vessel that is flexible enough to carry many
types of cargo. Such a multi-purpose ship is less
restrictive on the marketing efforts of the liner
firm. Nevertheless, the general-purpose ship can
never be as efficient as the specialized vessel.
   A different approach is to design a transitional
vessel to ease the move from one vessel technology
and cargo to another. In this way, the transitional
ship design can be used for a short time on a
particular trade route which is undergoing the
dynamics of changing vessel design. As soon as the
owner determines the best design for this trade

route, he constructs new ships of the appropriate specialized design. The transitional vessel is then placed on a different trade route after replacement by the new specialized ship. (Transitional vessels can also be converted to a specialized vessels at the appropriate time.)

As a technology matures, the problems change. For example, rather than a decision between a break-bulk cargo vessel and a full containership, later decisions have to do with the size of the containership, the size of the containers, and the number of special-purpose containers (e.g., refrigerated, liquid bulk). A liner operator may also wish to design a vessel that specializes in different cargos in each direction, for example, carrying containers one way and bulk commodities (and empty containers) in the opposite direction. Such a vessel is known as a con/bulker. As a vessel technology matures, management attention can focus more on management information systems, satellite communication networks, interfaces with rail and trucking systems, and computerized container control.

A reader analyzing a case study must consider many different factors in addition to the vessel technology. For example, how does a customer choose between liner firms on a particular trade route? Does the conference maintain a strong presence, so that all carriers charge the same price and a customer must choose a carrier based on factors other than published tariffs? Are there any independent or non-conference carriers on the trade route? How do competitors compare in terms of transit time, reliability, loss and damage, sailing frequency, itineraries, inland transportation services, through bills of lading, or computerized container control?

Other factors to be considered include: What role do governments play in subsidizing national-flag carriers or restricting competition? Will ports be able to provide the terminal facilities and services needed to handle the new vessels efficiently? Is there an imbalance of cargo on the trade route involved? How will this change in the future?

To analyze properly the problems of a liner firm, a reader must take into account many of the issues considered above, as well as the resources and personal desires of the management of that firm. A good analysis will integrate the many diverse topics mentioned into a meaningful evaluation.

FORMAT OF PART I

The first two chapters deal with the revolutionary change in the late 1960's from break-bulk cargo vessels to unitized cargo ships. The American Mail Line (AML) is planning for new construction of large efficient break-bulk cargo vessels, while Moore-McCormack Lines (MML) is expecting delivery of flexible vessels able to carry containers, wheeled vehicles over a roll-on/roll-off ramp, or break-bulk cargo. The two case studies provide a contrast in corporate financial strength, differences in trade routes (cargo types and trade imbalances), vessel designs, types of competition, and subsidy regulations. Common problems are potential transitional difficulties in introducing new technologies, need for new management control systems, and intermodal issues.

While the issues in these two case studies may seem outdated, they are not. Even in U.S. trade, the types of vessels described in Chapters 2 and 3 still operate today. More importantly, many less-developed countries (LDC's) are now just confronting the issues faced by AML and MML more than fifteen years ago. Consequently, the problems analyzed by some U.S. carriers many years ago are still current issues in some LDC's.

Similar reasoning applies to Chapter 4, dealing with government decisions to be made by the Commonwealth of Puerto Rico during the 1970's concerning the government ownership or control of its own liner fleet. In many parts of the world today, government policies concerning national-flag fleets and maritime subsidies are still openly debated. Chapter 4 has the added dimension of taking place within U.S. domestic trades where foreign-flag competition and U.S.-flag subsidized carriers are prohibited by the Jones Act.

In Chapter 5, American President Lines (APL) gives a preview of the problems of the 1980's. No one questions the feasibility of fully cellular containerships any more, and vessel designs have capacities of 2500 twenty-foot equivalent units (TEU) or more. As the industry has matured, the container revolution of the 1960's and early 1970's has changed to an evolution. Key issues relate to type of power plant, size of containers, and use of special-purpose containers (e.g., refrigerated). Important factors deal with sea-going labor unions, policies of various governments concerning the use of containers over their roads, and the needs and desires of customers.

Liner Shipping.

Cast Container Line (Chapter 6) finds a different way
to compete with modern containerships. Cast attempts
to compete against entrenched, financially stronger
conference carriers with a combination of con/bulker
technology, port labor agreements, limited itinerary,
inland truck network, and aggressive pricing. As a
shipping company carrying both liner and bulk cargos,
this case study helps to lead into Part II of the
book, Liquid and Dry Bulk Shipping.
     All in all, this section provides a contrast of
vessel technologies, government policies, competitive
strategies, and management skills and resources.

Chapter 2

AMERICAN MAIL LINE LTD.

In the summer of 1968, American Mail Line (AML), a Seattle-based U.S.-subsidized steamship operator, had five ships under construction at a cost--after construction differential subsidy (CDS)--of about $39 million. The management at AML was trying to determine the optimum scheduling and route structure for the line's fleet after these new ships went into service in late 1968 and 1969. The company currently ran (at a profit) a fleet of nine ships on the Far East Trade Route #29 and Trade Route #17, serving Indonesia, Malaysia, and India. The five new C-5 class ships were designed for Trade Route #29; on their delivery, four war-built C-3 class ships would be retired. (The "C" classification refers to the length of the cargo ship.)

AML ran two services called the "Short Run" and "Long Run." The Short Run consisted of routes to points in the Far East on Trade Route #29. The Long Run consisted of routes to the Bay of Bengal, Calcutta, and to other countries on Trade Route #17. The ships serving Trade Route #17 also called at ports on Trade Route #29. (Data on the ships, trade routes, and financial background of AML are contained in Exhibits 2.1 through 2.4.)

The new ships would not have cellular holds for containers; however, they were designed to carry 411 twenty-foot containers, 254 of which would be below decks. The containers, as well as the break-bulk cargo, could all be unloaded by the ship's conventional cargo-handling gear. Calculations comparing the C-4, or Mariner, against the new C-5 on various Short Run routes were made in which both ships carried only non-containerizable cargo (because of economical or physical characteristics). Exhibit 2.5 shows the summary of two such calculations for a Short Run routing known as Route A. Also shown are the summarized data from one simulated voyage of a C-5 carrying only containers on a shuttle run between Seattle and Japan.

Although the C-5 had capacity for both containers and break-bulk cargo, carrying both at the same time would necessitate extra stops in ports where terminal facilities were restricted to exclusively break-bulk or container cargo. However, in other ports, the break-bulk cargo could be loaded and unloaded into lighters simultaneously while the containers were being moved on and off a container dock.

AML was concerned about large amounts of cargo moving by rail to and from the Mid-West (particularly the Chicago area) through ports in California. Based on Bureau of Census data for 1966, outside consultants estimated that the market potential for the containerized cargo between Japan and a "corridor" between Seattle and Chicago was 2,100,000 measurement tons (MT) Eastbound and 1,000,000 MT Westbound.* AML currently carried less than 15% of this cargo Eastbound and practically none Westbound. At 22 MT per container, this market potential represented more than 95,400 container loads Eastbound and more than 45,400 container loads Westbound, annually. As of the fall of 1968, most all of AML's Westbound containerizable cargo consisted of military shipments. The commercial outbound commodities from the Pacific Northwest, such as wheat, wood pulp, lumber, flour, and aluminum, were not suitable for containerization. In contrast, it was estimated that over 90% of the Japanese exports to the Pacific Northwest were containerizable.

If rail service in the Northwest and AML ships were properly scheduled, inland cargo could move to Japan in one or two days less time than via the California route. A report recently completed by outside consultants told AML management that, "The

----

* A long ton weighs 2,240 pounds; a short ton, 2,000 pounds. A measurement ton is a space measurement of 40 cubic feet. The cargo is assessed a certain rate on every 40 cubic feet it occupies.

A revenue ton, or weight/measurement ton, is a means of assessing the cargo, either by weight or by volume, to give the carrier the greatest revenue. AML quotes rates on a revenue ton basis of either 2,000 pounds (Westbound) or 40 cubic feet (Eastbound).

forwarders in the overland area (including Chicago) are now consolidating for California because of the greater volumes moving in that direction for both domestic and international distribution." The report also stated, "The . . . rail lines have expressed concern that sailings to and from Pacific Northwest ports are far fewer than the number of sailings offered by competing systems, especially those serving the California ports. The California ports may have a sailing every two to three days." AML vessels sailed out of the Pacific Northwest for the Far East about every 10 to 12 days.

American Mail Line carried the majority of the U.S.-flag liner cargo through the Pacific Northwest ports on Trade Route #29. However, the U.S.-flag vessels carried less than 30% of the commercial liner dry cargo in this area, as shown in Exhibit 2.6. AML's future market share would be endangered by Japanese lines, which, after instituting a weekly container service in the fall of 1968 between California and Japan, planned in 1969 to begin a weekly container service between the Pacific Northwest and Japan, with ships carrying about 750 twenty-foot equivalent containers. The general cargo trade between the U.S. and Japan was growing at an impressive rate of about 12% per year in 1968.

Exhibit 2.1

American Mail Line Ltd.

TEN-YEAR SUMMARY OF OPERATIONS

Annual Report, 1967

	1967	1966	1965	1964	1963
Vessels Operated During the Year					
Owned vessels	9	9	9	7	7
Chartered vessels (A)			1	2	2
Total	9	9	10	9	9
Revenue from Vessel Operations	$28,090,956	$27,305,093	$24,705,314	$19,974,410	$18,686,440
Net earnings (B)	4,020,703	4,555,692	3,219,141	2,183,122	1,931,780
Special credits					
Net earnings and special credits	$ 4,020,703	$ 4,555,692	$ 3,219,141	$ 2,183,122	$ 1,931,780
Working Capital	$ 7,573,771	$ 8,084,107	$ 7,759,478	$ 6,289,825	$ 4,816,829
Ratio of current assets to current liabilities	2.67	2.53	2.97	2.96	2.60
Statutory reserve and related funds (including amounts accrued for deposit	$33,014,875	$ 8,211,100	$ 5,875,969	$ 5,253,036	$10,560,178
Vessels and equipment:					
Cost (including vessels under construction	46,303,629	37,051,186	36,684,350	35,765,311	29,927,432
Cost less depreciation	35,381,801	27,399,488	28,279,335	28,643,701	23,809,121
Long-term debt (Merchant Marine Bonds)	3,600,000				
STOCKHOLDERS' EQUITY (net worth)					
Capital stock – no par	3,614,313	3,614,313	3,614,313	3,614,313	3,614,313
Capital surplus	307,315	307,315	307,315	307,315	307,315
Retained earnings	32,472,313	29,227,949	25,448,596	23,005,794	21,599,011
Total stockholders' equity	36,393,941	33,149,577	29,370,224	26,927,422	25,520,639
Per share of capital stock (C):					
Net earnings	$ 5.18	5.87	4.15	2.81	2.49
Net earnings and special credits	5.18	5.87	4.15	2.81	2.49
Dividends paid	1.00	1.00	1.00	1.00	1.00
Stockholders' equity (book value)	46.88	42.70	37.83	34.68	32.87

	1962	1961	1960	1959	1958
Vessels Operated During the Year					
Owned vessels	8	6	6	6	8
Chartered vessels (A)	1	3	3	3	1
Total	9	9	9	9	9
Revenue from Vessel Operations	$15,448,985	$13,050,792	$15,437,657	$13,049,647	$12,293,232
Net earnings	1,073,062	770,392	1,493,646	1,197,322	1,088,482
Special credits (B)	496,043			1,657,513	
Net earnings and special credits	$ 1,569,105	$ 770,392	$ 1,493,646	$ 2,854,835	$ 1,068,842
Working Capital	$ 4,738,403	$ 4,239,912	$ 4,648,619	$ 4,301,199	$ 3,992,602
Ratio of current assets to current liabilities	2.67	2.89	2.52	3.10	3.57
Statutory reserve and related funds (including amounts accrued for deposit)	$ 4,120,102	$ 2,642,253	$12,421,032	$13,849,842	$13,357,516
Vessels and equipment:					
Cost (including vessels under construction	25,057,183	24,673,751	13,248,701	7,750,438	10,708,838
Cost less depreciation	19,977,695	18,995,430	8,112,937	3,106,797	3,389,925
Long-term debt (Merchant Marine Bonds)	37,800,000	9,800,000	10,600,000	11,400,000	12,200,000
STOCKHOLDERS' EQUITY (net worth)					
Capital stock – no par	3,614,313	3,614,313	3,614,313	3,614,313	3,614,313
Capital surplus	307,315	307,315	307,315	307,315	307,315
Retained earnings	20,443,570	19,650,804	19,656,751	18,939,444	16,860,948
Total stockholders' equity	25,365,198	23,572,432	23,578,379	22,861,072	20,782,576
Per share of capital stock (C):					
Net earnings	1.38	.99	1.92	1.54	1.40
Net earnings and special credits	2.02	.99	1.92	3.68	1.40
Dividends paid	1.00	1.00	1.00	1.00	1.00
Stockholders' equity (book value)	31.88	30.36	30.37	29.45	26.77

Source: American Mail Line Ltd., Annual Report, 1967.

(A) Where chartered vessels were operated only part of a year, these figures reflect the approximate number of full vessel-years.
(B) Capital gains on disposition of vessels.
(C) Per share amounts adjusted to basis of 776,839 shares outstanding at December 31, 1967.

American Mail Line Ltd.

Exhibit 2.2

SUMMARY OF BERTH SERVICE ACTIVITIES

The following recapitulation sums up our 1967 berth service activities as compared with those of the years 1966, 1965, and 1964:

	1967	1966	1965	1964
Number of completed voyages	39	37	39	36
Cargo (revenue tons)	921,816	929,400	900,168	742,016
Passengers	620	628	648	464
Mail (revenue tons)	850	697	1,017	498
Cargo revenue	$27,647,529	$26,782,039	$24,313,072	$19,694,149
Passenger revenue	276,999	283,875	286,422	200,436
Mail revenue	101,889	76,833	77,996	60,676
Miscellaneous	63,539	162,346	27,824	19,149
Total vessel revenue	$28,090,956	$27,305,093	$24,705,314	$19,974,410

An interesting item relating to gross revenues is the following recapitulation showing the spread between Commercial and Defense (MSTS) cargo carryings for the past three years:

Gross Freight Revenue	1967	1966	1965
Commercial	$21,462,295	$21,454,049	$20,633,819
Defense (MSTS)	6,185,234	5,327,990	3,679,253
Total	$27,647,529	$26,782,039	$24,313,072

Percentage of Total	1967	1966	1965
Commercial	77.63%	80.11%	84.87%
Defense (MSTS)	22.37%	19.89%	15.13%
Total	100 %	100 %	100 %

Source: American Mail Line Ltd., Annual Report, 1967

Exhibit 2.3

FLEET COMPOSITION
(ALL OWNED VESSELS)

	No. of Ships	Year Delivered	Type	Length Over all (feet)	Cargo Deadweight (tons)	Speed (knots)	Bale Capacity (cu. ft.)	Maximum** Container Capacity
Short run	5	1962-65	C-4***	564	13,200	20.5	768,585	237
Long run	4	1944-45	C-3	492	11,500	16	695,690	0
New vessels#	5	1968-69	C-5##	605	21,400	20.8	1,054,100	411###

*All ships have accommodations for twelve passengers.

**Standard 8'x8'x20' containers stowed in non-cellular spaces.

***Also called Mariner class.

#Dates of delivery for the five new vessels were 17 September 1968, 22 November 1968, 21 February 1969, 23 May 1969, and 22 August 1969.

##Also called Mailiner class.

###The 254 containers to be stored below deck will account for 487,680 cubic feet or almost 47% of the bale cubic.

American Mail Line Ltd.

Exhibit 2.4

SCHEDULE INFORMATION

Name of Service	Short Run	Long Run
Trade route number	29	17 (and parts of 29)
Approx. voyage time	59-75 days	110-120 days
Ships assigned to service	5 C-4's	4 C-3's
Places of call	U.S. Pacific Northwest	U.S. Pacific Northwest
	Japan	Japan
	Philippines	Philippines
	Hong Kong	Hong Kong
	Taiwan	Viet Nam
	Korea	Singapore
	Okinawa	Malaysia
		Indonesia
		Burma
		Ceylon
		India
		Pakistan
		California*

*Their present maritime subsidy agreement did not allow AML to load or unload cargo at California from the foreign areas of trade route number 29.

26

Exhibit 2.5

SAMPLE CALCULATIONS

Ship	Mariner	C-5	C-5
Route	Route A	Route A	Shuttle
Cargo(b)	Break-Bulk	Break-bulk	Container
Number of stops at ports	17	17	6
Days per voyage	60	60	22-23
Steaming time in days	29	29	20-21
Days in port	31	31	2-3
Revenue per voyage	$877,600	977,200	369,000
Net expenses per voyage	619,173	681,723(c)	270,803(d)
Profit before taxes	258,427	295,477	98,197
Taxes at 48%	124,045	141,829	47,134
10% surcharge	12,405	14,183	4,713
Total taxes	136,450	156,012	51,847
Net profit per voyage	121,977	139,465	46,350
Outbound-cargo carried(e)	14,200 S.T.	16,500 S.T.	100(f) containers
Outbound-space available	14,200 S.T.	21,500 S.T.	411 containers
Inbound-cargo carried(g)	11,700 M.T.	11,700 M.T.	411 containers
Inbound-space available	12,800 M.T.	17,400 M.T.	411 containers

FOOTNOTES

a Schematic diagrams of Route A and the shuttle route, and related data are shown in Exhibits 2.7 through 2.10. Both Route A and the shuttle route are within the Short Run portion of Trade Route #29.

b For these calculations, all cargo was divided into two exclusive categories: containerizable (physically and economically), and non-containerizable (or break-bulk). Therefore, there is no duplication of cargo between the break-bulk calculations and the container calculation.

American Mail Line Ltd.

Exhibit 2.5 Continued

c Net daily expenses including depreciation, interest, overhead, and operating costs for the C-5 are estimated to be about 8% higher than for the C-4.

d For the container operation, it was assumed that the total of agency fees, port charges, brokerage, and stevedoring, expressed as a percentage of the freight revenue, would be the same as for a normal C-4 operation.

e Because of the dense commodities carried on the outbound route, the ships are weight, rather than volume, limited. Consequently, cargo is measured in terms of short tons (ST).

f The outbound containers contain only military cargo.

g Because of the less dense nature of the inbound commodities, cargo is expressed in terms of measurement tons (MT).

ADDITIONAL NOTES

In order to perform sensitivity analysis on the simulated voyages in this exhibit, it is useful to make the following assumptions:

The combined incremental cost of both loading and unloading more break-bulk cargo is $21 per revenue ton. The incremental cost of both loading and unloading containers is $150 per container. Assume 12 long tons per container.

One port gang can load or unload 20 revenue tons per hour for break-bulk cargo and 8 containers per hour for containerized cargo.

Exhibit 2.6

COMMERCIAL CARGO SUMMARY: U.S.-FLAG PARTICIPATION
U.S. NORTHWEST/TR #29 AREAS CENSUS
(IN 000's LONG TONS)
WASHINGTON/OREGON/ALASKA

OUTBOUND	Total Liner Comm'l Dry Cargo	U.S.-Flag Liner Comm'l Dry Cargo	%U.S. Flag	American Mail Line Ltd. Annual Cargo Liftings Commercial	American Mail Line Ltd. Annual Cargo Liftings MSTS Cargo
1954	511	303	59.3	*	*
1955	627	496	79.1	*	*
1956	748	638	85.3	*	*
1957	787	609	77.4	*	*
1958	908	586	64.5	*	*
1959	828	365	44.1	*	*
1960	1,248	547	46.0	*	*
1961	1,541	550	35.7	*	*
1962	1,411	575	40.8	*	*
1963	1,805	678	37.6	201	34
1964	1,654	647	39.1	205	32
1965	1,237	480	38.8	219	59
1966	1,407	327	23.2	198	67
1967	1,413	266	18.8	168	90

INBOUND	Total Liner Comm'l Dry Cargo	U.S.-Flag Liner Comm'l Dry Cargo	%U.S. Flag	American Mail Line Ltd. Annual Cargo Liftings Commercial	American Mail Line Ltd. Annual Cargo Liftings MSTS Cargo
1954	185	127	68.6	*	*
1955	224	150	67.0	*	*
1956	270	186	68.9	*	*
1957	276	173	62.7	*	*
1958	250	97	38.8	*	*
1959	333	123	36.9	*	*
1960	274	102	37.2	*	*
1961	254	83	32.7	*	*
1962	327	83	25.4	*	*
1963	335	100	29.9	68	0.6
1964	445	149	33.5	81	0.1
1965	528	199	37.7	102	0.6
1966	566	194	34.3	92	0.2
1967	535	151	28.2	77	0.2

Source: MSB Docket No. S - 208
         American Mail Line

* Note: AML cargo data not available

American Mail Line Ltd.

Exhibit 2.7

PORTS OF CALL ON ROUTE STRUCTURE

Container Shuttle	Route A
Seattle (U.S.)	Columbia River Ports (U.S.)
Yokohama (Japan)	Puget Sound (besides Seattle)
Kobe (Japan)	Yokohama (Japan)
Nagoya (Japan)	Pusan (Korea)
Yokohama (Japan)	Inchon (Korea)
Seattle (U.S.)	Kaohsiung (Taiwan)*
	Hong Kong
	Keelung (Taiwan)
	Yawata (Japan)
	Kobe (Japan)
	Nagoya (Japan)
	Shimizu (Japan)
	Yokohama (Japan)
	Vancouver (B.C.)
	Seattle (U.S.)
	Columbia River Ports (U.S.)

----

* This port is replaced by Okinawa on alternate voyages.

Exhibit 2.8

EXPLANATION OF SYMBOLS FOR SCHEMATIC DIAGRAMS

◆   port of origin and final destination.

▭   name of port.

◯   port time in days.

▢   steaming time in days.

⬭   accomulated time from beginning of
         voyage.

Note: all times are given to nearest quater
       of a day.
       Diagrams are not to scale.

American Mail Line Ltd.

Exhibit 2.9

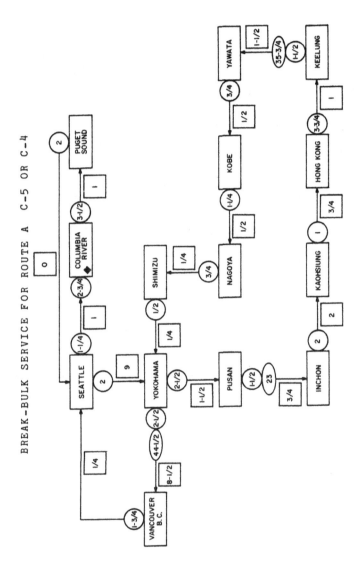

BREAK-BULK SERVICE FOR ROUTE A C-5 OR C-4

Exhibit 2.10

CONTAINER SHUTTLE

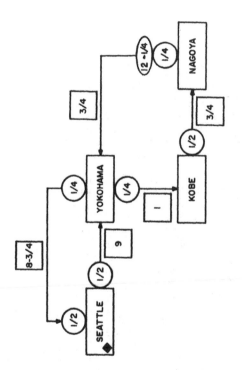

Chapter 3

MOORE-McCORMACK LINES, INC.:
ANALYSIS OF ROLL-ON/ROLL-OFF SHIPS

On April 26, 1968, the top management of Moore-McCormack Lines received an internally produced 1970-1979 cargo and profit analysis for four new roll-on/roll-off (also referred to as Ro-Ro) ships ordered in June 1966 and scheduled to enter service in 1969. Several preliminary profit studies had been completed before the ship design had been chosen, but the 1968 study was the first to include cargo data from the 1967 sailings.

The new ships were capable of carrying 830 twenty-foot equivalent unit (TEU) containers (8' x 8' x 20'), with a service speed of 25 knots. They had two features which distinguished them from ships being built by Moore-McCormack's major U.S. competition on the North Atlantic.

First, the Moore-McCormack ships had deck cranes, so that they could handle break-bulk cargo in the conventional manner.

Second, when the hatches were closed on the next-to-top deck, vehicles could be rolled aboard by means of a stern ramp. The stern ramp at each terminal would cost about $180,000. Containers would still be stored above and below this deck. This upper 'tween deck space could also be used for break-bulk cargo. When the hatches on this deck were raised, slides on the bottom of the hatches would serve as cellular holds for containers. With the hatches open, the ship could carry 830 TEU. With the hatches closed, the ship could carry 484 foreign cars and less than 600 TEU.

According to Moore-McCormack's manager of new construction, "At the time of the original design, the Military Sea Transportation Service, through the medium of an RFP (Request For Proposal), set forth certain requirements for charter of the roll-on/roll-off type vessel. This possibly influenced our thinking and led us to the design we now have". (An executive of Moore-McCormack estimated that the combination of deck cranes and Ro-Ro equipment accounted for the loss of about 200 TEU spaces. The deck cranes accounted for the vast majority of lost container space).

Moore-McCormack, unlike its U.S. competitors, could accept all types of cargo on their new ships. On the other hand, the major foreign competition would be operating ships with a higher roll-on/roll-off capacity than Moore-McCormack.

The extra features on the Moore-McCormack ships accounted for approximately $1 million (after subsidy) of the $8.15 million (after subsidy) cost per ship.

Although Moore-McCormack did not carry any regular vehicular traffic in early 1968, it was actively seeking such cargo for its new ships. Exhibit 3.1 shows information on the commercial imports and exports of vehicles.

NORTH ATLANTIC ENVIRONMENT

By the end of 1965, several companies had been making plans to provide container service on the North Atlantic, and at least two companies planned to use full containerships. In February 1966, Moore-McCormack started the first regularly scheduled container service on the North Atlantic by using up to 130 TEU as deck cargo on its modern conventional break-bulk, C-4 Constellation class vessels. The container capacity on these ships was later increased to 270 TEU. Moore-McCormack leased its containers rather than buying them.

Also in 1966, Sea-Land and American Export Isbrandtsen Lines (AEIL) entered the North Atlantic with full containerships. In addition, U.S. Lines and AEIL began to convert ships under construction to full containerships to be used on the North Atlantic.

Moore-McCormack operated three services, as shown in Exhibit 3.2. The new roll-on/roll-off ships were to be assigned to the American Scantic Line, which operated on the heavily containerized North Atlantic routes, replacing four Constellation class ships. By July 1968, the Moore-McCormack fleet consisted of 14 ships less than 8 years old and 24 ships over 20 years old.

Moore-McCormack Lines, Inc.

NEW VESSEL UTILIZATION

It was planned that the new roll-on/roll-off ships would operate a weekly service between six ports: Port Elizabeth (New York Harbor), Portsmouth (Hampton Roads area), and four foreign ports of call, depending on MarAd's reply to the trade route application for Trade Routes #7 and #9. The ports of Gothenburg and Rotterdam, however, were relatively certain to be included.

Exhibits 3.3 through 3.11 present excerpts from the report, "Ro-Ro Cargo and Profit Analysis, 1970-1979". In Exhibit 3.9, the values for the revenues and costs are based on average values. Exhibits 3.10 and 3.11 are based on various specific data for the trade routes and commodities involved. Consequently, the amount of contribution in Exhibits 3.10 and 3.11 is slightly different than if it had been calculated using the numbers in Exhibit 3.9. It should be noted that voyage cost simulations (Exhibits 3.10 and 3.11) were developed on the basis of carrying 40-foot containers.

A larger movement of commercial containers was expected Westbound than Eastbound. The majority of military containers was predicted to travel Eastbound. The voyage cost simulations assume an equal number of containers moving in the outbound and the inbound trade, thereby eliminating the need to ship empty containers. It was estimated that the total forty-foot container system described in Exhibits 3.10 and 3.11 would provide better profits than a system with either all 20-foot containers or a combination of 20-footers and 40-footers.

Transshipment costs refer to "substituted service" charges which were legal in many foreign countries, unlike in the United States. For example, if cargo existed at foreign Port A but the ship only stopped at nearby Port B, the steamship line could absorb the cost of transferring the cargo to Port B. The vessel expenses included:

1. Fuel
2. Crew and food
3. Operating subsidy
4. Administrative overhead including depreciation

No consideration was given to the outbound movement of military vehicles or military privately owned vehicles.

If the ship were fully utilized for 40-foot containers, the capacity would be 386 containers. (There were many places on the ship where a 20-foot container would fit but a 40-foot container would not.) If the roll-on/roll-off deck were fully used for foreign cars, this deck could carry 484 cars, and the remainder of the ship could carry about 259 forty-foot containers.

CORPORATE FINANCIAL DATA

Moore-McCormack Lines was investing in new vessels during a period of difficult financial conditions. The parent company, Moore and McCormack Co., Inc., had a return on investment of 1.9% in 1965, and 8.3% in 1966. The company showed a loss in 1967 and 1968. Exhibits 3.12 through 3.20 present excerpts from the 1967 Annual Report of Moore and McCormack Co., Inc. Although the firm owned some minor subsidiaries, Moore-McCormack Lines accounted for the vast majority of the financial data.

Moore-McCormack Lines, Inc.

Exhibit 3.1

DOMESTIC AND EXPORT FACTORY SALES FROM PLANTS LOCATED IN THE UNITED STATES
(IN THOUSANDS)

	Passenger Cars		Motor Trucks and Buses		Total Motor Vehicles	
	Total Domestic	Exports	Total Domestic	Exports	Total Domestic	Exports
1946	2,147	2,003 144	931	744 187	3,078	2,747 331
1950	6,657	6,504 153	1,296	1,145 151	7,953	7,649 304
1955	7,915	7,661 254	1,217	1,024 193	9,132	8,685 447
1960	6,669	6,525 145	1,164	948 216	7,834	7,473 361
1962	6,923	6,743 180**	1,167	1,029 138**	8,090	7,772 318**
1963	7,627	7,433 194	1,371	1,224 146	8,998	8,657 341
1964	7,741	7,543 198	1,483	1,320 163	9,223	8,862 361
1965	9,297	9,092 205	1,700	1,564 136	10,997	10,656 341
1966	8,587	8,326 261	1,673	1,548 125	10,260	9,874 386
1967	7,421	7,055 366	1,495	1,370 125	8,916	8,425 491

*Excludes factory sales to all federal government agencies.

**Starting with 1962, data not comparable with previous years.

Source: Automobile Manufacturers Association.

Exhibit 3.1 Continued

U.S. MOTOR VEHICLE IMPORTS BY COUNTRY OF ORIGIN 1967

| | Passenger Cars | | | | Trucks and Buses | | Automotive Parts Value |
| | New | | Used | | | | |
	Number	Value	Number	Value	Number	Value	
Austria	11	15,708	17	$ 24,487	33	$ 48,019	$ 114,292
Belgium	356	458,678	39	66,790	304	9,562,555	615,852
Canada	323,650	817,898,393			155,466	205,903,563	536,403,046
France	25,454	23,116,454	146	133,432	59	37,809	2,510,681
Italy	16,793	23,650,853	66	284,674	47	50,152	2,148,941
Japan	70,304	73,214,100	2	5,518	11,474	9,682,326	23,739,797
Malta	22	37,029					
Netherlands	232	276,664	1	472			370,330
Sweden	43,371	73,242,549	3	4,879	66	67,899	2,460,300
Taiwan	130	151,322			45	41,310	46,673
United Kingdom	67,928	103,388,227	193	223,799	231	709,866	15,182,923
West Germany	472,351	579,468,181	4,516	5,152,642	2,508	3,329,267	48,426,314
Other	18	44,476	9	12,114	4	14,323	2,451,925
Total	1,020,620	1,694,962,632	4,992	5,908,807	170,237	229,447,089	634,471,074

Source: Compiled by the Automobile Manufacturers Association from U.S. Department of Commerce data.

Moore-McCormack Lines, Inc.

Exhibit 3.2

CARGO SERVICES

Service	Trade Route No.	U.S. Coastal Area	Foreign Area
American Republics Line	1	Atlantic	East Coast South America
Robin Line	15A	Atlantic	South and East Africa
American Scantic Line	6	North Atlantic	Scandinavian and Baltic ports
	8	North Atlantic	Belgium and Netherlands
Also applied for but not yet approved	7	North Atlantic	German North Sea
	9	North Atlantic	Atlantic France and Northern Spain

Note: In addition to providing cargo service to the designated ports on these trade routes, Moore-McCormack also made permissive calls at a limited number of off-route ports.

Exhibit 3.3

ESTIMATED CONTAINER SERVICE TRADE ROUTES #5, #6, #7, #8, #9
1969

Lines	Weekly Sailings	Weekly Capacity 20-Foot Units	Annual Capacity 20-Foot Units
Container Marine/American Export	1	928	48,256
U.S. Lines	2	2,420	125,840
Atlantic Container Line	2	810	42,120
Sea Land*	1	788	40,950
Moore-McCormack Lines	1	830	43,166
Belgium Line	1	280	14,560
Finnlines	1	180	9,360
Other lines**	4	224	11,648
Total	13	6,460	335,900

*Assumes average capacity = 450 35-foot units.
 1-foot units = 1.75 20-foot units.

**Assumes about 60 20-foot units per line.

Note: Trade Route 5, the U.S. North Atlantic to the United Kingdom and Ireland, was included because of the potential diversion of containers to the other trade routes.

41

Exhibit 3.4

ESTIMATED CONTAINER SERVICE—TRADE ROUTES #5, #6, #7, #8, #9 1970

Lines	Weekly Sailings	Weekly Capacity 20-Foot Units	Annual Capacity 20-Foot Units
Total lines, 1969	13	6,460	335,900
Hamburg-American Line and North German Lloyd	1	620*	32,240
Belgium Line	1	620*	32,240
Atlantic Container Line	1	405	21,060
Total	16	8,105	421,440

*These vessels also carry break-bulk. The Belgium Line container capacity is estimated since published capacities are not available.

Note: It has been estimated that in 1970 the average 20-foot container will carry 12 long tons eastbound and 14 long tons westbound.

Exhibit 3.5

ESTIMATED IMPORTS
TRADE ROUTES #5, #6, #7, #8, #9
CALENDAR YEARS 1969-1979

Year	Long Tons (In Millions)
1969	4.4
1970	4.6
1971	4.9
1972	5.1
1973	5.4
1974	5.6
1975	5.8
1976	6.1
1977	6.3
1978	6.6
1979	6.8

Note: It was estimated that in 1970 the average 20-foot container would carry 14 long tons Westbound. It was also estimated that approximately 63% of import cargoes would be physically and economically containerizable by 1970. An additional 34% could be carried economically on pallets or "super-pallets," i.e., flats. This does not mean that they would not be carried on containers as well. For example, the cargo could be loaded onto pallets, and the pallets then loaded into containers for the oceanborne portion of the trip. The container could then be broken down at the port terminal on the other side, and the pallets dispersed for local delivery. The remaining 3% would be non-containerizable and non-palletizable, consisting mainly of vehicles and other large unwieldy equipment. This forecast did not include military cargo.

Moore-McCormack Lines, Inc.

Exhibit 3.6

ESTIMATED EXPORTS
TRADE ROUTES #5, #6, #7, #8, #9
CALENDAR YEARS 1969-1979

Year	Long Tons (In Millions)
1969	2.2
1970	2.3
1971	2.4
1972	2.5
1973	2.6
1974	2.7
1975	2.8
1976	2.9
1977	3.0
1978	3.1
1979	3.2

Note: It was estimated that in 1970 the average 20-foot container would carry 12 long tons Eastbound. It was also estimated that export cargo would be approximately 59% containerizable, that an additional 37% would be palletizable or flatable, and that the remaining 4% would be unwieldy independent units. This forecast did not include military cargo.

Exhibit 3.7

ESTIMATED MILITARY EXPORTS AND IMPORTS
TRADE ROUTES #6, #7, #8, #9
1970, 1975, 1979

Year	Exports	Imports
	(Long Tons in Thousands)	
1970	420	170
1975	210	50
1979	210	50

Note: It was estimated that about 55% of the military exports and about 85% of the military imports would be containerizable. Note that the weight is given in thousands of long tons rather than in millions.

Moore-McCormack Lines, Inc.

Exhibit 3.8

ESTIMATED MOORE-MCCORMACK MARKET SHARE*

Trade Routes	1970	1975	1979
Outbound			
6 & 8	16.0%	16.0%	16.0%
7	2.3	5.4	6.2
9	1.8	3.1	3.8
Inbound			
6 & 8	10.0%	6.7%	6.6%
7	1.6	of entire market	of entire market
9	2.5		

---

* The numbers in this exhibit have been disguised.

Exhibit 3.9

REVENUES AND COSTS

	Revenues per Unit	Cargo Cost	Container Costs	Brokerage and Commission
Outbound				
Commercial				
40' D.D.**	$ 930	$ 85	$ 190	$ 62
20' D.D.	615	85	168	48
40' P.P.***	1,300	510	110	70
Military & Mail				
40'	680	140	110	
20'	325	140	105	
Inbound				
Commercial				
40' D.D.	855	88	190	69
20' D.D.	475	88	168	61
40' P.P.	865	543	152	88
Military & Mail				
40'	680	140	110	
Cars	109	10		9

*The numbers in this exhibit have been disguised.

**Door-to-door.

***Pier-to-pier.

Note: Revenues per unit refer to the pier-to-pier charges paid by the shipper to Moore-McCormack. Loading and unloading charges make up the cargo cost. Container costs consist of the rental charges on a leased container or the depreciation, maintenance, and insurance charges on an owned container. The differences in the container costs between the door-to-door, military and mail, and pier-to-pier containers reflect the expected differences in turnaround time for each.

Door-to-door containers were loaded at the origin by the shipper and unloaded at the destination by the receiver. Therefore "cargo costs" for such shipments referred to the process of transferring full containers between the dock and the ship.

Pier-to-pier movements generally involved the consolidation of several small shipments at the pier. These shipments were loaded ("stuffed") by longshoremen into the containers at the origin port and unloaded at the destination docks prior to ultimate delivery. Thus, the pier-to-pier movements produced higher revenues per container (because of the multiplicity of small shipments), but entailed higher cargo costs.

Moore-McCormack Lines, Inc.

Exhibit 3.10

1970 RO-RO 28-DAY VOYAGE
A TOTAL FORTY SYSTEM

	Trade Routes 6 and 8	Trade Routes 6, 7, 8, 9
	Number of Units	Number of Units
Outbound		
Commercial		
40' D.D.	130	150
40' P.P.	70	75
Military & Mail		
40'	25	50
Inbound		
Commercial		
40' D.D.	140	150
40' P.P.	80	110
Military & Mail		
40'	5	15
Number of 40' containers each way	225	275
Contribution per voyage	$ 210,460	$ 247,750
Trans-shipment cost	40,000	40,000
Vessel expense	$ 171,500	$ 171,500
Profit per voyage	(1,040)	36,250
Contribution from 48 cars inbound	$ 39,600	$ 39,600
Adjusted profit per voyage	$ 38,560	$ 75,850

*The numbers in this exhibit have been disguised.

Note: Contribution refers to revenue minus the total cargo, container
and brokerage and commission costs. Trans-shipment costs refer to
"substituted service" charges.

48

Exhibit 3.11

RO-RO 28-DAY VOYAGE
A TOTAL FORTY SYSTEM
TRADE ROUTES #6, #7, #8, #9

	1975	1979
	Number of Units	Number of Units
Outbound		
Commercial		
40' D.D.	195	215
40' P.P.	80	110
Military & Mail		
40'	75	75
Inbound		
Commercial		
40' D.D.	205	240
40' P.P.	130	145
Military & Mail		
40'	15	15
Number of 40' containers each way	350	400
Contribution per voyage	$ 317,320	$ 366,640
Trans-shipment cost	40,000	50,000
Vessel expense	$ 171,500	$ 171,500
Profit per voyage	105,820	155,140

*The numbers in this exhibit have been disguised.

Note: Contribution refers to revenue minus the total cargo, container
and brokerage and commission costs. Vehicular traffic was excluded
from this forecast. Trans-shipment costs refer to "substituted
service" charges.

Moore-McCormack Lines, Inc.

Exhibit 3.12

ANNUAL REPORT, 1967
HIGHLIGHTS OF THE YEAR

Revenues	$ 96,802,000	$105,354,000
Expenses	103,872,000	104,859,000
Operating-Differential Subsidy	21,753,000	23,169,000
Vessel Depreciation	4,774,000	4,602,000
Overhead	13,400,000	13,369,000
Interest Expense-Net	60,000	7,000
Federal Income Taxes (credit)	(1,900,000)	1,913,000
Net Income (Loss) from Operations	(1,651,000)	3,773,000
Gain on Sale of Vessels		5,276,000
Net Income (Loss)	(1,651,000)	9,049,000
Per Share*		
Net Income (Loss) from Operations	($.69)	$1.58
Gain on Sale of Vessels		2.20
Net Income (Loss)	(.69)	3.78
Paid to Stockholders	1.00	.90
Book Value	43.89	45.55

*Based on shares outstanding at each year end.

50

Exhibit 3.13

NET INCOME (OPERATIONS)
AND DIVIDEND PAYMENTS
PER SHARE OF COMMON STOCK

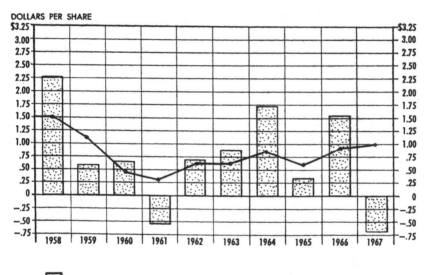

NET EARNINGS

DIVIDENDS
PAID PER SHARE
OF COMMON
STOCK

Moore-McCormack Lines, Inc.

Exhibit 3.14

STATEMENT OF CONSOLIDATED INCOME

	Year Ended December 31	
	1967	1966
Revenues	$ 96,802,441	$105,354,077
Expenses, other than vessel depreciation	(103,871,738)	(104,858,597)
Operating-Differential Subsidy, estimated (Note 2)	21,752,630	23,168,721
Vessel Depreciation	(4,774,398)	(4,601,974)
	9,908,935	19,062,227
Administrative and General Expenses	(13,399,963)	(13,368,350)
Interest Expense, less interest income of $829,214 and $820,353	(60,342)	(7,095)
Net income (loss) before provision (credit) for Federal income taxes	(3,551,370)	5,686,782
Provision (Credit) for Federal Income Taxes (Note 5)	(1,900,000)	2,562,300
Less-Investment Credit, including $537,000 in 1966 from carry forward from prior years	───────────	649,000
	(1,900,000)	1,913,300
Net Income (Loss) from Operations	(1,651,370)	3,773,482
Gain on Sale of Vessels	───────────	5,275,860
Net Income (Loss)-depositable in reserve funds $604,000 and $5,630,000 (Note 4)	($ 1,651,370)	$ 9,049,342

The accompanying Notes to Consolidated Financial Statements are an integral part of this statement.

Exhibit 3.15

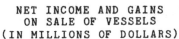

NET INCOME AND GAINS
ON SALE OF VESSELS
(IN MILLIONS OF DOLLARS)

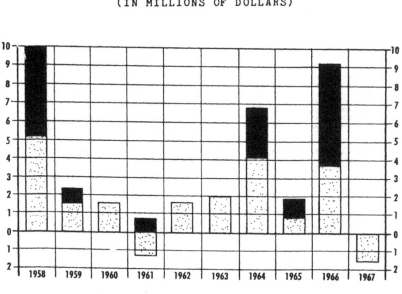

KEY

NET INCOME

GAINS

Moore-McCormack Lines, Inc.

Exhibit 3.16

CONSOLIDATED BALANCE SHEET
DECEMBER 31, 1967 AND 1966

ASSETS

	1967	1966
CURRENT ASSETS		
Cash	$ 3,635,355	$ 5,088,823
Marketable securities--at cost, which approximates market.	1,527,127	4,302,551
Receivables, net	11,624,896	12,270,877
Federal income tax refund, estimated	1,273,000	
Accrued operating-differential subsidy (Note 2)	11,244,069	11,750,499
Other current assets	1,882,766	1,662,932
	31,187,213	35,075,682
Less-Estimated deposits to reserve funds.	7,991,821	5,643,682
	23,195,392	29,432,000
STATUTORY RESERVE FUNDS (Note 4):		
Cash, U.S. Government securities and mortgage notes	32,882,466	10,894,159
Estimated deposits to be made. . .	7,991,821	5,643,682
	40,874,287	16,537,841
VESSELS AND OTHER PROPERTY, at cost (Notes 6 and 7):		
Vessels.	144,128,588	142,290,377
Other property and equipment . . .	6,643,550	6,034,655
	150,772,138	148,325,032
Less-Reserves for depreciation . .	54,684,766	49,535,096
	96,087,372	98,789,936
Vessels under construction	3,989,651	748,861
	100,077,023	99,538,797
OTHER ASSETS (Note 1)	5,666,727	4,011,522
	$169,813,429	$149,520,160

Exhibit 3.16 Continued

LIABILITIES AND STOCKHOLDERS' EQUITY

	1967	1966
CURRENT LIABILITIES:		
Notes payable to bank, current portion	$ 4,866,000	$ 366,000
Accounts payable and accrued liabilities	12,055,619	10,968,902
Prepaid passenger revenue	2,394,345	2,510,356
Federal income taxes	_____	__2,183,266
	19,315,964	16,028,524
NET UNTERMINATED VOYAGE REVENUE (excess of revenue over expense on voyages in progress)	3,832,862	4,014,250
LONG-TERM DEBT (Note 7)	39,300,151	17,682,461
RESERVE FOR CLAIMS	2,508,327	2,818,868
CONTINGENT LIABILITIES (Note 11)		
STOCKHOLDERS' EQUITY:		
Common stock, par value $5.00 per share Authorized 2,750,000 shares (Note 8) Issued 2,430,934 shares and 2,429,514 shares	12,154,670	12,147,570
Capital surplus (Note 9)	22,157,523	22,152,908
Earned surplus (Notes 4 and 5)	__71,282,460	__75,324,571
	105,594,653	109,625,049
Less: Treasury stock at cost— 41,800 shares and 37,300 shares	____738,528	____648,992
	104,856,125	108,976,057
	$169,813,429	$149,520,160

Moore-McCormack Lines, Inc.

Exhibit 3.17

STATEMENT OF CONSOLIDATED EARNED SURPLUS

	1967	1966
Balance, Beginning of Year	$75,324,571	$68,438,876
Net Income (Loss)	(1,651,370)	9,049,342
	73,673,201	77,488,218
Less-Dividends paid $1.00 and $.90 a share	2,390,741	2,163,647
Balance, End of Year (Notes 4 and 5)	$71,282,460	$75,324,571

Exhibit 3.18

STATEMENT OF CONSOLIDATED SOURCE
AND APPLICATION OF FUNDS

	YEAR 1967	
	General Funds	Statutory Reserve Funds
	(In thousands)	
Funds Provided By:		
Net income		$ 604
Long-term debt		26,000
Depreciation	__587	__4,774
	$ 587	$31,378
Funds Used For:		
Net loss	$2,255	
Cash dividends	2,391	
Investment in vessels and other property	783	5,026
Reduction of long-term debt	_4,500	__2,016
	$9,929	$ 7,042
Net Increase (Decrease) in Funds	(9,342)	24,336

*Principally invested in marketable securities.

The accompanying Notes to Consolidated Financial Statements are an integral part of these statements.

Moore-McCormack Lines, Inc.

Exhibit 3.19

NOTES TO CONSOLIDATED FINANCIAL STATEMENTS

NOTE 1: PRINCIPLES OF CONSOLIDATION

The consolidated financial statements include the accounts of Moore and McCormack Co., Inc. and its subsidiaries, Moore-McCormack Lines, Incorporated (referred to herein as "Lines"); Wood Flong Corporation; Tidewater Terminals, Inc.; Trident Leasing Co., Inc.; Commercial Steamship Co., Inc.; Moore and McCormack Belgique S.A.; Mormac-BBN Corporation; and Moore-McCormack Administradora S/A.

The consolidated financial statements do not include the wholly-owned foreign subsidiaries of Lines. Investments in and advances to these subsidiaries are carried at $1,375,222 which approximates their underlying book value. Operating results of these subsidiaries are not significant in relation to the consolidated operating results.

NOTE 2: OPERATING-DIFFERENTIAL SUBSIDY ACCRUALS

Lines' current operating-differential subsidy agreement, under the Merchant Marine Act of 1936, as amended, provides for subsidized operations to December 31, 1977. Subsidy accruals are based on final rates or Lines' estimate thereof. Management is of the opinion that the amount of subsidy, when finally determined, will not be less than the amount accrued. Collections of subsidy are limited to amounts billed on final or tentative rates accepted by Lines. A portion of the balance will be billed and collected after additional final rates are determined and the remainder after final audit and accounting with the Maritime Administration.

NOTE 3: RECAPTURE OF OPERATING-DIFFERENTIAL SUBSIDY

Operating-differential subsidy is subject to recapture by the United States to the extent of one-half of the amount by which the net profits from subsidized operations on a cumulative basis for a ten-year period exceed 10% per annum of capital necessarily employed. Lines' estimate of capital necessarily employed for 1967 is $101,000,000. No

Exhibit 3.19 Continued

provision for recapture is required for the ten-year period ended December 31, 1967.

NOTE 4: STATUTORY RESERVE FUNDS

The Merchant Marine Act of 1936, as amended, and the operating-differential subsidy agreement require deposits in statutory reserve funds of 1) earnings from subsidized operations in excess of 10% per annum of capital necessarily employed, 2) income received on reserve fund securities, 3) an amount equal to depreciation provided on owned subsidized vessels, if earned, and 4) proceeds of insurance, indemnities, or sale of subsidized vessels. In addition, earnings otherwise available for distribution to stockholders may be voluntarily deposited with the approval of the Maritime Administration. Earnings which are deposited are restricted as to dividends. The Act and the agreement limit dividends which may be paid from subsidized earnings to 10% per annum of capital necessarily employed. Under these provisions, approximately $68,700,000 of consolidated earned surplus at December 31, 1967 is restricted as to cash dividends.

NOTE 5: FEDERAL INCOME TAXES

Earnings subsequent to January 1, 1947, which have been, or will be, deposited in the reserve funds have not been subject to Federal income taxes. Such earnings, unless withdrawn under certain conditions for general use, will not be subject to Federal income taxes until termination of subsidized operations. At December 31, 1967, consolidated earned surplus included approximately $59,000,000 of such earnings on which no Federal income taxes have been paid.

NOTE 6: VESSEL-REPLACEMENT PROGRAM

Lines is committed under its operating-differential subsidy agreement to a vessel replacement program. Under this program, Lines contracted for four new vessels in 1966 and is required to contract for 21 additional freighters by 1972.

Moore-McCormack Lines, Inc.

Exhibit 3.19 Continued

NOTE 7: LONG-TERM DEBT

	1967	1966
Payable from Statutory Reserve Funds:		
U.S. Government Insured Merchant Marine Bonds--		
5%, due 1978	$ 5,729,000	$ 6,403,000
4.2%, due 1983	6,839,000	7,380,000
5.75%, due 1987	25,342,000	-
Deferred ship purchase payments	88,651	231,961
	$37,998,651	$14,014,961

Notes Payable to Bank:

Due Date	Interest Rate		
Feb., 1968	5.5 %	$ 1,000,000	-
Mar., 1968	6 %	500,000	-
Mar., 1968	6 %	1,000,000	-
May, 1968	5.75%	2,000,000	2,000,000
May, 1972	6 %	1,350,000	1,650,000
May, 1972	6.25%	200,000	240,000
May, 1972	6.5 %	117,500	143,500
		6,167,500	4,033,500
Less: Current Portion		4,866,000	366,000
		1,301,500	3,667,500
TOTAL LONG-TERM DEBT		$39,300,151	$17,682,461

The bonds payable from the statutory reserve funds
are insured under Title XI of the Merchant Marine Act
of 1936, as amended, and are subject to semi-annual
redemptions. The bonds are secured by first
preferred ship mortgages upon various vessels.
    The notes payable to bank due May, 1972 are
payable in quarterly installments, of which $366,000
will be paid in 1968.

60

Exhibit 3.19 Continued

NOTE 8: STOCK OPTION PLANS

The following table sets forth certain pertinent information on the Company's stock option plans for certain officers and key employees:

	1962 Plan
Options exercisable at December 31, 1966	6,740
Options exercisable during 1967	(1,420)
Options exercisable at December 31, 1967	5,320
Expiration date for options	Oct. 22 1969

NOTE 9: CAPITAL SURPLUS

The increase during 1967 represents the excess of amounts received over par value of common stock issued upon exercise of stock options.

NOTE 10: LONG-TERM LEASES

The annual obligation for office and pier space under leases expiring beyond three years is approximately $1,400,000 per annum.

In addition, Lines is committed to annual rentals of approximately $2,400,000 for container and related equipment leases.

NOTE 11: CONTINGENT LIABILITIES

Claims for approximately $600,000 have been filed against Lines for recovery of repairs and damages to a vessel, incurred subsequent to its sale in 1964.

The resultant amount of liability is not presently determinable, but it is the opinion of management that the outcome will not materially affect the Company's consolidated financial position as of December 31, 1967.

Moore-McCormack Lines, Inc.

Exhibit 3.19 Continued

Lines is a guarantor on $1,800,000 of notes payable by Container Terminals N.Y. Inc., an affiliated company.

NOTE 12: PENSION PLAN

The Company amended its office employees' pension plan in 1967. As of December 31, 1967, unfunded past service costs amounted to approximately $3,000,000. The Company is providing for normal costs currently and is amortizing past service costs over thirty years.

Exhibit 3.20

TEN-YEAR COMPARISON OF FINANCIAL DATA

(In thousands of dollars)

	1967	1966	1965	1964	1963	1962	1961	1960	1959	1958
Vessels, less depreciation	90,668	93,612	97,463	95,161	85,883	77,776	81,036	74,999	60,805	55,748
Reserve Funds—principally for vessel replacement	40,874	16,538	12,774	13,895	18,972	18,215	13,954	22,057	25,659	29,408
Debt—principally ship mortgages	39,300	17,682	19,598	19,119	17,647	9,724	13,075	14,796	2,317	1,589
Stockholders' equity	104,856	108,976	102,038	101,298	96,314	95,664	95,388	96,626	96,144	96,436
Per Share*	43.89	45.55	43.33	43.65	41.97	41.70	41.58	42.12	41.91	42.04
Net income (loss) from operations	(1,651)	3,773	834	4,039	2,020	1,652	(1,301)	1,513	1,414	5,228
Per Share*	(.69)	1.58	.35	1.74	.88	.72	(.57)	.66	.62	2.28
Gain on sale of vessels		5,276	1,115	2,695			752		876	4,825
Per Share*		2.20	.47	1.16			.33		.38	2.10
Dividends	2,391	2,164	1,403	1,965	1,377	1,376	688	1,032	2,581	3,441
Per Share*	1.00	.90	.60	.85	.60	.60	.30	.45	1.13	1.50

*Based on shares outstanding at each year end.

Chapter 4

PUERTO RICO: LINER SERVICE WITH THE MAINLAND

In the spring of 1974, the government of the
Commonwealth of Puerto Rico was deciding what role--
if any--to play in the liner service between Puerto
Rico (P.R.) and the mainland of the U.S. The
initiation of service by a new competitor,
Transamerican Trailer Transport (TTT) with new roll-
on/roll-off (Ro-Ro) containerships, had brought
overcapacity to the U.S. North Atlantic/P.R. trade.
In addition, there was the danger that overcapacity
might lead to financial ruin for existing
competitiors. (Sea-Land and Seatrain competed with
World War II tonnage converted to lift-on/lift-off
[Lo-Lo] containerships; Trailer Marine Transport
[TMT] used tugs and barges to Jacksonville and
Miami.)
    The Office of the Governor had received reports
on the liner service, including those by a management
consulting firm and others by a banking institution.
Excerpts from these reports provide the information
detailed in the remainder of this chapter.

HISTORICAL PERSPECTIVE

Characteristics of the Puerto Rico/North Atlantic Trade Route

The character of the Puerto/North Atlantic trade route has largely determined the kind of service offered in the past; similarly, it will be a deciding influence in shaping the alternatives available for the future. The main features which characterize this route are the following:

> **Fairly stable annual cargo flows and predictable growth:** Large annual variances can be caused by swings in the overall U.S. economy, as exemplified by the 1970 economic recovery, but excluding this one source of instability, flows have maintained a steady rhythm of growth, as shown in Table 4.1.

TABLE 4.1

Rate of Increase in Tonnage Shipped by Vessel, U.S. to Puerto Rico
(1970-1972)

1970	17%
1971	4%
1972	4%

Source: U.S. Department of Commerce

> **High degree of imbalance in flows:** Although Northbound and Southbound tonnage data are not published, value data are. The value differential indicated by the Department of Commerce between Southbound and Northbound carrying has fluctuated between 10.7:1 and 13.4:1 over the period from 1968 to 1972.

> **Broad cargo mix:** A broad mix is especially found on the Southbound run, where the cargo ranges from substantial volumes of high-value/high-cube consumer products (such as automobiles) to large volumes of low-value/high-density commodities (such as grains).

> **Short ocean transit:** Excluding, perhaps, some ocean-carrying among the British Isles and island-to-island carriage in Japan, this

route probably represents a unique combination of high volume movement and short-transit mileage.

Insulation from foreign competition: Under the Jones Act, carriage on this route is considered to be domestic in nature and is restricted to U.S.-flag vessels. As such, control over rates has been placed in the hands of the Federal Maritime Commission (FMC).

Impact of Containerization on Puerto Rico/North Atlantic Trade, 1955-1968

The technology of containerization was originated, tested, and perfected on this route, primarily because the route attracted the attention of trucking companies and carriers of railroad cars. The system developed by these carriers was a drastic departure from the traditional economics of break-bulk cargo carrying. First of all, it required a much more capital-intensive system, with more complex costly vessels and terminal facilities, as well as substantial investment in the containers themselves. Second, the savings in cargo-handling charges and the enhanced utilization of vessels through faster port turnaround created cost economies that more than offset the capital cost burden on each unit handled.

The innovating companies, Sea-Land and Seatrain, were actually able to minimize much of the cost impact of containerization's high capital costs. They achieved this by converting relatively old, fully depreciated, break-bulk vessels or World War II tankers for container carrying.

Advent of TTT and Its Effect on the Current Situation

The initiation of TTT service on the Puerto Rico/ North Atlantic trade route in 1968 upset the competitive balance that existed between Sea-Land and Seatrain in two ways:

1. The vessels introduced by TTT provided faster port-to-port service at the same rate. Many shippers saw this as a way of getting more for their money; thus, TTT tended to establish a more selective, higher-rated, cargo mix.
2. Each TTT vessel represented a very considerable increment in total carrying capacity on the route, both for containers

and automobiles, in contrast to the relatively gradual increments that Sea-Land and Seatrain had been making. This led directly to overcapacity on the route, which was compounded by Sea-Land's own tendency to add larger ships as a means of lowering unit costs.

In addition, TTT was unique in that it was the first truly capital-intensive container carrier on the route. By using new ships, rather than fully depreciated converted vessels, its internal economics were quite distinct from those of the earlier carriers.

The combination of these factors has largely shaped the current situation on the route, one which is marked by:

1. Surplus capacity.
2. Carrier profit deterioration which is traceable to under-utilized capacity and the impact of sharp rises in costs.
3. The presence of a "mature" system in which the intrinsic technological efficiencies now appear to have absorbed cost increases to the maximum extent possible.

Varying Economic Impact on Three Carriers

The influence of the economic factors that have emerged, particularly in the previous three years, has varied considerably from carrier to carrier.

1. Seatrain

Seatrain has suffered most from the drastic changes in the competitive environment on the route, even though its vessels, if used at high levels of capacity, are likely to be the lowest cost containerships.

Under the impact of competitive change, Seatrain has the least to offer potential shippers. Its vessels are the slowest on the route, and its sailing frequency the lowest. This leads almost inevitably to its having the lowest load factors and the poorest cargo mix.

In 1972, Seatrain's pre-tax operating loss for Puerto Rican service reached $10.9 million. (Even if this figure is influenced by some distorted allocation of corporate costs, Seatrain's losses clearly must have been substantial.) The company certainly did not maintain a positive cash flow, since its losses surely exceeded depreciation allowances; it may not even have recovered its direct costs for Puerto Rican service.

Seatrain's financial difficulties on the Puerto Rican service represent only one element in a larger corporate financial problem. The firm's overall pre-tax loss in 1972 on all of its container operations has been estimated at $40 million, and this has not been fully offset by profits on chartering. The corporation recorded a $10.5 million net loss in 1972; consequently, its corporate life is clearly in jeopardy.

If Seatrain's operations to and from Puerto Rico continue to drain corporate resources strongly, there is a high likelihood of route abandonment. Indeed, there are strong rumors that Seatrain intends to do this in February, 1974. However, at present Seatrain appears not to have clear alternatives for using its physical resources--vessels and containers--currently dedicated to this route.

2. Sea-Land

Although Sea-Land shares with Seatrain the competitive disadvantage of slow transit, its sailing frequency compares favorably with that of TTT. Consequently, neither its cargo mix nor its load factors are distributed as severely.

Although Sea-Land's 1972 pre-tax loss of $5.4 million, also possibly overstated, was of considerable proportion, Sea-Land probably achieved break-even levels of cash flow. Its Puerto Rican service made normal contributions to the overall corporate overhead.

It appears unlikely that Sea-Land will cease servicing this route. Rate increases are likely to make the route once again satisfactorily profitable. In addition, like Seatrain, Sea-Land does not appear to have any obvious alternatives for using its vessels and containers elsewhere. Finally, Sea-Land may be attracted by the possibility of monopolizing the route which, even with close FMC supervision over rates, would be likely to increase profitability greatly.

3. TTT

TTT appears to be the carrier which has been the least seriously affected by the changes in the competitive environment, many of which, of course, were caused by its own introduction of service. In 1972, TTT's profits represented a probable after tax return on shareholders' equity of approximately 10%.

To a great extent, this level of profitability was traceable to TTT's unique cargo mix. Until 1973, more than 25% of the firm's revenue were generated by automobile carrying, an area in which it enjoyed substantial dominance of the new car portion.

TTT has forecasted break-even performance for 1973, but underlying this we see considerable possible instability, based on the following factors:

a. TTT is the only one of the three carriers with extremely high capital costs.

b. TTT is the only carrier entirely dependent upon Puerto Rico service and thus is unlikely to be able to absorb losses for more than the shortest periods of time.

c. TTT is highly debt-leveraged; although the methods used in its vessel chartering and container financing may give it a relatively low effective interest rate, TTT's owners' equity still represents only about 3% of its real asset base.

d. TTT faces major cash drains associated with its need to move to new terminal facilities in New York and its need to satisfy retroactive assessments of the New York Shipping Association.

e. TTT is highly dependent upon revenues from automobile carrying, an area in which effective unit rates have slipped by nearly 20% in the previous two years and in which TTT was, during the first half of 1973, utilizing about 40% of its carrying capacity.

To an even greater degree than the other two firms, we find the situation of TTT to appear somewhat precarious because of: 1) its short-term cash pressures, 2) the unlikelihood of its finding any other comparably attractive use for its new and custom-configured vesels, and 3) its narrow capital structure.

Summary

On balance, the methods of transportation and the structure of the transportation system have served the interest of both the Commonwealth and the carriers satisfactorily in the past.

However, the existing system, as it stands, is a mature one that will be sensitive to cost increases, and these will have to be reflected in the rates charged.

In addition, the unstable financial factors cited for two of the three carriers will create strong risks of short-term service disruptions if one or both of these carriers decides to abandon service on the route.

MAJOR STRATEGIC ALTERNATIVES

There are three major types of strategic alternative open to the Commonwealth. These alternatives focus on either technology or policy, but by no means are they exclusive of one another; in fact, there is the clear possibility of combining options.

These major alternatives are the following:

1. Leave the technological aspects of the shipping "system" largely as they are and either:

    a. Do almost nothing except increase the Commonwealth's efforts to influence the FMC toward weighing the economic objectives of the Commonwealth more heavily in its rate-making deliberations, or

    b. Acquire one of three carriers providing service on the route, and attempt to use it to exert pressure on the other carriers to maintain low rates.

2. Change the technological aspects of the "system" by either:

    a. Replacing the present container fleet with new, larger, faster containerships, or

    b. Finding a new, lower cost means of handling the most essential forms of cargo carried on the route.

3. Monopolize service on the route, running the Commonwealth-owned company as a "public instrument," in the public interest much like a public utility.

I.   A Proposal to Purchase Existing Carriers

The following proposal has been prepared as a workable and practical plan for the creation of a

Puerto Rican merchant marine. As an initial investment, approximately $60 million would be required for working capital and acquisition of certain assets. It would appear that funds for future capital requirements would be provided from operations.

This study has been prepared assuming the existing rate structure. The only rate increases provided are those which cover actual labor and operating expense increases. This procedure results in substantial savings to the Commonwealth and sufficient cash to replace all existing vessels (except the roll-on/roll-off vessels) with modern high-speed containerships. The existing capacity would be almost doubled by 1985.

Estimated revenues, cash available from operations and capital requirements are shown in Exhibit 4.1. It is assumed that operations commence July 1, 1974. The net savings which result (after payment for management services) could be utilized in many ways, including additions to working capital, the reduction of rates, and expansion of marine services.

II. Markets

A. **Existing Services**: Marine service to Puerto Rico is currently provided by three major private carriers plus one barge operator under the U.S. flag as required by the Jones Act. The approximate weekly carrying capacity currently provided from various U.S. ports is shown in Exhibit 4.2.

In addition, service is provided from the West Coast to Puerto Rico by Sea-Land Service on a weekly intercoastal sailing. Sea-Land Service and Seatrain also operate between Puerto Rico and many islands in the Caribbean.

In order to evaluate the sufficiency of the service currently being provided, it is necessary to estimate the total present market between the United States and Puerto Rico. Estimates for the Southbound market for 1974 are presented in Exhibit 4.3.

The existing service to Puerto Rico being provided by the four carriers, therefore, exceeds the projected 1974 Southbound demand by 1,053 containers per week. As such, the average vessel utilization Southbound will be 75%.

B. **Projections of Future Requirements**: Historical trends in the volume of traffic to Puerto Rico have been analyzed in order to project the anticipated growth in the volume of waterborne freight moving between Puerto Rico and the United States mainland. The market has been projected for the next 12 years to develop an estimate of the traffic that will require service by the proposed merchant marine. This market projection appears in Exhibit 4.4 in annual container loads.

Exhibit 4.4 indicates a growth in physical volume of approximately 8% per year.

III. Operations

A. Present Vessel Schedules: The following is an analysis of the vessels and schedules currently being provided by the carriers (excluding TMT):

1. Seatrain Lines: Seatrain Lines is currently operating three 480 forty-foot container vessels in the Puerto Rico service. These vessels are deployed as follows: San Juan --New York--San Juan--Baltimore--Charleston --San Juan on a 21-day cycle. Thus, one vessel calls at each listed port every seven days.

2. Transamerican Trailer Transport: TTT currently operates three vessels in the trade in two independent deployments. One vessel operates San Juan--Baltimore--San Juan on a 7-day run. The other two vessels operate San Juan--New York--San Juan on a 7-day turn, providing two sailings per week.

3. Sea-Land Service: Sea-Land Service operates vessels in three different deployments:

   a. Four 360 thirty-five-foot container vessels operate on a 28-day turn from San Juan--New York--San Juan--New York --San Juan--Baltimore--San Juan. This deployment results in two 360 sailings from New York and one 360 sailing from Baltimore each week. Approximately 200 loads per week are also carried Southbound on an intercoastal sailing from New York--San Juan--San Francisco.

   b. Three 332 thirty-five-foot container vessels operate on a 21-day turn from San Juan--Charleston--Jacksonville-- San Juan--Miami--Jacksonville--San Juan. This deployment results in one sailing from Charleston and Miami and two sailings from Jacksonville per week.

c. The third deployment consists of two 274 thirty-five-foot capacity vessels in the Gulf Coast/Puerto Rico trade. One vessel operates on a 12-day turn between Mobile and San Juan, and the other operates on a 12-day turn between New Orleans and San Juan.

B. Proposed Vessel Deployment: It is proposed that the Commonwealth consider acquiring the use of the following ships from the major carriers:

TTT: Three roll-on/roll-off vessels (a fourth vessel could be acquired and deployed elsewhere through a subcharter until growth in the Puerto Rico trade requires its use).
Seatrain Lines: Three 480 forty-foot container vessels.
Sea-Land Service: Three 609 thirty-five-foot container vessels and two 360 thirty-five-foot container vessels. (The plan also contemplates operations from Sea-Land Service to charter or purchase additional vessels if required in the startup phase of the Commonwealth's merchant marine or prior to delivery of newly constructed vessels.)

This fleet of vessels would be deployed as follows:

1. Three 609 Vessels: New York--San Juan--New York--San Juan--New York on a 21-day turn, resulting in two sailings per week.
2. One TTT Vessel: New York--San Juan--New York on a 7-day turn, resulting in one sailing per week.
3. One TTT Vessel: New York--Ponce, P.R.--New York on a 7-day turn, resulting in one sailing per week.
4. One TTT Vessel: San Juan--Miami--Jacksonville--San Juan on a 7-day turn, resulting in one sailing per week.
5. Three 480 Vessels: San Juan--Baltimore--San Juan--Charleston--Jacksonville--San Juan on a 21-day turn, resulting in two sailings per week.
6. One 360 Vessel: San Juan--Mobile--San Juan on a 12-day turn.

7. **One 360 Vessel**: San Juan--New Orleans--San Juan on a 12-day turn.

This deployment results in the capacities per week shown in Table 4.2.

TABLE 4.2

New York	1,818
Baltimore	480
Charleston	240*
Jacksonville	390* **
Miami	150 **
Mobile	210
New Orleans	210
TOTAL:	3,498

The above deployment would result in a capacity reduction of 706 loads Southbound per week and add vessel service to Ponce.

C. **Port Facilities**: It is proposed that the Commonwealth's fleet be operated out of facilities which are restricted in their use to the Puerto Rico trade. Initial analysis indicates that the following facilities would most adequately serve the needs of the Commonwealth's fleet:

New York: It is proposed that the operation be conducted out of Sea-Land's recently vacated facility at Port Elizabeth, N.J. Roll-on/roll-off sailings would also be made from this facility. Ramps for roll-on/roll-off service would be moved from TTT's Staten Island facility and the lease of the Staten Island facility terminated, if possible. Seatrain Lines would discontinue operations to Puerto Rico at their present facility.

---

* One 480 sailing, split evenly between Charleston and Jacksonville.

** One roll-on/roll-off (300-container capacity assumed), split evenly between Jacksonville and Miami.

Puerto Rico: Liner Service with the Mainland

Baltimore: All operations would be consolidated
at the existing Sea-Land facility. Sea-Land
could operate their continuing services from
either TTT's or Seatrain's present facility.

Charleston: The existing Sea-Land terminal would
become the terminal for the proposed service.
Additional parking would be required in 1975.

Jacksonville: Either the existing Sea-Land
facility, or a newly constructed port facility,
would be moved from TTT's Baltimore facility.

Miami: Roll-on/roll-off ramps would have to be
purchased for use at the existing Sea-Land
facility.

New Orleans: A recently vacated Sea-Land facility,
or a newly constructed port facility, would be
utilized. A shore crane would be required for a
360-container vessel.

Mobile: The existing Sea-Land facility would be
utilized with the addition of a shore crane.

San Juan: It is proposed that all operations be
conducted at the existing, adjacent Sea-Land and
TTT facilities. The existing Seatrain facility
would be utilized by Sea-Land for its continuing
services. (No acquisition costs have been
included for the Seatrain facility.) A second
Sea-Land facility for its Gulf Coast/ Puerto
Rico operations would be closed.

Ponce: A suitable site for roll-on/roll-off ramps
and trailer parking would be required.

The total estimated capital expenditures
required through 1985 for relocation and improvements
to facilities is $53,250,000. A list of these
expenditures is shown in Exhibit 4.5.

D. Equipment Requirements: Equipment needs have been
estimated as follows:

Concerning the roll-on/roll-off vessels, TTT's
existing equipment pools would either be acquired or
leased on a long-term basis, with additional
requirements to be provided by other carriers on a
daily basis.

75

Sea-Land and Seatrain vessels require the equipment shown in Exhibit 4.6. These requirements are based on Sea-Land's historical experience in the various ports.

Of the total container requirements, it is estimated that the quantities of specialized equipment shown in Table 4.3 would be required to support the proposed service:

TABLE 4.3

	Approximate Percentage	Units
Refrigerated	11.0%	1,300
Tanks	1.5	200
Containers	4.0	500
Flats	0.5	50
Other	2.0	250
TOTAL	19.0%	2,300

Equipment requirements could be reduced if effective collection procedures were instituted for demurrage. Shippers would thus be encouraged to return equipment promptly for reloading. In addition, pre-loading of cargoes and inland penetration of equipment could be minimized to reduce equipment requirements.

Additional equipment will be required in future years as new vessels are acquired and as existing equipment is retired. Estimated additional equipment needs and replacements are shown in Exhibit 4.7. It is assumed that 10% of the containers initially required would be replaced each year for 10 years. A pool of 1,854 containers and 1,236 chassis is assumed for each of nine new containerships. Cost of new equipment is escalated at 5% per year.

In addition, in 1980, TTT's equipment currently under long-term lease would have to be replaced. The estimated cost would be $16,750,000: 1,500 forty-foot trailers at $8,500 each and 200 reefers at $20,000 each.

E. Other Areas of Benefit: Major savings could be accomplished in other areas besides consolidation of facilities, reduced number of vessels, and optimization of equipment usage. These might include reduced credit losses (bad debts), reduced sales and administrative expense, and the elimination of unprofitable competitive practices.

F.   Cost of Implementation: Substantial costs will be incurred in the implementation of this plan, principally in the consolidation of facilities, general offices, and equipment.   These costs are estimated to be $2-5 million.   This should be a one-time expenditure.

G.   Future Vessel Requirements: An   orderly construction program is required to provide for the replacement of the containerships initially placed in service by the Commonwealth and for the growth in physical volume anticipated in the trade.   Based on a hypothetical 618 forty-foot container-capacity, 26-knot vessel, one additional vessel would be required each year from 1978 through 1985, except for 1983, when two vessels would be needed.   Estimated vessel costs are shown in Exhibit 4.8.

IV.   Management and Organization

It is proposed that the fleet be owned and directed by a newly created public authority of the Commonwealth, the Puerto Rico Maritime Shipping Authority.   It is suggested that the Board of Directors of the Authority be composed of leading citizens of Puerto Rico.   It is understood that the Authority will contract with an independent concern to manage and operate the fleet after the basic principles of operation are established by the Authority.
      Sea-Land Service has offered to provide such services to the Authority for a fixed fee (subject to escalation) plus an incentive based on actual cost savings. If Sea-Land is selected as manager/operator, it would form a separate subsidiary strictly for the purpose of fulfilling this contract.
      Under Sea-Land's offer, the Authority would enter into a long-term management contract with a reasonable cancellation clause.   The annual payment for management services would be equal to a fixed $7.5 million, escalated at 4% per year plus an incentive payment of 15% of the actual cost savings in that year.

V.   Financial Consequences

A.   Estimated 1974 Financial Results: In 1973, the total revenue of the three major carriers serving Puerto Rico was estimated to be $165,000,000. It is quite likely that, in the aggregate, these carriers broke even in 1973. Total costs are therefore assumed to equal revenues.

It is estimated that total revenues will be $198 million in 1974, after making allowances for the pass through of additional bunker costs and the growth of physical volume in the trade. A detailed analysis of operating costs for 1974, assuming the Commonwealth's adoption of the proposed plan, is shown in Exhibit 4.9. Detailed breakdowns of various costs are shown in Exhibit 4.10.

B.   Projected Financial Results: The projected financial results for the years 1974 through 1985 are shown in Exhibit 4.11. Cash flow projections are shown in Exhibit 4.12. Initial capital requirements to implement the proposed service are estimated at approximately $60 million. Initial capital requirements would include the purchase of TTT and possibly TMT, the acquisition of miscellaneous assets of Sea-Land Service and Seatrain Lines (not including Seatrain's San Juan terminal), $2.5 million of consolidation expenses, and approximately $25-30 million of working capital.

Exhibit 4.1

PREDICTED CASH FLOW (IN THOUSANDS)

Year	Revenues	Cash Available from Operations(2)	Capital Requirements(3)	Net Available
Initial Capital			$ 60,000	$(60,000)
1974-6 Months (1)	$ 99,000	$ 20,371	7,500	12,871
1975	220,526	51,453	8,340	43,113
1976	245,453	63,057	8,395	54,662
1977	273,212	75,619	8,716	66,903
1978	305,491	79,518	75,390	4,128
1979	342,280	84,465	76,149	8,316
1980	381,149	109,372	93,374	15,998
1981	427,836	130,786	82,322	48,464
1982	480,901	138,862	88,263	50,599
1983	537,204	147,952	171,905	(23,953)
1984	601,596	162,159	97,910	64,249
1985	670,485	182,862	93,223	89,639
	$4,585,133	$1,246,476	$871,487	$374,989

(1) Assumes one-half of revenues and operating costs projected for 1974.
(2) After allocations to depreciation reserve. Does not reflect payments for management services rendered.
(3) Includes capital items related to terminals and equipment as well as vessels.

Puerto Rico: Liner Service with the Mainland

Exhibit 4.2

EXISTING SERVICE

Port	Carrier	Weekly Sailings	Weekly Container Equivalents
New York	Sea-Land Service	3	820(1)
	TTT	2	600(2)
	Seatrain Lines	1	480
			1,900
Baltimore	Sea-Land Service	1	360
	TTT	1	300(2)
	Seatrain Lines	1	240(3)
			900
Charleston	Sea-Land Service	1	166(4)
	Seatrain Lines	1	240(3)
			406
Jacksonville	Sea-Land Service	2	408(4)
	TMT	NA	90
			498
Miami	Sea-Land Service	1	90(4)
	TMT	NA	90
			180
Mobile	Sea-Land Service	.58(5)	160
New Orleans	Sea-Land Service	.58(5)	160
Total Weekly Containers to Puerto Rico			4,204

(1) Two 360 sailings plus 200 containers on an intercoastal sailing less 100 spaces utilized by Caribbean loads.
(2) One roll-on/roll-off vessel assumed equivalent in carrying capacity to 300 containers.
(3) One 480 sailing split evenly between Baltimore and Charleston.
(4) One 332 sailing split evenly between Charleston and Jacksonville; one 332 sailing split between Miami/Jacksonville 90/242.
(5) One 272 sailing every twelve days.

Exhibit 4.3

1974 ESTIMATED SOUTHBOUND CONTAINER MARKET
(CONTAINERS PER WEEK)

New York	1,528
Baltimore	473
Charleston	217
Jacksonville	351
Miami	157
Mobile	214
New Orleans	211

TOTAL	3,151

Exhibit 4.4

PROJECTED ANNUAL CONTAINER TRAFFIC
EAST AND GULF COASTS TO PUERTO RICO

1974	163,852
1975	173,732
1976	184,548
1977	196,196
1978	208,728
1979	222,728
1980	237,068
1981	253,084
1982	270,348
1983	289,172
1984	209,504
1985	331,708

Exhibit 4.5

ESTIMATED FACILITIES EXPENDITURES

Year	Port	Item	Estimated Cost
1974	New York	Relocated Roll-on/Roll-off Facilities	$ 500,000
	Baltimore	Relocate Roll-on/Roll-off Facilities to Jacksonville	500,000
	Ponce	Add Roll-on/Roll-off Ramps	750,000
	Miami	Add Roll-on/Roll-off Ramps	750,000
	Mobile	Add Container Crane	1,500,000
	New Orleans	Add Container Crane	1,500,000
1975	Charleston	Add 200 Parking Spaces	250,000
1978	Charleston	Add Container Crane	1,500,000
	Jacksonville	Add Container Crane, 200 Parking Spaces	2,000,000
	Mobile	Add Container Crane	1,500,000
	New Orleans	Add Container Crane	1,500,000
1979	Baltimore	Add Two Container Cranes, 100 Parking Spaces	3,500,000
1981	New York	Add Container Crane	1,500,000
			17,250,000
		Miscellaneous Improvements	36,000,000
		Total Expenditures	$53,250,000

Note: $2,000,000 per year is provided for miscellaneous improvements through 1981; after 1981, $5,000,000 per year is provided.

Exhibit 4.6

CONTAINER AND CHASSIS REQUIREMENTS

Vessel Complements:		35'	40'
3-480 Vessels			1,440
3-609 Vessels		1,827	
2-360 Vessels		__720	_____
		2,547	1,440

Land Pools:

Containers

		35'	40'
New York	1,218 x 1.45	1,776	
Baltimore	480 x 1.8		864
Charleston	240 x 1.3		312
Jacksonville	240 x 1.46		350
Mobile	360 x 1.18	425	
New Orleans	360 x 1.44	518	
San Juan	40- 960 x 1.5		1,440
	35-1,638 x 1.5	2,457	_____
		5,176	2,966
		7,723	4,406/12,129

Chassis

	35'	40'
Total Containers	7,723	4,406
Less Vessel Complements	2,547	1,440
Net Chassis Requirements	5,176	2,966
Stevedore Chassis	378	212
Maintenance Chassis	_275	_160
Total Chassis Required	5,829	3,338/ 9,167
Total Units		21,296

Puerto Rico: Liner Service with the Mainland

Exhibit 4.7

EQUIPMENT ADDITIONS AND REPLACEMENTS

Year	Additions	Replacements	Total	¢	Cost
1975		1,200	1,200	$3,500	$ 4,200,000
1976		1,200	1,200	3,675	4,410,000
1977		1,200	1,200	3,860	4,632,000
1978	3,090	1,200	4,290	4,052	17,383,000
1979	3,090	1,200	4,290	4,254	18,250,000
1980	3,090	1,200	4,290	4,467	19,163,000
1981	3,090	1,200	4,290	4,690	20,120,000
1982	3,090	1,200	4,290	4,925	21,128,000
1983	6,180	1,200	7,380	5,171	38,162,000
1984	3,090	1,200	4,290	5,430	23,295,000
1985	3,090	_____	3,090	5,701	17,616,000
	27,810	12,000	39,810		$188,359,000

Plus 45% Specialized Equipment   84,762,000

                                              $273,121,000

Exhibit 4.8

ESTIMATED VESSEL CAPITAL COSTS

Basis: 1979 price of 618 forty-foot capacity, 26-knot vessel is $35 million, with price escalation at 6% per year.

1978	$ 41,685,000
1979	44,187,000
1980	46,838,000
1981	49,648,000
1982	52,627,000
1983	111,570,000
1984	59,132,000
1985	62,680,000
	$468,367,000
Average Cost:	$ 52,041,000

Exhibit 4.9

1974 PROFORMA INCOME STATEMENT
(IN THOUSANDS)

<u>Revenues</u> $198,000

<u>Operating Expenses</u>:

Vessel Operating	29,419	
Fuel Surcharge*	15,520	
Stevedoring	13,587	
LTL Cargo Handling	8,267	
Terminal Costs	17,364	
Maintenance	7,910	
Sales & Administration	4,000	
Mayaguez Absorption	3,000	
Cargo Claims	___990	
		100,057
		97,943

<u>Charter and Leases</u>:

Facilities	5,582	
Vessels	18,901	
Equipment	18,457	
		_42,940
		55,003

<u>Royalties</u>:

Containerization	3,000	
NYSA Hourly	2,500	
NYSA Tonnage	_8,385	
		13,885
Depreciation Reserve		____375
Cash Available from Operations**		$40,743

----

* Equivalent to $8 per barrel.

** Available for capital expenditures, management payments, and additions to working capital.

86

Exhibit 4.10

1974 VESSEL EXPENSE DETAIL
(PER DAY)

Vessel Type	Roll-on/Roll-off	609	480	360	618
Bunker Use/Barrels Per Day	795	380	380	325	770
Crew/Number of Men		37	37	41	32
Labor Costs:					
Wages		$ 1,085	$ 1,085	$ 1,136	$ 1,050
Overtime		792	792	738	700
Fringe	------	1,518	1,518	1,572	1,450
Total	$4,358	3,395	3,395	3,446	3,200
Subsistence	150	140	140	154	150
Supplies	150	150	150	150	150
Fuel @ $11.00 Per Barrel	8,745	4,180	4,180	3,575	8,470
Insurance	1,524	582	582	388	1,920(1)
Maintenance	1,402	627	627	578	800
Miscellaneous	300	276	276	276	300
Total Daily Operating Cost	16,629	9,350	9,350	8,567	14,990
Charter Hire(2)	5,123	5,562	4,384	3,288	7,671
Total Daily Vessel Cost	$21,752	$14,912	$13,734	$11,855	$22,661

(1) 2% of $35,000,000.
(2) Charter hire is based on $20,000 per space over six years for the 360, 480, and 609 vessels. The roll-on/roll-off vessels are at actual charter rates. The 618 container vessel is based on a 25-year leveraged lease at a constant annual payment of 8% of the cost of $35,000,000. This calculation has been made for comparative purposes in the event the Commonwealth leases the vessels instead of purchasing them.

Exhibit 4.11

PROJECTED INCOME STATEMENT
(IN THOUSANDS)

	1974	1975	1976	1977	1978	1979
Revenues(1):						
1974 Base Revenue	$198,000	$198,000	$198,000	$198,000	$198,000	$198,000
Addition Volume-8%		15,840	32,947	51,423	71,377	92,927
Rate Increase due to Expense Increase		6,686	14,506	23,789	36,114	51,353
Total	198,000	220,526	245,453	273,212	305,491	342,280
Operating Expenses(1):						
Vessel-1974 Rate	29,419	29,419	29,419	29,419	32,642	35,865
Fuel Surcharge-74 Rate	15,520	15,520	15,520	15,520	17,768	20,017
All Other-1974 Rate	55,118	59,527	64,290	69,433	74,987	80,986
Total	100,057	104,466	109,229	114,372	125,397	136,868
Estimated Escalation		6,686	14,506	23,789	36,114	51,353
Total	100,057	111,152	123,735	138,161	161,511	188,221
Charters and Leases:						
Facilities	5,582	5,582	5,582	5,582	5,582	5,582
Vessels	18,901	18,901	18,901	18,901	18,901	18,901
Equipment	18,457	18,457	18,457	18,457	18,457	18,457
Total	42,940	42,940	42,940	42,940	42,940	42,940
Total Expenses	142,997	154,092	166,675	181,101	204,451	231,161
Depreciation	2,375	1,096	1,836	2,607	7,637	12,769
Royalties	13,885	13,885	13,885	13,885	13,885	13,885
	40,743	51,453	63,057	75,619	79,518	84,465

	1980	1981	1982	1983	1984	1985
Revenues(1):						
1974 Base Revenue	$198,000	$198,000	$198,000	$198,000	$198,000	$198,000
Addition Volume-8%	116,201	141,337	168,484	197,803	229,467	263,664
Rate Increase due to Expense Increase	66,948	88,499	114,417	141,401	174,129	208,821
Total	381,149	427,836	480,901	537,420	601,596	670,485
Operating Expenses(1):						
Vessel-1974 Rate	34,732	37,955	41,178	40,715	41,634	40,251
Fuel Surcharge-74 Rate	20,367	22,517	24,864	26,032	27,171	27,200
All Other-1974 Rate	87,465	94,463	102,020	110,181	118,996	128,515
Total	142,564	154,935	168,062	176,928	187,801	195,966
Estimated Escalation	66,948	88,499	114,417	141,401	174,129	208,821
Total	209,512	243,434	292,479	318,329	361,930	404,787
Charters and Leases:						
Facilities	5,582	5,582	5,582	5,582	5,582	5,582
Vessels	12,256	5,610	5,610	5,610	5,610	5,610
Equipment	10,879	3,300	3,300	3,300	3,300	3,300
Total	28,717	14,492	14,492	14,492	14,492	14,492
Total Expenses	238,229	257,926	296,971	332,821	376,422	419,279
Depreciation	19,663	25,239	39,183	42,546	49,130	54,459
Royalties	13,885	13,885	13,885	13,885	13,885	13,885
Cash Available from Operations(2)	109,372	130,786	138,862	147,952	162,159	182,862

(1) Revenues: Additional revenue due to growth in physical volume of the traffic at 8% per year has been included at the 1974 rate level. Rate increases equal to estimated variable cost increases have been included. This is about 3 1/2% per year.

Expenses: Operating expenses are shown at 1974 cost levels adjusted for expected volume increases and the vessels deployed in the service. In addition, escalation in variable costs have been estimated at 8% per year based on 80% of total operating expenses.

(2) Available for capital expenditures, management payments and additions to working capital.

Exhibit 4.12

CASH FLOW STATEMENT (IN THOUSANDS)

Year	Cash Available from Operations(1)	Capital Expenditures				Net Available (Cumulative)
		Vessels	Equipment	Facilities	Total	
Initial Capital					$ 60,000	$(60,000)
1974-76 Months	$ 20,371	$	$	7,500	7,500	(47,129)
1975	51,453		6,090	2,250	8,340	(4,016)
1976	63,057		6,395	2,000	8,395	50,646
1977	75,619		6,716	2,000	8,716	117,549
1978	79,518	41,685	25,205	8,500	75,390	121,677
1979	84,465	44,187	26,462	5,500	76,149	129,993
1980	109,372	46,838	44,536	2,000	93,374	145,991
1981	130,786	49,648	29,174	3,500	82,322	194,455
1982	138,862	52,627	30,636	5,000	88,263	245,054
1983	147,952	111,570	55,335	5,000	171,905	221,101
1984	162,159	59,132	33,778	5,000	97,910	285,350
1985	182,862	62,680	25,543	5,000	93,223	374,989
	$1,246,476	$468,367	$289,870	$53,250	$871,487	

(1) After Allocations to depreciation reserve. Available for capital expenditures, management payments and additions to working capital.

Chapter 5

AMERICAN PRESIDENT LINES, LTD.

In March 1979, the management of American President
Lines (APL) was completing a determination of the
characteristics of new containerships to be built.
Within several weeks, they would be concluding
contracts with a shipyard for the construction of
these ships. Although the main parameters of these
fully cellular vessels had been set, a final analysis
was being made to determine the exact power plant and
the degree to which 45-foot containers (8' wide and 9
1/2' high) would be used on the vessels.

BACKGROUND

American President Lines, Ltd., is a fully integrated
intermodal transportation company. One of the oldest
U.S.-flag carriers, dating back to 1848, APL's modern
fleet is concentrated in the Pacific Basin, where its
marketing and operations efforts are primarily
directed toward the containerized movement of cargo
by sea and land (see Exhibit 5.1). The largest
single U.S.-flag trans-Pacific container shipping
line, the company serves the growing Pacific Basin
markets with routes from the U.S. West Coast as far
as the Arabian Gulf, and intermodal activities
spanning North American to the Atlantic Seaboard.

In the mid-1973, APL became a wholly owned
subsidiary of Natomas Company, a San Francisco-based
energy, transportation, and real estate enterprise.
Under its direction, APL has developed into one of
the financially strongest shipping lines in the
American trades. APL's net income has more than

————————————————

Some of the information is this case study has been
disguised.

American President Lines, Ltd.

tripled from $13,105,000 in 1976 to $46,195,000 in 1978. (See Exhibits 5.2 and 5.3.) Yet the basic fleet of 17 containerships and 5 break-bulk cargo vessels has remained the same.

FLEET REPLACEMENT

All existing APL vessels had been built with construction-differential subsidy (CDS) and were run with the aid of operating-differential subsidy (ODS). One of the terms of the ODS contracts was to replace vessels at the end of their statutory life of 25 years. APL was required to enter into contracts for a minimum of two new vessels by December 31, 1978. The U.S. Maritime Administration (MarAd), who ran the subsidy program, granted APL a ninety-day extension. If APL received the maximum amount of CDS, 50% of the total shipyard price, the cost to APL of the three new vessels, would be half the total cost of approximately $272 million.

The new containerships were classed as C-9 vessels by MarAd, signifying that they were between 800 and 899 feet in length. With a carrying capacity of the equivalent of 2500 twenty-foot equivalent units (TEU), these vessels would be the largest containerships built in the U.S.; each ship would carry up to 35% more cargo than APL's next largest vessel. (See Exhibit 5.4.)

REFRIGERATED CONTAINERS

The C-9 vessels were designed with flexibility in mind. Of the 2500 TEU container capacity, nearly one-third or 400 forty-foot equivalent units (FEU) would be outfitted with refrigerated container receptacles. (See Exhibit 5.5 for vessel particulars.) In 1979, each of the company's containerships in service could carry between 150 and 175 forty-foot refrigerated containers. APL's three C-8 class vessels were being modified to increase that capacity to 250-300 refrigerated containers per vessel. Of course, any container slot equipped for a refrigerated container could also accept a non-refrigerated container. Similarly, refrigerated containers could also be used as a normal non-refrigerated container, if desired.

In 1978, APL began an equipment expansion program to establish the largest refrigerated cargo system of any single carrier in the Pacific Ocean.

APL officials noted that this was one of the company's top priorities, and this aim would be attained in 1982 when the C-9's entered APL service.

Of the 400 FEU refrigerated-container capacity on the C-9 vessels, 136 forty-foot units would be stored below deck, while 264 others would be stored above deck. These containers included the latest solid state circuitry and large compressors to ensure a constant temperature, within plus or minus one degree Fahrenheit. The compressor and the container's insulation can even maintain a constant minus 15 degrees Fahrenheit when the outside temperature is as hot as 120 degrees Fahrenheit, which occurs in areas APL serves, such as the Arabian Gulf and Southeast Asia.

Most of the goods shipped in refrigerated containers were U.S. agricultural products bound for Asian markets. The degree to which this trade was increasing could be found by examining trans-Pacific export statistics. U.S. sales alone were expected to increase from $8.5 billion in 1976 to nearly $17 billion by the end of fiscal 1981. Even with APL's investments to expand its refrigerated cargo capacity, including the new C-9 vessels, APL still would not be able to handle all its orders during the peak citrus season.

VESSEL DESIGN FLEXIBILITY

As far back as 1976, APL was looking at various vessel design options. The design for the C-9 class vessels included a structure that could be modified with the minimum of lost volume, to enable the carriage of non-standard-length 45-foot containers. There was a good deal of flexibility built into the vessel design in that all the transverse bulkheads could be moved to allow 45-foot containers to be stored below deck. Storage of 45-foot containers above deck would also be possible, since 44 feet were allocated to each row of containers. This would allow 45-footers to be stacked in alternate rows alongside 40-footers with virtually no loss of space. Any of APL's current vessels could accommodate 45-foot containers above deck.

Over-the-road limits in the U.S. trucking industry allow 45-foot units. Since the U.S. domestic market favors volume rather than weight, 45-foot trailers are more appealing than smaller containers.

American President Lines, Ltd.

Although there were no 45-foot marine containers or chassis in use in 1979, APL was considering their development, because of their 27% greater volume over the industry-standard containers (40' x 8' x 8 1/2'). APL owned or leased long-term nearly 36,000 containers and truck chassis. (See Exhibit 5.6.) APL also used varying numbers of containers and chassis (approximately 4,000 units) under short-term arrangements. (The cubic capacity and new cost of each size container are shown in Exhibit 5.7. The costs of various sizes of chassis are also included.)

If APL should elect to introduce the industry's first 45-foot containers, there was a question of how they should be used. A container passing through the APL system was called a "CFS container" or a "CY container". A CFS container passed through container freight stations where stuffing and stripping services were provided. At the origin of the trip, the customer's shipment would go to an APL container freight station (CFS) where it would be loaded with shipments of many other customers into an APL container. At the destination of the trip, each customer shipment would be unloaded at another APL CFS. Customer shipments would move to and from the CFS via a pickup and delivery service which might, or might not, be in an APL container. While a CFS was typically located at an APL waterfront terminal, in the case of APL's U.S. East Coast service, the CFS was located at an eastern city that was the terminus of the transcontinental railroad service.

The CY container moved through APL container yards in a door-to-door service. Once the customer loaded the APL container at his "door", it passed through the APL container yards without being opened, until it arrived at the "door" at its destination. A customer would get three days of "free time" in addition to the day of arrival before he would have to pay demurrage on the container. An APL container yard and container freight station were typically located together at the same location.

The 45-foot containers, when used in place of 40-foot containers aboard ship, would speed the loading and unloading of vessels because the same amount of cargo could be carried by a fewer number of containers. The 45-foot units were especially well-suited to the carriage of high-volume LCL (less-than-container-load) cargo out of the Far East. APL's Eastbound cargo was consumer-oriented and typically included electronic equipment, toys, garments, shoes, furniture, machinery, and plastic goods. APL transported nearly half of this cargo from U.S. West

Coast ports by land to the East Coast. Eastbound cargo was generally higher-valued and brought higher shipping revenues than did Westbound cargo.

U.S. Westbound exports included much of the raw materials used for Asian exports. APL's Westbound cargo typically included cotton, resins, leather, machinery, lumber, military cargo, and refrigerated agricultural and meat products.

From the standpoint of competition, APL may well gain a competitive advantage on its rivals. The extra cubic capacity that the 45-footers offered over standard 40-foot boxes would undoubtedly prove popular with shippers of the high-volume cargoes out of the Far East.

Shippers could stuff more cargo in each box, thereby reducing the total number of containers to be shipped. This would amount to savings in drayage costs for shippers that must truck the containers to the terminal for loading. APL felt that, because the 45-foot boxes would be popular and also because of their increased capacity, they would stand to gain a larger share of the market.

APL has concentrated much of its resources in the "Big Four" Asian areas of Hong Kong, Japan, Taiwan, and South Korea. With the help of government-supported export programs, these countries had experienced tremendous growth in the past decade. In 1979, they represented 85% of APL's demand.

Taiwan, Korea, the Philippines, and Singapore presented no problems to the use of 45-foot containers. Japan, on the other hand, had strict government regulations forbidding the use of 45-foot equipment. Hong Kong had no regulatory restrictions, but many of its roads were too narrow to accommodate their use. In response to this problem, APL could limit the use of 45-foot containers to CFS's, where they would typically not have to leave APL waterfront terminals.

Though the new units were non-standard, both in length and in height (9' 6 1/2" high), APL had been careful to minimize handling problems. By setting the lifting points some 2' 6" from each end, the 45-foot box could be handled like a 40-foot box with a normal 40-foot spreader.

Terminal Problems
If APL should go ahead with the production of 45-foot containers, they would also need to provide 45-foot chassis for use in the terminals. Terminal operators had identified a number of potential problems. In particular, they pointed out that 45-foot containers

would complicate unloading because the containers would have to be coordinated with 45-foot chassis. They also said that since stacking areas were very much tied to 20-foot/40-foot modules, the extra five feet of space required could well make them difficult to accommodate. Even if the units were left on chassis, the extra five feet could prove to be a problem.

Rail Transportation

Because cargo not only has to be transported from port to port but also to and from inland cities, shipping involves more than just ocean-going vessels. APL has developed a system that allows shippers to deal solely with APL instead of having to deal individually with trucking companies, railroads, and airlines. By establishing a transcontinental land transportation system from U.S. West Coast ports to U.S. East Coast population centers, APL had greatly reduced its Asia-to-New York cargo transit time over that of the all-water route.

On average, APL's service provided faster transit by approximately seven days compared to the all-water competition, and faster service by approximately three to four days compared to water-land competition between Asia and North American East Coast markets. APL was able to cut transit time because it leased its own trains and operated its own inland terminals, documentation handling, and management systems.

In 1977, APL shipped approximately 33,000 containers to and from inland U.S. points. This number was expected to increase to 60,000 by 1981 and even further in 1982, when new ship capacity was added.

APL feels most of the advantages to be derived from the use of 45-foot containers will be attained during the transcontinental rail portion of the container's trip. The 45-foot containers were designed to fit on existing 89' 4" standard intermodal railcars, either in the container on flat car (COFC) mode or the trailer on flat car (TOFC) mode. This would permit one 40-foot container and one 45-foot container to ride together, instead of two 40-footers. In effect, five feet of additional container would be riding the rails for free under the existing rail tariffs. Additionally, a 45-foot program could substantially reduce APL's equipment repositioning costs by reducing the number of empty containers shipped cross-country. Each year, the railroads ship empty domestic piggyback or "pig" trailers Eastbound from Los Angeles; the units were over-the-road trailers owned by the railroad. Once these pigs arrived fully loaded on the West Coast, they would be unloaded and reloaded into an APL container before being placed aboard the ship. Some new rail equipment was being designed to accommodate 100% forty-five-foot units, while others were being designed for 50% forty-five-footers initially, with conversion to 100% forty-five-footers possible in the future.

Since handling and transportation costs were largely determined on a unit basis rather than by the size of the containers, the larger boxes were expected to provide significant savings and help hold the line on rapidly rising costs. It was predicted that in 1982, when the C-9's were delivered, it would take a fleet of roughly 1100 forty-five-footers to serve fully the major CFS's in Boston and New York via transcontinental rail service.

The 45-footers would be constructed of aluminum with steel end-frames and were designed for a payload of 64,300 lbs. However, typical over-the-road limits were only 50,000 lbs. Of course, if the container was put on a railroad flat car or did not go outside the container terminal, then the over-the-road limit was irrelevant. Nor would the over-the-road limits be a problem when the containers were loaded with high-volume/low-density Asian cargoes bound for U.S. markets. A problem could arise however, in the over-the-road portion of Westbound movements of dense U.S. raw materials en route to U.S. West Coast terminals for shipment. In short, Eastbound cargo movements tended to cube out while Westbound cargo movements tended to weight out.

Forecasts for box shipping looked good. The major container shipping trades were expected to grow at an average annual rate of 5% over the next five years. The strongest growth would be in the North American/Asia trades, precisely APL's interest, because of Asia's rapid industrial growth. Nearly 70% of Asia's containerized imports were industrial supplies and materials. Growth for this trade was expected to increase by an average of 6.5% annually between 1980 and 1986.

APL'S INTEREST IN THE DIESEL

APL's interest in the diesel engine as a potential prime mover for its new C-9 class vessels stemmed from the superiority of the diesel's fuel consumption. APL would be the first U.S.-flag operator to use a domestically built, low-speed diesel engine. It went without saying that being the "first" in anything was a risky proposition. With only thirty days to determine the type of power plant to be placed in the ships, APL had to decide whether these risks were outweighed by the lure of potential savings.

The propulsion-plant design selected for the new vessels was originally to be selected from a group of three alternatives. The first of these three was a conventional single-screw steam turbine. All of APL's other 22 vessels were steam-powered; therefore, the steam turbine plant would be considered the base case to which the other two would be compared. The other two alternatives were both low-speed marine diesel engines. One of these would use a single engine turning a single screw, and the other would use twin diesels turning twin screws.

The conventional steam turbine would be the least risky alternative for APL because steam turbine technology had already reached an advanced stage in the United States. The U.S. had always stressed steam propulsion because higher horsepowers were attainable with steam than with diesel. In 1979, 90% of the U.S. fleet was steam-powered, in contrast to the world fleet, 80% of which was powered by diesel engines.

The twin-screw diesel alternative posed the problems of a loss in hull efficiency and of adding manning requirements. The losses incurred owing to these two weaknesses outweighed any potential gains to such an extent that APL's engineering staff concentrated their efforts on the comparison of the single-screw diesel and steam turbine alternatives.

Space requirements for the single-screw diesel and steam plants were virtually the same and, therefore, had no impact on the decision. From a ship handling standpoint, the diesel was a superior installation to the steam turbine. Response times for bridge instructions are about equal for both installations; the advantage of the diesel comes in its astern mode. The diesel is capable of developing 100% power in reverse, while the steam turbine can only develop about 60%.

The quality of marine bunkers was certain to deteriorate in the future. This would have an impact on both steam and diesel propulsion units, but particularly on diesel plants. APL, being a West Coast operator, should not be seriously affected by degrading oil quality because of the multitude of straight-run West Coast refineries, resulting in a reasonable abundance of non-cracked fuel. The C-9's had enough fuel capacity to load for a round trip. Thus, deteriorating fuels did not appear significant in APL's case, but they could present problems for other diesel operators.

In their efforts to determine the type of plant to be used, APL classified the key considerations into two groups. The first group consisted of cost factors relating to the operation of a diesel plant. Such factors were the capital cost differential, fuel and lubricating oil consumption, and engine maintenance.

The second group consisted of training and manning requirements for a diesel vessel as well as overall engine reliability. Although somewhat qualitative in nature, these factors were equally important in arriving at a decision.

CAPITAL COST DIFFERENTIAL

Obtaining accurate figures regarding the capital-cost differential of the steam and diesel alternatives was difficult because of the uniqueness of the proposal. The proposed type of large, low-speed diesel had never been manufactured by a U.S. licensee.

In an effort to develop low-speed diesel components in the U.S. fleet, the U.S. Maritime Administration would permit a portion of the diesel engine to be manufactured abroad and assembled in U.S. shipyards. This policy would be acceptable for the first several low-speed, diesel-propelled ships but would not be allowed indefinitely.

Since APL would be the first U.S.-flag operator of a domestically built low-speed diesel, they would be allowed to take advantage of having many of the engine parts shipped to the U.S. for assembly by the U.S. licensee. APL hoped the engine would be 50-60% of Swiss manufacture. Based on the APL study, it was estimated that foreign construction of the diesel plant would cost approximately half of the domestic construction cost.

However, the question arose as to whether the Maritime Administration would subsidize the full cost of the engine or only the cost of those parts in the engine which were manufactured domestically. With a subsidy rate of 0.4998 and the full cost of the engine subsidized, the diesel contract change cost would amount to $4,843,153, as shown in Exhibit 5.8. MarAd would make its decision on the subsidy rate and

American President Lines, Ltd.

the percentage of the diesel to be subsidized before
APL would sign construction contracts. It might seem
that obtaining CDS on foreign parts was "excess"
subsidy. However, even with maximum CDS, the net
cost to APL of the diesel engine with subsidized
Swiss parts was higher than the lower prices
available in Japan to its foreign-flag competitors.

FUEL AND LUBRICATING OIL CONSUMPTION

The cost of fueling the slow-speed diesel, with its
specific fuel consumption of 0.346 lb/BHP-hr (see
Exhibit 5.9), was significantly lower than that of
the steam plant. It was this superiority in the
specific fuel consumption (SFC) of the diesel that
generated large annual savings in fuel costs.
Exhibit 5.10 shows the estimated annual fuel
operating costs associated with the diesel and steam
alternatives.
Lubricating oil consumption, on the other hand,
was significantly greater for a diesel engine than
for a steam turbine. Lubricating oil requirements
for a steam plant are for machinery bearings and
gearing. The diesel, in addition to having the
aforesaid lube oil requirements, needs to supply oil
to the engine cylinder walls to reduce piston-ring
and cylinder-wall wear. Exhibit 5.9 shows that the
specific fuel consumption for cylinder oil is 0.70
g/BHP-hr, while the specific fuel consumption of
crankcase oil is 0.05 g/BHP-hr.
Diesel cylinder oil was nearly one and one-half
times as expensive as the diesel crankcase oil.
Exhibit 5.11 shows calculations for estimating the
annual lube oil cost of diesel plant operation.

MAINTENANCE

Upon comparing the maintainability of the steam
turbine alternative and the diesel alternative,
several distinct differences arose, the most
significant difference being that the diesel
alternative required a higher level of skilled
attention at a higher cost than the steam turbine.
This was offset somewhat by the advantage of the
diesel's unmanned engine room, enabling the engine
crew to perform engine maintenance during their watch
schedule.
The diesel has the added advantage of having
replaceable parts, which permits wear-prone moving

parts to be removed and replaced by new parts while the old parts are refurbished. Thus, engine downtime is considerably less for a diesel engine than for a steam turbine. Exhibit 5.12 shows typical downtimes for specific engine repairs for steam and diesel propulsion plants.

Sulzer Diesel Engine Manufacturing Company has guaranteed APL a zero maintenance and repair cost for the first three years of engine operation. Thereafter, a $6.00/BHP-year maintenance and repair (M&R) cost was expected (in 1980$). Annual inflation of 8% advances this cost to $8.82 for each of the engines' 43,200 BHP. 1982 M&R costs for diesel plant auxiliaries were estimated at $174,960. The steam plant M&R cost estimate was based on a two-year average of APL's Seamaster class vessels and amounted to $152,798.

OTHER COST FACTORS

Due to a four-month extended delivery period associated with the installation of the diesel plant, a one-time penalty of $171,383 (1982$) in operating costs would be assessed. This represented the loss in profit due to the delivery delay.

Another factor in assessing the costs associated with the diesel alternative was the increase in insurance payments due to the increased capital cost of the ship. There would be a 1980 insurance increase of $4,800 per million dollars of price differential.

Exhibit 5.13 considers the relevant economic cost factors associated with the steam and diesel alternatives, and forecasts the resulting cash flows over a 25-year period. The 25-year period was consistent with the expected economic life of the ship and assumed no residual value at the end of the period.

Possible manning/wage savings existed with the diesel alternative. Since no agreements with the cognizant maritime unions had been reached pertaining to a decrease in the number of crew members on the diesel vessel, it was assumed there would be no difference in manning levels. However, if it was possible to reduce manning on the diesel vessel, significant savings would be attained. APL hoped to outfit the diesel vessel with 33 crew members as opposed to 38 or 40 on the steam ship (see Exhibit 5.14). If MarAd subsidized 30 of these crew members at the existing 66% level, annual savings of $114,381 would be reached. If all 33 were subsidized, the savings will be even greater, amounting to $212,337 below that of a steam vessel (see Exhibit 5.15).

TRAINING AND MANNING

Important problems to be avoided were those that would occur subsequent to the delivery of the ship. The relative scarcity of trained, experienced U.S. marine diesel engineers posed an operational risk to American President Lines. In 1979, there was a sufficient number of adept diesel engineers to satisfy fleet requirements because the number of diesel-propelled vessels was so small. However, this supply might not be satisfactory when the number of diesel ships in the U.S. fleet grew in the future.

APL expected to incur a front-end training cost of $156,000 for each of the three ships. The $156,000 represented a one-time cost of $66,000, plus a $30,000 annual training cost for each of the first three years of operations. Those ratings to be trained included two Chief Engineers, two First Assistant Engineers, and two Second Assistant Engineers. APL operating personnel had expressed confidence that their anticipated recruiting and training programs, coupled with high-quality shipboard and shoreside supervision, would minimize the operational risks associated with the diesel alternative.

In 1979, diesel engineers were paid a 10% premium over steam engineers. However, APL looked towards the elimination of this premium through informal conversations with union leaders.

APL could attain a significant savings in maintenance and repair work done onboard the diesel ship as opposed to the steam ship. The engineering crew would accomplish a greater portion of engine maintenance while steaming because of the diesel's advantage of an unmanned engine room. All ratings were thus on day work. Also, the time span of various jobs from engine stop to start is enough so that the engineering crew can accomplish the work in scheduled port time. Thus, APL can have most of the mandatory engine maintenance work done at sea by the crew, whose wages were subsidized, as opposed to having the work done onshore where the wages were not subsidized. See Exhibit 5.16 for the cost per man-hour of an onboard rating as compared to shipyard M&R billing rates.

SUMMARY

Thus, with only 30 days left, APL had to decide on the type of propulsion unit to be placed in the new C-9 vessels. The decision pertaining to the use of 45-foot containers was not as immediately crucial, but like the diesel alternative, would represent a bold step for U.S.-flag shipping.

American President Lines, Ltd.

Exhibit 5.1

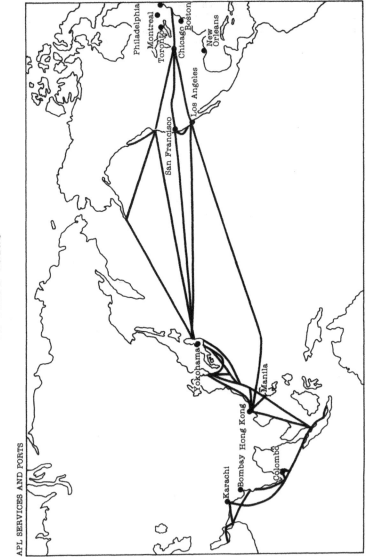

APL TRADE AREAS

APL SERVICES AND PORTS

Exhibit 5.2

FIVE-YEAR SUMMARY OF OPERATIONS
AND FINANCIAL REVIEW
(IN THOUSANDS)

	1978	1977	1976	1975	1974
Operating Revenues	$407,564	352,538	287,144	202,769	234,565
Operating Expenses	$303,478	288,451	249,630	177,981	198,429
Operating Profit	$104,086	64,087	37,514	24,788	36,136
% of Revenues	25%	18%	13%	12%	15%
Operating Differential Subsidy	$ 26,561	29,257	36,828	30,933	29,981
Gain (Loss) on Disposition of Ships	$ (210)	(2,633)	4,450	0	3,375
Profit Before Depreciation, Interest and Administrative Expenses	$130,437	90,711	78,792	55,721	69,492
Admin. & General	$ 51,397	38;337	32,448	30,610	25,308
Depreciation & Amortization	$ 20,765	20,948	20,066	18,426	17,980
Interest Expense	$ 9,080	9,632	10,423	10,780	11,543
Income Before Income Taxes	$ 49,195	21,794	15,855	(4,095)	14,661
Provision for Income Taxes	$ 3,000	3,418	2,750	(759)	4,561
Net Income (Loss)	$ 46,195	18,376	13,105	(3,336)	10,100

American President Lines, Ltd.

Exhibit 5.3

FIVE-YEAR SUMMARY OF CORPORATE CHARACTERISTICS

SELECTED OPERATING DATA (In Thousands)

	1978	1977	1976	1975	1974
Revenue Tons	5,267	4,947	4,125	3,433	3,171
Capital Expenditures	$19,358	16,741	15,577	18,868	28,786
Cash Flow From Operations	$70,223	41,284	33,548	15,345	27,846

FINANCIAL POSITION AT YEAR END (In Thousands)

Cash & Temporary					
Investments	$66,180	56,965	25,324	20,009	21,823
Current Liabilities	$73,922	62,591	48,963	50,808	43,656
Working Capital	$(10,398)	12,796	6,436	(15,012)	57
Property & Equipment	$205,700	209,219	216,606	230,888	233,069
Long Term Debt	$120,336	140,166	142,988	149,734	158,559
Shareholders' Equity	$165,536	133,076	121,591	108,672	112,179
Total Assets	$366,274	340,839	320,238	311,706	321,862

STATISTICS AND KEY RATIOS

Employees	2,328	2,012	2,121	2,090	2,337
Current Ratio	0.9	1.2	1.1	0.7	1.0
Debt Equity Ratio	0.68	0.97	1.12	1.31	1.34
Return On Average					
Shareholders' Equity	31%	14%	11%	(3%)	9%
Return On Average Assets	13%	6%	4%	(1%)	3%
Return On Revenues	11%	5%	5%	(2%)	4%
Number Of Active Ships					
Container	15	15	17	18	18
Breakbulk	5	5	5	5	5

106

Exhibit 5.4

VESSELS IN OPERATION

FULLY CONTAINERIZED	VESSELS	YEAR CONSTRUCTED	YEAR CONVERTED	DESIGN CONTAINER CAPACITY (IN TEUs)
C-8s*	PRESIDENT GRANT	1971	1978	1856
	PRESIDENT HOOVER	1971	1978	1856
	PRESIDENT TYLER	1971	1978	1856
Pacesetters	PRESIDENT JEFFERSON	1973		1504
	PRESIDENT JOHNSON	1973		1504
	PRESIDENT MADISON	1973		1504
	PRESIDENT PIERCE	1973		1504
Seamasters	PRESIDENT FILLMORE	1968	1972	1094
	PRESIDENT McKINLEY	1968	1972	1094
	PRESIDENT TAFT	1967	1972	1094
	PRESIDENT VAN BUREN	1967	1972	1094
C-6s**	PRESIDENT TRUMAN	1962	1971	1124
	PRESIDENT EISENHOWER	1962	1972	1108
	PRESIDENT ROOSEVELT	1961	1971	1108
Master Mariner	PRESIDENT POLK	1965	1972	839
BREAKBULK/CONTAINER				
C-5s**	PRESIDENT ADAMS	1968		332
	PRESIDENT CLEVELAND	1969		332
	PRESIDENT JACKSON	1968		332
	PRESIDENT TAYLOR	1969		332
	PRESIDENT WILSON	1969		332

Note: Three new C-9 containerships will be delivered in 1982. The design capacity of each will be 2500 twenty-foot equivalent units (TEUs).

*The C-8's were converted barge-carriers of the LASH design, formerly owned by Pacific Far East Lines.

**In 1973, APL acquired American Main Lines (AML). The C-6s (which originally were C-4s that were jumbo-ized and containerized) and the C-5s were part of the AML fleet.

American President Lines, Ltd.

Exhibit 5.5

VESSEL PARTICULARS

Name: PRESIDENT LINCOLN   Class: C9
             ASI Hull 2329   Service: Containership

             PRESIDENT WASHINGTON
             ASI Hull 2330

             PRESIDENT MONROE
             ASI Hull 2331

Type: C9-M-132b

Builder: Avondale Shipyards, Inc., Avondale, LA.
          Expected Delivery Dates: 2329 - May 1982
                           2330 - August 1982
                           2331 - November 1982

Gross Tonnage: 40490 (Approx.)   Net Tonnage: 29000 (Approx.)

ABS Classification: +Al E Container Carrier +AMS +ACCU

	English	Metric
Length, Overall	860' - 0"	262.13m
Length, Between Perpendiculars	810' - 0"	246.89m
Beam, Molded	105' - 9"	32.23m
Depth, molded to Upper Deck at side	66' - 0"	20.12m
Draft, full load	35' - 0"	10.67m
Displacement, full load	49500 L.T.	50286mt
Lightship Weight (approx.)	19157 L.T.	19461mt
Permanent ballast	1889 L.T.	1919mt
Deadweight, excluding ballast (approximate)	30343 L.T.	30825mt
Height, Baseline to Top of Foremast	170' - 0"	51.83m
Height, Baseline to Top of Range Light	152' - 0"	46.33m
Max. Service Speed at Full Load Draft	23.9 Knots	
Cruising Range - at Max. Draft & SHP	22020 Miles	40810km
- at Avg. Draft & Speed	29700 Miles	55040km

Passengers   1 - Owner
                      2 - Riding technical

Cargo Oil Capacity   None
Built-In Reefer Capacity   None
Reefer Container Receptacles 264 on deck
                         136 in Hold 4 (Total 400)
Container capacity   1250 FEU

Exhibit 5.6

FLEET SUMMARY

Equipment Type	Total
20' Dry Containers	6,559
40' Dry Containers	14,727
20' Reefer Containers	144
40' Reefer Containers	3,451
20' Flatrack Containers	321
40' Flatrack Containers	79
40' Rag Top Containers	73
20' Bulk Containers	50
40' Ventilated Containers	2
20' Garment Containers	88
40' Garment Containers	170
SUB-TOTAL:	25,664
20' Chassis	1,902
40' Chassis	7,920
SUB-TOTAL:	9,822
TOTAL FLEET:	35,486
Aggregate Fleet Capacity	31,720 FEU

American President Lines, Ltd.

Exhibit 5.7

CONTAINER CHARACTERISTICS

	Dry20' Steel	Dry 40' 8'-6"	Dry 40' 9'-6 1/2"	Reefer 40'	Dry 45' 9'-6 1/2"
TARE WT. (lbs.)	5,400	6,570	7,080	10,670	8,160
MAX GROSS (lbs.)	44,800	67,200	67,200	67,200	72,800
PAYLOAD (lbs.)	39,400	60,630	60,120	56,530	64,640
CUBIC CAPACITY (cubic feet)	1,160	2,398	2,715	2,035	3,035
NEW COST* ($)	2,500	6,400	6,600	21,000	8,200

CHASSIS COST*

	Domestic	Asia
40-Foot	$6,200 A	$9,400 C
45-Foot	$7,182 B	$9,816 D

Notes: A = Theurer, f.o.b. NJ
        B = Fruehauf, f.o.b. Fresno
        C = Korea
        D = Taiwan

* Costs are estimated for delivery of equipment in 1982 to coincide with delivery of C-9's.

Exhibit 5.8

INCREMENTAL CAPITAL COST TO APL OF USING
DIESEL VS. STEAM PROPULSION PLANT

If Diesel Plant is Not Subsidized
(But Steam Plant is Subsidized)

Total Cost (Unsubsidized Diesel Plant)	$30,731,809
Total Cost (Subsidized Steam Plant)	- $10,528,898
Incremental Capital Cost	$20,202,911

If 100% of Diesel Plant is Subsidized at 49.98% Rate

Subsidized Diesel Cost ($30,731,809 x .5002)	$15,372,051
Subsidized Steam Cost	- $10,528,898
Incremental Capital Cost	$ 4,843,153

American President Lines, Ltd.

Exhibit 5.9

POWER PLANT OPERATING PROFILE AND
FUEL RELATED FACTORS

		Steam Plant	**Diesel Single Screw**
HP at Sea		36,000 HP	36,000 HP
HP Maneuvering		9,000 HP	9,000 HP
Time at Sea: Eastbound Westbound		131 days 131 days	131 days 131 days
Time Maneuvering		15 days	15 days
Time in Port		73 days	73 days
SFC at Sea	Eastbound Westbound	.457 lb/HP-hr .527 lb/HP-hr	.346 lb/HP-hr
SFC Maneuvering		.750 lb/HP-hr	.373 lb/HP-hr
Electrical Load at Sea: Eastbound Westbound		1,596 KW 5,186 KW	1,596 KW 5,186 hr
Electrical Load Maneuvering		4.125 KW	4.125 KW
Electrical Load in Port		3,191 KW	3,191 KW
Turbo-Generator SFC		1.50 lb/HP-hr	N/A
Waste Heat Boiler Diesel Generator SFC		N/A N/A	1,000 KW .480 lb/KW-Hr

CONSUMED PETROLEUM PRODUCT COSTS

Main Plant-Fuel Oil Costs
    1980 $130/ton (steam)   10% annual escalation
                 $134/ton (diesel)

Main Plant #2
Marine Diesel Oil Costs
    1980 $155 (assumes 4:1 mix)   10% annual escalation
Diesel Cylinder Oil Costs $4.24/gal. with sfc of .70 g/BHP-hr (1980)
Diesel Crankcase Oil Costs $2.83/gal. with sfc of .05 g/BHP-hr
Diesel Generator Crankcase Oil Costs $3.22/gal. with sfc of .005 lb/KW-hr

Exhibit 5.10

ANNUAL FUEL OPERATING COSTS

STEAM PLANT

1. At Sea:
   a. Eastbound:
   $$\frac{(131\ days)(.457\#/SHP/hr)(24\ hr/day)(36,000\ SHP)(130\$/LT)}{2,240\ \#/LT} = 3,001,902$$

   b. Westbound:
   $$\frac{(131)(527\ \#/SHP/hr)(24)(36,000)(130)}{2,240\ \#/LT} = 3,461,712$$

2. Maneuvering: $\dfrac{(15)(.75\ \#/SHP/hr)(24)(9,000)(130)}{2,240\ \#/LT} = 141,027$

3. Electrical $\dfrac{(73)(1.5\ \#/KW/hr)(24)(3.191)(130\ \$/LT)}{2,240\ \#/LT} = 486,685$
   Load in Port:

	Total FO Cost	7,091,326
	1982	8,580,505

DIESEL PLANT

1. At Sea:
   $$\frac{(262\ days)(.346\ \#/BHP/hr)(24\ hr/day)(36,000\ BHP)(134)}{2,240\ \#/LT} = 4,685,413$$

2. Maneuvering: $\dfrac{(15)(.373)(24)(9,000)(134)}{2,240\ \#/LT} = 72,295$

3. Electrical Load:

   a. At Sea Eastbound $\dfrac{(131)(.48)(24)(596)(155)}{2,240} = 62,238$

   b. At Sea Westbound $\dfrac{(131)(.48)(24)(4,186)(155)}{2,240} = 437,126$

   c. Maneuvering $\dfrac{(15)(.48)(24)(4,125)(155)}{2,240} = 49,323$

   d. In Port $\dfrac{(73)(.48)(24)(3,191)(151)}{2,240} = 185,689$

	Total FO Cost	5,492,084
	1982	6,545,423

American President Lines, Ltd.

Exhibit 5.11

ANNUAL LUBRICATING OIL OPERATING COSTS
BASE CASE

Steam Plant:

The total annual cost of lubricating oil for the steam plant has been estimated at $33,008 based on the escalation of lube oil costs at an eight percent level:

Total Cost 1982 . . . $38,500

Diesel Plant:

1. Cylinder Oil
   a. At Sea:

   $$\frac{(\$4.24/gal)(0.7g/BHP/HR)(36,000\ HP)(262\ days)(24HR/day)}{(7.4\#/gal)(454g/\#)}$$

   $= \quad \$199,982$

   b. Man: $\quad \dfrac{(4.24)(0.7)(9,000)(15)(24)}{(7.4)(454)}$ $\quad = \quad \$2,862$

2. Crankcase Oil
   a. At Sea: $\quad \dfrac{(2.83)(.05)(36,000)(252)(24)}{(7.4)(454)}$ $\quad = \quad \$9,534$

   b. Man: $\quad \dfrac{(2.83)(.05)(9,000)(15)(24)}{(7.4)(454)}$ $\quad = \quad \$\ 136$

3. DG Crankcase Oil
   a. At Sea Eastbound: $\quad \dfrac{(3.22)(.005)(596)(131)(24)}{(7.4)}$ $\quad = \quad \$4,077$

   b. At Sea Westbound $\qquad\qquad\qquad\qquad\qquad$ $\$28,634$

   c. Man $\qquad\qquad\qquad\qquad\qquad\qquad\qquad$ $\$3,231$

   d. Port $\qquad\qquad\qquad\qquad\qquad\qquad\qquad$ $\$12,163$

Main Engine Lube Oil 1980	$212,514
1982	$247,876
Diesel Generator Crankcase Oil 1980	$48,105
1982	$56,110
Total 1982 Lube Oil Cost	$303,986

Exhibit 5.12

DOWNTIME COMPARISONS

<u>Downtime for Specific Major Breakdowns On Steam-Powered Vessels</u>:

a.   Boiler burn down (approx.)   3 weeks

    Scavenger fire   6 days

b.   Open turbine engines in response to
    blade failure

    Open   2 days

    Effect Repair   2 days

    Close   2 days

    Later Permanent Repair   <u>4 days</u>

               TOTAL: 10 days

<u>Downtime For Specific Major Breakdowns On Diesel-Powered Vessels</u>:

a.   Rebuild 1/2 engine inluding new liners,
    pistons, bearings, etc.   5 days

American President Lines, Ltd.

Exhibit 5.13

FORECAST OF ANNUAL CASH FLOWS

Benefit		Diesel Single Screw
1	1982	1,504,194
2	1983	1,850,325
3	1984	2,043,123
4	1985	2,023,612
5	1986	2,225,973
6	1987	2,470,830
7	1988	2,742,621
8	1989	3,044,310
9	1990	3,379,184
10	1991	3,750,894
11	1992	4,050,966
12	1993	4,375,043
13	1994	4,725,047
14	1995	5,103,050
15	1996	5,511,294
16	1997	5,952,198
17	1998	6,428,374
18	1999	6,942,644
19	2000	7,498,055
20	2001	8,097,899
21	2002	8,745,732
22	2003	9,445,390
23	2004	10,201,021
24	2005	11,017,103
25	2006	11,898,571

Note: Calculations assume 8% annual escalation on lube oil, insurance, maintenance and repairs; and 10% annual escalation on fuel oil.

Exhibit 5.14

COMPARISON OF MANNING CHARACTERISTICS

	Diesel	Steam
Master	1	1
Chief Mate	1	1
2nd Mate	1	1
3rd Mate	2	2
Purser	1	1*
P.E.O.	1	1
Bosun	1	1
A.B.	6	6
O.S.	3	3
Chief Engineer	1	1
1st Engineer	1	1
2nd Engineer	1	1
3rd Engineer	2	2
Electrician	1	1
2nd Electrician		1*
Reefer	1	1
Jr. Engineer	3	4
Wiper		2*
Steward	1	1
Cook	1	1
2nd Cook	1	1*
Utility	1	2
Pantry	1	1
Waiter	1	1*
TOTAL:	33	38

----

* One unsubsidized rating.

American President Lines, Ltd.

Exhibit 5.15

ANNUAL SUBSIDY FOR STEAM SHIP

Manning	Annual Cost of Wages	Annual Subsidy For 33 Ratings	Annual Cost Net Subsidy	Subsidy As % of Cost
Total				
38	$2,273,681	$1,350,500	$923,181	
Subsidized				
33	$2,058,548	$1,350,500	$700,048	66%

Diesel

Proposed crew on the diesel vessel is 33, of which 30 are subsidized.
The same wages and subsidy as derived for steam were used for the diesel
vessel.

Manning	Annual Cost of Wages	Annual Subsidy For 30 Ratings	Annual Cost Net Subsidy	Subsidy As % of Cost
Total				
33	$2,090,718	$1,281,918	$808,800	
Subsidized				
30	$1,950,965	$1,281,918	$669,047	66%

DIESEL: Proposed crew of 33 of which 33 are subsidized

Manning	Annual Cost of Wages	Annual Subsidy For 30 Ratings	Annual Cost Net Subsidy	Subsidy As % of Cost
Total				
33	$2,090,718	$1,379,874	$710,844	66%

Exhibit 5.16

COMPARISON OF SHIPBOARD AND SHIPYARD
LABOR COSTS

The cost per man hour of an onboard rating as compared to shipyard
M&R billing rates are as follows:

	Before Subsidy*	Net Subsidy	Billing Rate
Chief Engineer	$52.41	$10.98	$23.00/24.00
1st Engineer	34.24	7.19	23.00/24.00
2nd Engineer	30.22	6.33	23.00/24.00
3rd Engineer	23.95	4.90	23.00/24.00
Electrician	12.23	2.57	23.00/24.00
Reefer	11.93	2.51	23.00/24.00
Jr. Engineer	10.83	2.27	23.00/24.00

*Wages, fringes, non-watch, earning allowance (no overtime)

Chapter 6

CAST CONTAINER LINE

The story of Cast Container Line* (Cast) was supposed
to be different. Its founder, Frank Narby, was
supposed to be quicker and smarter. For 14 years
Frank Narby, Eurocanadian Shipholdings Ltd. (ECS),
and its wholly-owned subsidiary, Cast, waged a war
for market share on the North Atlantic. But like so
many before him, Frank Narby and his maverick ECS
came to rest in Bankruptcy Court. Why?

In 1969, Narby established Cast to carry
containers and bulk in specialized dual-purpose ships
between Canada and Northern Europe. Cast was to be a
no-frills, non-conference operator with regular,
dependable service at rock-bottom prices. The idea
of combining a container-liner service with a bulk
service was not new, but it had never been so
effectively used.

Cast had the following advantages over other
North Atlantic operators:

1. The North Atlantic bulk trade was strong;
   with Cast's ships loaded with bulk, the
   containers could piggyback on deck or in
   holds at little extra cost.
2. Cast was no-frills, one-route (Montreal to
   Antwerp), and had a single box rate with
   volume discounts. Conference lines had up
   to 3,000 different tariffs and many routes,
   which created high administrative costs.
3. Cast operated as an intermodal carrier,
   owning trucking fleets on both sides of the
   Atlantic. Each stage of the operation was
   a separate profit center.

---

* Cast is not an acronym--Frank Narby's leg was in a
cast when he formed the company in 1969.

4. Cast could offer single intermodal (door-to-door) rates. Conferences in the U.S. international trade could not offer intermodal rates. Individual carriers could offer intermodal rates and had to register all rates with the Federal Maritime Commission (FMC).

5. Cast could pull cargo from within the U.S., using its own trucking firm, without any FMC regulation.

6. Cast did not own any vessels; all were time chartered.

7. Cast marketed directly to shippers, bypassing freight forwarders.

Cast Container Line, Cast trucking operations, and other supporting businesses were all subsidiaries of Eurocanadian Shipholdings Ltd. (ECS). ECS was incorporated in Bermuda and headquartered in Fribourg, Switzerland. Frank Narby's Dolphin Investments, also incorporated in Bermuda, owned 70% of ECS. Helix Investments, a Canadian corporation, owned the rest.

ECS OWNERS

Frank Narby began his shipping career with a Greek company in Alexandria. After the fall of King Farouk in 1952, he moved to Canada. There he worked for Federal Commerce and Navigation (FCN), owned by another Egyptian family, the Pathys. He spent 15 years with FCN. When his ambitions were blocked by members of the Pathys family, he quit. For the next two years he worked on setting up Cast and finding backers.

Ben Webster, "...one of Canada's leading Venture Capitalists" and scion of Canada's wealthy Webster family, whose original money was made in coal, became Narby's backer. Webster's Helix Investments put up $485,000 in initial equity.

THE BEGINNING

1970
Cast's first year in the business, 1970, produced $17 million in contracts. The majority of these were from large corporations such as Ford and Dupont, and from the carrying of asbestos. Cast carried 14,000 TEU.

1975

By 1975, Cast was carrying 38,000 TEU and had contracts worth nearly $90 million. Profits were around $10 million. By this time, ECS had also moved into the pure bulk field by time chartering bulkers and putting them on the spot market.

With business booming, Frank Narby decided it was time for him to concentrate on expanding ECS and to let the day-to-day control of Cast and the bulk operations go to his executives. His time and energy would be needed to spearhead the growth that was so essential for Cast's survival.

As Frank Narby said:

> Cast must get bigger to survive....All our resources are going to build up Cast as a large unit by one means or another....Shipping is the most intensely competitive international business that exists. It is a business that lends itself to large-scale operations. There are easily acquired economies of scale if you can develop a large enough share of the market....Ultimately there will be only large operators.

Narby's quest for market share and growth was just beginning. The first five years were a test, a way to build his confidence, and a time to build an equity base.

THE GROWTH YEARS (1975 - 1977)

To help broaden ECS's equity base and gain the financial muscle of a large, state-owned corporation, ECS sold Canadian National Railway (CNR) an 18% stake for $12 million. Robert Bandeen, the tight-fisted president of CNR who brought CNR into profitability after 50 years of losses, saw Cast as the perfect vehicle to extend CNR's transportation business. It was also a way for CNR to compete with Canadian Pacific (CP), its chief competitor in the rail business. CP ships controlled the largest fleet in Canada.

Rather than lease more ships and build from the bottom up, Narby decided to buy his growth. Manchester Lines (ML), which served the Montreal-U.K. route, was his target. The majority owner of ML was Furness Withy (FW), a U.K. corporation. Narby bought up all the shares of ML not held by FW. Narby then made an offer to FW. It was rejected, leaving ECS as the sole minority owner.

Even after he lost to FW, Narby still wanted ML. He carried the battle one step further and began buying up shares of ML's parent, FW.

By the end of 1976, Narby had control of 24.9% of FW. To defend itself, FW took its case to the U.K. Monopolies Commission. A ruling in January that ECS must reduce its stake in FW to 10% ended Narby's two-year battle.

With the ML route closed, Cast leased another vessel to call at Liverpool. The new route would be Montreal-Antwerp-Liverpool. This would give Cast a direct link to the U.K. and give Cast two routes.

1976 was another banner year for ECS's operations. Cast had contracts of $100 million and profits of $12 million. The parent company was also doing very well. Tight cost controls, a mark of the ECS companies, were continuing to be effective. ECS still did not own a single vessel.

Cast had continually chartered larger and larger ships. The average ship now had a 600 TEU capacity. "But this is still far too small and can't compete with 2000 TEU ships", said Narby.

As the FW battle cooled, Cast became embroiled in a dispute with the Maritime Employers Association (MEA) that represented longshoremen in the port of Montreal. MEA increased Cast's assessment by $400,000 to cover costs of retirement benefits to redundant longshoremen. What created the problem was that the $400,000 was due to a change in how assessments were calculated. The total collected was not going to change; Cast's competitors would simply pay less. Cast had little representation on the MEA board that decided these issues; it was a case of "taxation with no representation".

Narby told the MEA that if the assessments were not changed, Cast would move to the Port of Halifax. Since Cast did 40% of the containerized volume in Montreal and employed 75 longshoremen, Cast's case was strong. The MEA refused, and as of April 2, 1977, the first Cast vessel arrived in Halifax. By May, Cast had switched four out of its six vessels to Halifax.

The Provincial Government of Quebec stepped in at this point for fear of losing Cast completely. Out of the discussions came a two-part agreement: (1) A panel would be established to study MEA affairs; (2) If Cast was unhappy with the outcome, the Provincial Government would help Cast set up a new terminal at Becancour--outside MEA jurisdiction.

Cast was soon back in Montreal, and $3 million poorer for the fight.

NEW GROWTH STAGE (1978 - 1979)

1978
The beginning of 1978 marked an abrupt change in ECS policy. Cast bought three vessels in January:

    CAST OTTER: 43,580 DWT; 712 TEU; con/bulker.
    CAST SEAL: 51,000 DWT; 750 TEU; con/bulker.
    CAST BEAVER: 51,000 DWT; 750 TEU; con/bulker.

The policy had been to time charter only, to keep costs down. The stated reason for the change was availability of vessels at low prices.
In August Cast bought CAST SEAL's sister ship:

    CAST DOLPHIN: 51,000 DWT; 768 TEU; con/bulker.

ECS was now operating 20 vessels total, in both the liner and bulk trades, and in both the Atlantic Basin and the Arabian Gulf.

1979
In May, 1979, ECS purchased two ore-bulk-oil ships (OBO's) from Silver Line. The two vessels were: the 142,000 DWT SILVER BRIDGE and the 101,000 DWT THISTLE STAR. Total cost was $26 million. These two vessels represented another major change in policy as ECS moved into the tanker market.
By June, Cast had five owned and one chartered vessel for the Montreal-Antwerp route. The vessels averaged 750 TEU. The Westbound U.K. leg was cancelled due to labor problems. A feeder ship making runs between Antwerp and Bristol took up the slack.
Furness Withy once again became the target of Narby's expansion, only this time Narby teamed up with Paul Bristol, president of KCA International, an offshore drilling concern. Bristol wanted FW's Kingsnorth Marine Drilling. If Bristol and Narby could gain control, Bristol would take the drilling rigs and Narby the ships. Bristol owned 3.73% of FW and Narby owned 18.4%. Together they were still unable to gain control of FW. Narby sold his 18.4% stake to the C.Y. Tung Group. C.Y. Tung was able to gain control and add Manchester Lines to his fleet.
In October, Cast ordered three new 70,000 DWT con/bulkers, purposed-designed to replace three of

the present vessels on the Montreal-Antwerp route.
The three new vessels were:

CAST CARIBOU: 70,000 DWT;   1466 TEU;   delivery
               December 1981.
CAST POLARBEAR: 70,000 DWT;   1466 TEU;   delivery
               June 1982.
CAST BEAVER: 70,000 DWT;   1466 TEU;   delivery
               June 1983.

The vessels were from the III Maj yard and cost
$27 million each. The terms were 20% on delivery,
with 80% financed over ten years at 9% through the
Yugoslavian government.

The North Atlantic liner trades were heading
into even more troubled waters as 1979 ended. The
combination of over-tonnaging and the beginning
economic slowdown meant the competition for market
share would soon turn to an all-out rate war.

QUANTUM GROWTH (1980 - 1981)

As part of Robert Bandeen's plans to push CNR's
position in ECS to 50%, CNR bought $42 million worth
of preferred shares. The shares carried the option
of being convertible to common stock before the end
of 1983. This would increase CNR's stake to 26%.

Sea-Land Service launched another legal attack
against Cast through the FMC. This was only one in a
number of earlier attempts to get Cast under FMC
regulation. In Congress, bills were being put foward
to stop the diversion of U.S. cargo through Canada.
There was a lot of talk and paper movement, but Cast
was not worried, being a Canadian corporation.

The box rate charged by Cast in the fall of 1980
was $1,700 Eastbound and $1,400 Westbound.

From October of 1980 to October of 1981, Frank
Narby went on a buying spree that committed ECS to
over half a billion dollars in loans. The
acquisitions included the following:

1. When Seatrain abandoned the North
    Atlantic routes, Cast paid $5 million
    to pick up 20 Seatrain offices in the
    U.S. and Europe.
2. Cast ordered six vessels from Hyundai
    for $270 million.
    a. Three con/bulkers similar to the ones
        on order at III Maj, each 70,000
        DWT, 1466 TEU, 14-knots.

CAST HUSKY: delivery June 1982.
CAST MUSKOX: delivery October 1982.
CAST OTTER: delivery November 1982.

b. Three OBO's of 150,000 DWT at $60 million apiece. Terms:

Three con/bulkers and one OBO, with the same terms as III Maj.
One OBO, 50% on delivery, 50% long-term.
One OBO, 100% on delivery.

3. 2000 x 40-foot containers from Seatrain.
2000 x 40-foot containers new.
2000 x 20-foot containers new.
4. $10 million in port improvements for Montreal, Antwerp, and Ipswich.
5. $20 million for trucks and chassis.
6. A $165 million package from Anglo-Nordic, included:

1 ULCC of 240,000 DWT
1 OBO of 240,000 DWT
4 OBO's of 160,000 DWT
2 con/bulkers of 61,338 DWT

With this purchase, ECS became the largest owner of OBO's in the world.
7. $5 million to buy St. Lawrence Stevedoring Co. (SLS).
Frank Narby bought SLS because of a deep-water coal berth it owned. When the predicted coal boom came, ECS would be perfectly situated to move coal out of the Mid-West using CNR's rails, his coal berth, and his ships.
8. Cast signed a 15-year agreement with the Port of Ipswich to help revamp the container terminal there--cost: 1.8 million pounds.

Between October 1979 and October 1981, ECS bought 23 ships, doubled the trucking fleet to 128 trucks and 455 chassis, doubled the number of containers, improved port facilities, and bought a coal berth--the cost: approximately $750 million. That was quite a bill to run up, especially when the original investment ten years earlier was only $485,000.

In 1981 another bill, the Biaggi Bill, was put before Congress to stop Cast from diverting U.S. cargo. Again, the Bill was just noise.

The C.Y. Tung Group formed the St. Lawrence Consolidated Service (SLCS) in March 1981. C.Y. Tung, which controlled both Dart Containerline and Manchester Line, set up a consortium with C.P. Ships and Compagnie Maritime Belge. The outcome was a united effort by the four companies in both the Canadian and U.S. trades. This consortium was a surprise to everyone.

THE FALL

The decline of ECS began before the buying spree ended. ECS was a victim of high costs and expensive money, the very factors that enabled it to grow in the first place. In the beginning ECS chartered its vessels and controlled costs, offering shippers no frills and cheap rates. Now, after three years of buying: $265 million in con/bulkers, $308 million in OBO's, and $400 million in container services. The high costs were sinking ECS. The bulk market had no bottom in sight, and ECS's vessels sat waiting for the big boom to make a killing on the spot market.

December 1981: ECS sold most of the Anglo-Nordic vessels to help ease the cash flow problems. Then ECS time chartered the same vessels back again to continue using them as they had.

1982

January 1982: ECS's cash problems became public knowledge as things began to unravel with its most powerful backer, CNR. CNR put Cast on a straight cash basis for all freight bills ($400,000/week) and called in $4 million of outstanding freight bills.

Robert Bandeen, CNR president, then lost a boardroom battle in mid-January to turn the $42 million worth of preference shares into equity. Bandeen quit, leaving CNR with an 18% equity stake and $42 million of preference shares in ECS.

February 1982: Cast closed sales offices in New York City, St. Louis, Cleveland, Hamburg, Le Havre, and Manchester. All six were part of the Seatrain deal a year earlier. Cast also added a "recession emergency surcharge" to all rates, amounting to an 8-9% increase.

March 1982: Frank Narby offered to sell 50% of Cast for $100 million. The current crisis was a $50 million capital progress payment due on the three OBO's at the Hyundai yard. ECS's exposure in the bulk market continued to keep it cash-starved. Transatlantic grain rates had fallen from $23/ton in 1980 to $7/ton, so that even the con/bulkers were in trouble. Coal, which was to have saved the day, went bust.

April 1982: The combined exposure of the Royal Bank of Canada (RBC), Bank of Montreal, and Chemical Bank to ECS was $130 million. Without some type of rewritten debt, ECS was sunk.

Chemical Bank (CB) decided it was best to deal independently. The deal CB proposed was that ECS agree to sell the three vessels CB had loaned against to specified groups, that they be managed by Skaarup, and then optionally leased back to ECS. The loan was for $37.1 million; the vessels sold for $29 million. Chemical took a loss, but not a bath. The vessels involved were:

```
CAST SKVA:    105,000 DWT OBO
CAST GANNET:  105,000 DWT OBO
CAST BEAR:     62,000 DWT con/bulker
```

ECS took $37.1 million off its balance sheet and still had use of its vessels. Frank Narby accepted the deal within minutes.

May 1982: The major Canadian creditors--RBC, Bank of Montreal and CNR, and South Korean Hyundai--got together and rescheduled ECS's debt. The cost to ECS was a smaller fleet and less equity in the new buildings, but considering the circumstances, ECS made out quite well.

Canadian creditors:

1. Took over ownership of three con/bulkers (Hyundai-built) and leased them to Cast for 20 years.
2. Accepted moratoriums worth $10 million on ships already afloat.
3. Accepted an option to buy 75% of Cast within three years.
4. Bought terminal equipment on Canadian soil for $15 million cash.

This deal, plus the Chemical deal, lifted $195 million, or approximately 45% of short-term and medium-term debt, off ECS's back.

Since the Canadian triumvirate was willing to stand behind three of the con/bulkers and one of the OBO's at Hyundai, Hyundai was willing to extend long-term financing to the other two OBO's. The terms were 20% on delivery, 80% over ten years at 9%.

April 1982: Cast's troubles and the heated North Atlantic competition drove Cast's annualized carriage down to a 50,000 TEU annualized rate in December of 1981. By April of 1982, the volume had rebounded to a 75,000 TEU annualized rate, still well below the 110,000 TEU for 1981 and the 90,000 TEU for 1980.

August 1982: Cast announced its intention to join four Canadian North Atlantic Conferences. Present members included Atlantic Container Line, C.P. Ships, Dart Containerline, Hapag-Lloyd, and Manchester Lines. Speculation had it that pressure from Cast's financiers was the reason behind the move.

September 1982: The tentative agreement between Cast and the Conferences stated that Cast would:

1. Use only five of six new con/bulkers.
2. Cut down aggressive Mid-West marketing.
3. Be guaranteed $350 per TEU on 30,000 TEU's.

The Conferences would then increase rates averaging 20-30%, and set minimum box rates of $1,200.

Cast's larger customers were paying $700 per box. The $1,200 minimum would effectively raise their rates 70%. Kurien Jacob, Vice-President of Cast North America Ltd., led 34 other Cast employees out and into forming Sofati Container Line (SCL) to take advantage of this situation. SCL had the backing of Michel Gaucher, owner of Sofati Ltd., a Canadian engineering and construction group. SCL's first sailing was set for late October, 1982.

The structure of SCL was patterned after Cast in its early days. SCL would charter three vessels averaging 500 TEU, keep all costs and overheads to a minimum, and offer no-frills rates. SCL would have a 40,000 TEU two-way, annual slot capacity with three 500 TEU vessels. These vessels were pure containerships.

Two other lines also began container services on these routes in September: Soviet Artic Lines and American Coastal Lines.

The rate war of the previous two years was only a skirmish compared to what followed with three new independent lines.

October 1982: Cast ended talks with the Conferences and cancelled all agreements. Conference rate increases due to take effect on December 1 were cancelled.

SCL's first sailing averaged 30% of capacity each leg on the Montreal-Antwerp-Tilbury route.

Average rates were $870/box. It was said, however, that Cast was offering rates as low as $350/box to keep its large-volume shippers away from SCL.

December 1982: Kersten Hunik & Co., a Rotterdam shipping and agency firm, invested $1 million to become a minority shareholder (less than 20%) in SCL. More important than the money was the marketing help it could offer in Europe. Rates were averaging $625/TEU.

1983

January 1983: Seven North Atlantic Conferences considered merging to gain an upper-hand in the present rate war.

February 1983: ECS sales figures came out for 1982: sales of $354.9 million; losses of $35 million. 1981 sales were $365 million, with a $35.2 million profit. Cast had sales of $250 million.

ECS's fleet totaled 16 vessels: five con/bulkers and eleven OBO's, down from a high of 40 in 1980/81.

SCL's vessels have been fully booked, and SCL was looking for larger vessels. Rates were averaging $600/TEU.

TABLE 6.1

CANADIAN CONTAINER MARKET
(APPROXIMATIONS)

Cast	90,000 TEU	33-25%
Sofati	30,000 TEU	10%
Artic Line & Polish Ocean	20-25,000 TEU	8%
SLCS	150,000 TEU	50%

CNR and Cast began secret negotiations. It was said that CNR was seeking to protect its $60 million investment in ECS by taking control of the Cast subsidiary.

March 1983: The Canadian North Atlantic Conferences gave member lines "limited independent action" in rate-setting to counter the present competition.

April 1983: SCL chartered two 800 TEU capacity sisterships to replace two of the present 500 TEU vessels. Rumors abound that SCL is in financial trouble.

While negotiations were continuing with Cast, CNR began an attempt to take over SCL. The potential outcome became even more confusing since Cast's major creditors were pressuring Cast to set up some kind of rationalized service with SCL.

The bulk cargoes between Canada and Europe dwindled to nothing. All Cast's credit lines with suppliers were now gone. Rates were averaging $500/TEU.

May 1983: Trans-Freight Lines, the major non-conference operator on the North Atlantic joined the North Atlantic Conferences.

THE FINAL DAYS

June 1983: The Royal Bank of Canada (RBC) said it was going to pull the plug on ECS and Cast. RBC's exposure was estimated at $270 million.

June 20, 1983: Talks between CNR and Cast collapsed.

June 21, 1983: RBC issued a statement saying it would continue to support Cast, but not ECS. ECS was forced into receivership. RBC was appointed receiver.

July 1983: Sofati was said to be losing $250,000/month.

July 3, 1983: The III Maj yard repossessed CAST POLAR BEAR and CAST CARIBOU. Both vessels were impounded at the Yugoslav yard. Cast began negotiations to get the two new con/bulkers back.

August 5, 1983: The restructuring of Cast was made public. The parent company, ECS, filed for bankruptcy. All of Cast's assets were purchased from ECS by the RBC for their fair market value, $8.6 million. Cast would continue operating, but now under the control of RBC. Cast was reincorporated as Cast (1983) Ltd.

Cast's debt equaled $55.5 million. Breakdown of the debt was: $27.5 million unsecured and accounts payable; $23.6 million due to ECS affiliated companies; and the rest secured.

RBC set up a trust which would receive 20% of after-tax income from Cast (1983) Ltd. for five and one-half years or until $10 million had been set aside. This fund, plus the assets sold, would give the 327 unsecured creditors 20 to 40 cents on the dollar. RBC's reason for setting up this fund was "goodwill".

Klaus Gausing was named CEO of Cast (1983) Ltd.

August 8, 1983: Newly incorporated Cast (1983) bought Sofati Container Line (SCL) from Michel Gaucher for $5 million.

August 18, 1983: ECS filed its final bankruptcy notice.

August 26, 1983: RBC finalized an agreement with III Maj to get CAST POLAR BEAR and CAST CARIBOU back to sea.

September 1983: Cast (1983) announced it would boost rates by 30% as of November 1. Rate increases worked out to $150 for 20-foot boxes, and $250 for 40-foot boxes.

October 1983: Both U.S. and Canadian North Atlantic Conferences announced 12.5-15% rate increases effective January 1.

The Canadian Bank Act states that a bank cannot hold more than 10% of the common shares in a company that is being restructured for longer than two years. Bank insiders said there are special provisions which would allow the bank to hold Cast (1983) longer if necessary.

Observers felt that RBC has already reached an agreement with CNR. Cast (1983) was losing an estimated $3 million a month.

TIME LINE

1969	Eurocanadian Shipholdings Ltd. (ECS) and its subsidiary Cast were formed.
1970	First year of Cast operating.
1975	ECS began attempted takeover of Manchester Lines (ML).
1976	Canadian National Railway (CNR) bought 18% of ECS for $18 million.
	ECS failed at ML takeover, began buying shares in parent, Furness Withy (FW).
1977	U.K. Monopolies Commission ruled ECS must reduce holdings in FW from 26% to 10%.
	Dispute began with Maritime Employers Association (MEA); some vessels switched from Montreal to Halifax.
1978	MEA backed down, and Cast returned to Montreal.
	Cast bought its first vessels.
	Parent, ECS, began to get big in the bulk markets.
1979	ECS bought its first OBO's.
	Another attempt was made on FW, another loss.
	ECS's 18.4% of FW sold to the C.Y. Tung Group.
	Cast purchased three con/bulkers from III Maj.
1980	Cast bought Seatrain's sales offices for $5 million.
	CNR invested $42 million for preferred shares, with an option to switch it to equity shares by 1983.
	Cast began purchases at Hyundai--three con/bulkers and three OBO's.
	Cast bought a $165 million package from Anglo-Nordic.
	Cast bought St. Lawrence Stevedoring Co. (SLS) for $5 million.
1981	C.Y. Tung Group led formation of St. Lawrence Coordinated Service (SLCS).
	Cast spent $10 million on port improvements.
	Cast spent $20 million to expand the trucking fleet.

Cast Container Line

1982

<table>
<tr><td>January</td><td>Cast's cash flow problems became public.
Robert Bandeen lost boardroom battle to turn CNR's $42 million in preference shares to common equity.</td></tr>
<tr><td>February</td><td>Narby offered to sell 50% of Cast for $100 million.</td></tr>
<tr><td>April</td><td>Cast and Chemical Bank reached accord on $37.1 million loan.</td></tr>
<tr><td>May</td><td>$100 million came due for OBO's at Hyundai.
Royal Bank of Canada (RBC), Bank of Montreal (BM), and CNR reached an agreement with Cast over their $130 million exposure.
Hyundai agreed to long-term financing of two OBO's.</td></tr>
<tr><td>August</td><td>Cast agreed to join Canadian Conference.</td></tr>
<tr><td>September</td><td>Thirty-seven Cast employees left to form Sofati Container Line (SCL).</td></tr>
<tr><td>October</td><td>Cast pulled out of Conference agreements.
SCL began operating.
Soviet's Artic Line began operating.</td></tr>
</table>

1983

January	Cast and ECS reported losses of $35 million on sales of $355 million.
February	Cast and CNR began secret negotiations.
March	Canadian North Atlantic Conferences gave member lines "limited" right to set rates independently.
April	SCL acquired larger vessels for increased demand.
	CNR began attempt to take over SCL.
	Cast lost all credit lines with suppliers.
	Cast's creditors were pressuring for some kind of rationalization with SCL.
June	RBC statement withdrew support from ECS, while continuing to support Cast.
	CNR-Cast negotiations collapsed.
	ECS placed under receivership.
July	III Maj repossessed two con/bulkers it built for Cast.
August	ECS filed for bankruptcy.
	Cast bought by RBC and reincorporated as Cast (1983) Ltd.
	Cast (1983) Ltd. bought SCL for $5 million.
	III Maj yard released two con/bulkers to the RBC.
September	Cast announced rate increases of 30%, effective November 1.
October	Conferences announced rate increases of 12.5-15%, effective January 1, 1984.

Cast Container Line

Exhibit 6.1

CAST FLEET-ARRIVALS FIXTURES AND DEPARTURES
POST JANUARY 1980

Ship	DWT	Owner	Remarks
CAST BEAVER*	51 666	Regal Marine	sold with t/c back
CAST DOLPHIN*	52 019	Ocean Tramping	⌈sold $27m en bloc
CAST ORCA*	51 890	Ocean Tramping	⌊both with ch. back
CAST OTTER*	44 279	Marlion	8.5m with 3 yr. ch. back
CAST SEAL*	51 920	Ocean Tramping	$11.5 with 2 yr. ch. back
CAST CORMORANT	155 106	Cast	ex Nordic Clipper
CAST FULMAR	161 805	Cast	ex Nordic Crusader
CAST GANNET	104 750	Chemical Bank	bought by Cast 1980
CAST GULL	145 057	Cast	
CAST HERON	161 798	Cast	ex Nordic Chieftain
CAST KITTIWAKE	162 465	Cast	ex Nordic Challenger
CAST SHEARWATER	104 749	Mightious (Teh Hu)	$18.5m with 5 yr. ch. back
CAST RAZORBILL	103 078	First TS	
CAST PETREL	145 015	Cast	
CAST PUFFIN	145 015	Cast	
CAST SKUA	104 749	Chemical bank	bought by Cast in 1980
CAST TERN	103 018	P.S. Li	$17m with 5 yr. ch. back
CAST NARWHAL	268 728	Cast	ex Nordic Conquerer
CAST BEAR	62 322	Chemical Bank	ex Nordic Mariner
CAST PORPOISE	45 499	Russ	ch. now redelivered
CAST TROUT	4 676		feeder on charter
CAST WALRUS	19 775	Ahlers	ch. now redelivered
CAST ELK	61 308	Bethlehem Steel	ex Nordic Merchant
CAST CARIBOU	70 200	Cast	Yugoslav newbuilding

*Container/bulkers sold with charter back phased to introduction of six
con/bulker newbuildings from Yugoslavia and South Korea. Total
realized $60-70m.

Chemical Bank ships wiped out $37m debt to the bank.
Anglo Nordic Ships bought 1980 for $165m, with VLCC Nordic Commander
laid up.

Source: Seatrade, May 1982

Exhibit 6.2

CHARACTERISTICS OF
NORTH EUROPE/EAST COAST NORTH AMERICA TRADE

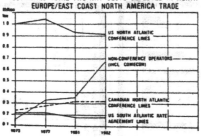

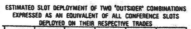

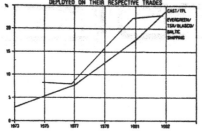

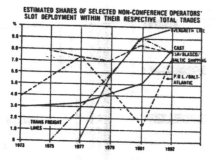

Source: "Lloyd's Shipping Economist," November 1981.
Reprinted with permission.

137

Exhibit 6.3

CONTAINER TRADE VOLUMES

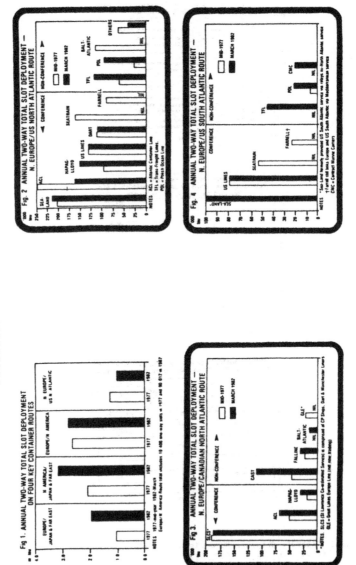

Source: "Lloyd's Shipping Economist," March 1982.
Reprinted with permission.

Exhibit 6.4

ANNUAL TWO-WAY TOTAL SLOTS ADDED
TO EUROPE/NORTH AMERICA TRADE
SINCE MID-1977

Operator	TEU
Trans-Freight Lines (TFL)	147,472
Sea-Land Service	129,064
Hapag-Lloyd	85,748
Polish Ocean Lines (POL)	84,240
Cast	66,267
Maersk Line	62,400
Atlantic Cargo Service (ACS)	43,992
Contract Marine Carriers (CMC)	40,456
Costa Line	38,168
Cie. Maritime Affretement (CMA)	31,200
Zim Container Service	27,456
Jugolinja	21,112
Euro-Pacific	17,472
Nedlloyd Lines	17,212
Gulf Europe Express	16,900
D'Amico	16,744
Nordana Line	13,728
Ibero Lines	13,624
Falline	7,800
Splosna Plovba	3,640
Waterman Lines	3,120
Star Shipping	2,288
TOTAL:	890,103

Note: Maersk and Nedlloyd slots are one-way (Westbound) from the Mediterranean.

Source: "Lloyd's Shipping Economist," March 1982.

Cast Container Line

Exhibit 6.4 Continued

ANNUAL TWO-WAY TOTAL SLOTS WITHDRAWN
FROM EUROPE/NORTH AMERICA TRADE
SINCE MID-1977

Operator	TEU
Seatrain Lines	213,824
Farrell Lines	148,928
Balt-Atlantic Line	95,576
Atlantic Container Line (ACL)	71,448
Balt-Gulf Line	38,272
Great Lakes Europe Line	21,320
Prudential Lines	20,800
Norwegian America Line	20,384
Black Sea Shipping Co.	19,136
Italia Line	10,816
Others	46,800
SUB-TOTAL:	707,304
Waterman Lines	155,376
TOTAL:	862,680

Note: Waterman Lines' additional new 158,496-slot
capacity service has been postponed/abandoned.

Source: "Lloyd's Shipping Economist," March 1982.

140

Part II

LIQUID AND DRY BULK SHIPPING

A major difference between liner and bulk shipping is the method of competition. While conference liner firms compete in terms of such factors as transit time, sailing frequency, and itinerary, bulk carriers mainly compete on price. One might think that such a straightforward approach would lead to an equally straightforward analysis of bulk carrier problems. However, such is not the case.

For example, take the problem of vessel replacement. The owner must consider when to dispose of his existing vessel and replace it with a newer one. The viability of the existing ship is dependent on its operating costs and the demand for its services. Operating costs are affected by the potential increase in maintenance and repair costs over time. The owner will want to compare his crew and fuel costs to what would be possible on a new vessel. The owner also wishes to know the revenue he can receive by scrapping or selling his existing vessel.

A potential investment in a new or second-hand liquid or dry bulk vessel is influenced by the government subsidies and financing terms available. The attractiveness of adopting a new or different technology in propulsion system (e.g., diesel engine vs. steam turbine) or vessel design (e.g., tug-barge combination vs. self-propelled ship) depends on such factors as the economics involved and the attitude of the sea-going labor union. To some extent both liner and bulk shipping firms share similar types of labor union problems in introducing new technology.

While liner firms are common carriers, offering their services to the public with published tariffs and sailing schedules, bulk vessel owners have more options as contract or private carriers. A shipowner should consciously decide on the type of risk-return scenario he wishes. For example, he could charter out the vessel for its useful life before he has it built. In this way he has little or no risk. However, his return on investment (ROI) will also be low. On the other hand, he can build a new vessel on speculation with no usage guaranteed--a high-risk situation. Of course, if a shipping boom occurs, his ROI may also be very high, since his vessel will be available to the highest bidder.

The risk-return scenario chosen by the ship owner depends on the individual business environment. Within a company that uses bulk vessels to move its own cargo (e.g., an oil company), marine transportation may be thought of as a "necessary evil" used to deliver its product. Such a private carrier may wish to have no risk, by keeping its own bulk vessels fully utilized with its own cargo. A publicly held bulk shipping company, with no cargo of its own, must carry the cargo of others to stay in business. The manager of this company must make a high enough ROI to attract and maintain investors but a low enough risk to keep his job.

A privately held business may be run by an entrepreneur who must only answer to his own conscience. The risk-return scenario chosen by this shipowner will reflect his personal attitude towards risk and his financial position.

. All shipowners are concerned with the future demand for their vessels. In the past, many shipping booms have occurred in conjunction with wars or canal closing--events that are generally impossible to predict. Bulk vessel demand is also affected by worldwide economic conditions (e.g., economic booms, high oil prices, drought),·also difficult to foresee with any high degree of accuracy.

As with liner firms, bulk vessel owners must be concerned with government policies and subsidies. Even government tax laws can impact the operations of a tanker owner.

In conclusion, while bulk shipping differs from liner shipping in many respects, the issues are still complex. The reader must carefully integrate the diverse factors involved to arrive at an appropriate evaluation.

FORMAT OF PART II

Chapters 7 through 13 deal with bulk shipping from the point of view of a publicly held shipping firm (Ogden Marine), oil companies (Triton Oil and Venture

Oil), privately held (Laval Maritime) and closely held (Legrand Shipping) shipping firms. In Chapter 7, Ogden Marine proposes a methodology for investing in new vessels. In the following chapter, Ogden has an opportunity to apply this methodology to the Jones Act liquid bulk trade. The vessel design under consideration can carry petroleum products or chemicals with a capacity of more than 42,000 deadweight tons (DWT). The modern diesel propulsion plant envisioned would appear to be far superior to the steam turbines in most of the existing Jones Act fleet. Ogden is faced with a dilemma in choosing a risk-return scenario because there is not a great demand to charter these proposed vessels.

In Chapter 9, Triton Oil is considering a new vessel of more than 55,000 DWT. Because the vessel will move the company's oil, there does not seem to be a risk of vessel usage. However, the firm must choose between conventional self-propelled tankers and tug-barge combinations.

Chapter 10 is a technical note dealing with tanker freight rate indices and terminology. This chapter will be helpful in understanding the remaining chapters in Part II. In addition, the reader can evaluate how the tax laws described would apply to alternatives open to Venture Oil in Chapter 11. Venture Oil has a vessel apparently in need of repair or replacement. The ship is used to lighten a large tanker bringing in crude oil from overseas. Building an offshore terminal is also an alternative for consideration.

Chapter 12 considers a speculative investment in a huge 330,000 DWT tanker for a privately owned company. Although there is no market demand for this vessel, Laval Maritime may have negotiated a deal too good to refuse. The entrepreneurial instincts of the potential owner must be analyzed in conjunction with the possible cash flow outcomes.

The final case study in Part II allows the reader to compare liner and bulk shipping operations within the same company. Legrand Shipping is a family-controlled firm that has problems in both its liner and bulk divisions. An analysis of key issues shows the reader a comparison of industry characteristics, problems, and solutions in these industry segments.

Chapter 7

FLEET INVESTMENT ANALYSIS:
A PROPOSED METHODOLOGY FOR OGDEN MARINE, INC.

INTRODUCTION

The object of this study is to develop a methodology
to assist the Odgen Marine, Inc. (OMI) management in
analyzing hold/sell decisions for vessels in the
fleet shown in Exhibit 7.1.   One aspect of this
methodology is to determine which ships should be
analyzed on a regular basis. The overall approach
includes required charter rate calculations that
serve as useful guidelines when applied jointly with
other qualitative criteria.
       This report first describes the operation of the
international vessel sale and purchase market. Next,
the factors which determine the marketability of any
given vessel are presented. The entire OMI fleet is
then examined in light of the sale and purchase
market, and the marketability criteria set forth
above. Finally, a procedure for conducting a
periodic analysis of the fleet is proposed.

THE INTERNATIONAL SALE AND PURCHASE MARKET

The international sale and purchase market is global
in scope, with centers of activity in New York,
London, Oslo, and Hong Kong. The value of a vessel
follows the spot charter market very closely; prices
may double or be halved in a matter of months. As

This case was written by Richard T. du Moulin and
adapted for classroom use by Henry S. Marcus.

Copyright (c) 1981 by the President and Fellows of
Harvard College. Reprinted by permission of the
Harvard Business School.

the charter market rises, more buyers perceive profitable opportunities and compete for available tonnage. Meanwhile, owners become reluctant to sell vessels which are now positioned for a better market. Therefore, less tonnage is offered, and the price, hence value, of existing tonnage increases.

As the high spot charter rates persist, vessel prices become firmer, and buyers begin to consider the option of ordering new construction. When comparing existing ships to new construction, potential buyers consider three important factors:

1. Most newbuilding vessels are available with government-subsidized financing, often taking the form of artificially low interest rates, whereas used tonnage must obtain financing at less favorable rates.
2. A charter-free vessel is available for immediate employment, whereas delivery of new construction might take as long as two or three years.
3. Only newbuilding vessels can be precisely tailored to owner's specifications (e.g., power plant specifications, cargo handling gear, etc.).

Depending on the weighting of these criteria, it is possible that a used vessel can be more or less valuable than a newbuilding. Therefore, in addition to the economics of shipyard labor, material, overhead, and profit, new construction prices are affected by the sale and purchase market of used ships.

THE MARKETABILITY OF VESSELS

Several factors greatly influence the marketability of any vessel. Aside from physical characteristics, the most important factor is whether or not the vessel has a charter. The rate level of the charter above or below the present market is secondary to the fact that a vessel with a long charter becomes more of a financial deal and less of a true shipping deal. As the length of the charter increases, the value of the vessel decreases relative to the value of the earnings stream and currency hedges that might be inherent in the charter. Since a buyer generally has more faith in the market than a seller, the existence of a charter blocks a potential buyer's access to the market in which he has confidence. In addition, the buyer would discount the residual value of the vessel at the end of the charter more heavily than would the seller.

An owner might be motivated to sell a chartered vessel because the cash flow is close to break-even, or perhaps negative. Naturally, a buyer is very difficult to find. The sale of such a vessel would require that the seller absorb the present value of the cash losses as well as lose most of the residual value.

There are several other practical difficulties associated with the sale of a vessel under charter:

1. Most time charters contain a clause which makes any sale subject to charterer's approval.

2. A seller knows his vessel and places a certain value on the knowledge of its condition and performance. The buyer, however, cannot be as certain as the seller and therefore reduces the ship's value.

3. U.S.-flag vessels financed under Title XI must receive Maritime Administration approval of the buyer to ensure discharge of the remaining debt.

4. The owner of a U.S.-flag vessel must be a U.S. citizen, thus limiting the field of potential buyers and necessitating another Maritime Administration approval.

5. Companies owning U.S.-flag vessels often have restrictive clauses in their union agreements.

In summary, only a vessel without a charter, or a vessel with a short-term charter, can be considered as a readily marketable candidate for sale.

EXAMINATION OF THE OMI FLEET

The OMI fleet can be divided into four sectors: bareboat charters, long-term charters, short-term charters, and spot vessels. The primary characteristics of each category will be examined in order to evaluate the marketability of its vessels.

BAREBOAT CHARTERS

Bareboat charters usually extend through a majority

of a vessel's useful life. They are purely financial propositions, totally disconnected from the shipping markets. In the case of OMI, the vessels were contracted with the shipyard and simultaneously bareboat-chartered at a rate providing an expected return on the investment. The owner has no operational risk or responsibility; the charterer provides the crew and assumes all operational costs.

As financial propositions, bareboat charters are occasionally sold for financial reasons. A lucrative bareboat charter may be sold to improve the corporate balance sheet or foreign exchange exposure.

When selling such a vessel, the major points of negotiation are: cash flow, discount rate, residual value, and currency denomination. If the owner should sell a bareboat charter, the asset play on the vessel at the completion of the charter is lost. The buyer will discount the residual value of the vessel to scrap, even though its value at the end of the bareboat charter is substantially greater.

As an example, in 1978 OMI sold three vessels which were under 15-year bareboat charters with hire payable in yen. Although they would have been only 15 years old at the end of the charter (1989) and worth a considerable sum as trading vessels, they were assigned a present residual value equal to scrap. Of the final sale price for the three-ship package, the value of the ships themselves represented approximately 7%.

For the above reasons, vessels on bareboat charter are rarely sold; they are therefore not included in the analysis of hold/sell decisions. OMI owns four such vessels: OGDEN JORDAN, OGDEN SENEGAL, OGDEN CONGO, and OGDEN GENERAL. The charters expire in 1989, 1989, 1989, and 1990, respectively.

LONG-TERM TIME CHARTERS

The second category of vessels includes those under long-term time charter. Long-term charter may be defined as any charter in excess of about three years. In a time charter, the vessel owner undertakes both financial and operational responsibilities, including crew, insurance, stores, supplies, subsistence, and maintenance.

The value of a vessel with a long-term charter is the sum of the present value of the cash flow from the time charter, and the residual value of the vessel. In determining the cash flow, careful analysis must be made of expected operating costs and any escalation provisions in the charter party. This cash flow is then present-valued at a mutually agreeable discount rate (a financial calculation). A buyer would again attempt to treat the vessel's residual value as scrap, whereas the seller would try to value it as an operating ship. The result would be a diminished valuation of the vessel and the loss of "asset play" by the owner, similar to the bareboat charter category.

Vessels with long-term charters are therefore not analyzed in this report. These vessels include OGDEN CHAMPION, OGDEN WABASH, and OGDEN BRIDGESTONE. The charters expire in 1984, 1985, and 1988, respectively.

SHORT-TERM TIME CHARTERS

The third category of vessels includes those on short-term time charter, defined as those time charters with between six months and three years remaining. The values of these vessels reflect the more persistent movements of the spot charter market. Due to the relatively short period of the remaining charter, a potential buyer can identify a horizon and is therefore able to match the value of the asset against his assessment of the future market. A realistic determination of residual value is therefore possible. For vessels on short-term time charter, the asset value has greater weight than the cash flow of the charter.

When considering the purchase of a vessel on short-term time charter, a potential purchaser also has the option of ordering new construction with a delivery approximating the availability of the chartered vessel. The buyer will compare the existing vessel's price, specifications, and available financing against those obtainable in newbuilding tonnage.

Most of the vessels in the OMI fleet are in the short-term time charter category: OGDEN CHALLENGER, CONNECTICUT, OGDEN WILLAMETTE, OGDEN CHARGER, OGDEN LEADER, OGDEN AMAZON, OGDEN DANUBE, OGDEN THAMES, OGDEN FRAZER, OGDEN CLIPPER, OGDEN OTTAWA, and OGDEN EBRO.

Since their values are strongly related to the sales, purchases, and new construction markets, these vessels are included in the analysis of hold/sell decisions.

SPOT VESSELS

The fourth category of vessels to be examined contains those either trading spot or with less than six months to run on their present charters. The values of these vessels fluctuate with the spot charter market. All the differing views of the future freight market are distilled in the sale and purchase market. If one owner has a substantially more optimistic view of the market than another owner, a vessel may change hands, because two parties value the asset differently.

If an owner believes there will be a downturn that is not generally perceived by the rest of the market, he has two options:

1.   Sell the vessel.
2.   Charter the vessel long-term.

Chartering long-term is essentially the sale of a portion of the vessel's useful economic life while retaining the residual value. In evaluating sale vs. chartering, the owner must compare the age of the vessel to the estimated duration of the depressed market. If the vessel can command a charter of sufficient length and still retain trading value at the end of the charter, the owner should seek a suitable charter. If the vessel has reached an age such that it is not able to secure long-term employment, perhaps it should be sold.

The following vessels are in the spot category and are included in the hold/sell analysis: OGDEN SAGUENAY, OGDEN EXPORTER, OGDEN IMPORTER, OGDEN SUNGARI, and OGDEN NELSON.

The four old U.S.-flag bulk carriers also trade spot. Since it is apparent that these vessels are nearing the end of their useful lives, their market values are only incrementally above scrap. Management is subjecting them to continual scrutiny, so further hold/sell analysis is unnecessary.

PROCEDURE FOR ANALYSIS

In order to provide for orderly management review, it is proposed that an investment analysis be prepared on an annual basis and presented at the annual Board meeting. Directed at those vessels trading in the spot market or under short-term charter, this analysis will include both required charter rate calculations and qualitative evalutions of the

Fleet Investment Analysis

vessels and their market segments.

REQUIRED CHARTER RATES

As part of the investment analysis, numerical calculations of required charter rates should be derived as follows (for a sample analysis, see Exhibit 7.2):

1. Examine the sale and purchase market and estimate the current charter-free price for each vessel.
2. Subtract the scrap value from the price to determine the present investment in the vessel as an operating entity.
3. Calculate the annual revenue required to recover this investment during half of the vessel's remaining economic life.
4. Add the annual operating cost of the vessel to the required revenue.
5. Basis the vessel's deadweight and estimated operational days/year, derive the required time chartered rate.
6. Compare the required rate with:

    a. That vessel's current rate, if under short-term time charter.
    b. Spot rates.
    c. One, two, and five-year rates*.
    d. Ten-year payout rate based on a newbuilding contract price.

7. As a reference, compare the charter-free market price of each vessel with its book value.

QUALITATIVE EVALUATION

Following the above material analysis, a more general qualitative evaluation of each vessel and market segment must be made, paying particular attention to:

----

* These market rates should not be confused with OMI's formal budget numbers. Market rates are the current rates, assuming immediate vessel availability, whereas budget numbers include considerations of existing charter commitments, expected off-hire, and OMI's chartering strategy.

1. Future market trends.
2. Age, condition, and technical obsolescence of company vessels.
3. Age and technical profiles of the relevant competition; backlog of newbuilding orders.
4. Impending regulatory changes.
5. Fit of the vessels in the fleet based on the principles of:

   a. Portfolio management.
   b. Admissible risk (i.e., the maximum risk OMI can tolerate on a vessel deal).
   c. Opportunistic nature of shipping.
   d. Principle of speculative acquisition (see Exhibit 7.3 for explanation).
   e. Environmental risk.

6. Book profit or loss that might result from a sale. (While this is not a relevant consideration when evaluating the market, the impact of a sale on earnings-per-share cannot be ignored.)

CONCLUSIONS

The goal of this investment analysis is to develop a management tool that is useful in deciding whether to hold or sell ships. The existence of a charter on a vessel shifts the emphasis on the analysis from an estimation of that vessel's future trading value to a determination of cash flows resulting from past chartering decisions. Therefore, to realistically analyze OMI's vessels in light of the international shipping markets, this study will concentrate on those vessels which are charter-free or short-term chartered. As vessels approach the end of long-term charters, they will then be included in the analysis.

It is important to realize that the required charter rate analysis is only a helpful guideline, and that qualitative evaluation based on management's continuous interaction with the shipping market is the key element to successful implementation of OMI's strategy.

Exhibit 7.1

OGDEN MARINE FLEET SEPTEMBER 1978

Vessels	Type	Registry	Year Built	Deadweight Tonnage	Basic Trade
TANKERS					
OGDEN SUNGARI	Tanker	Liberian	1975	271,575	Crude oil
OGDEN NELSON	Tanker	Liberian	1972	266,120	Crude oil
OGDEN BRIDGESTONE	LPG Tanker	Panamanian	1973	48,706	LPG
OGDEN GENERAL	LPG Tanker	Liberian	1975	49,094	LPG
OGDEN SAGUENAI	Product Tanker	Liberian	1976	39,105	Oil products
OGDEN OTAWA	Product Tanker	Liberian	1976	39,105	Oil products
OGDEN CHAMPION	Product tanker	U.S. (Jones Act)	1969	37,874	Coastwise oil products
OGDEN WABASH	Product tanker	U.S. (Jones Act)	1969	37,853	"
OGDEN WILLAMETTE	Product tanker	U.S. (Jones Act)	1969	37,853	"
CONNECTICUT	Product Tanker	U.S. (Jones Act)	1958	38,240	"
OGDEN CHALLENGER	Product Tanker	U.S. (Jones Act)	1960	35,112	"
			Total	900,637	
BULK CARRIERS					
OGDEN THAMES	Bulk Carrier	Liberian	1971	60,762	Iron ore
OGDEN DANUBE	Bulk Carrier	Liberian	1971	60,524	Coal
OGDEN AMAZON	Bulk Carrier	Liberian	1973	60,247	Grain
OGDEN FRASER	Geared Bulk Carrier	Liberian	1973	33,822	
OGDEN CLIPPER	Geared Bulk Carrier	Liberian	1963	26,800	Grain
OGDEM EXPORTER	Geared Bulk Carrier	Liberian	1966	26,701	Fertilizer
OGDEN IMPORTER	Geared Bulk Carrier	Liberian	1966	26,701	Scrap
MERRIMAC	Geared Bulk Carrier	U.S. (unsubsidized)	1962*	26,216	Coal and Grain
TRAVELER	Geared Bulk Carrier	U.S. (unsubsidized)	1962*	25,977	"
COLUMBIA	Geared Bulk Carrier	U.S. (unsubsidized)	1962*	24,318	"
POTOMAC	Geared Bulk Carrier	Liberian	1962*	23,846	"
OGDEN JORDAN	Car/Bulk Carrier	Liberian	1974	37,411	Coal
OGDEN SENEGAL	Car/Bulk Carrier	Liberian	1974	37,411	Grain
OGDEN CONGO**	Car/Bulk Carrier	Liberian	1974	37,411	Cars
OGDEN EBRO	Ore/Bulk/Oil Carrier	Liberian	1978	70,747	Crude oil, iron ore
			Total	578,894	
			GRAND TOTAL	1,479,531	26 vessels

*Year rebuilt; originally built 1945
**50% owned

Exhibit 7.2

SAMPLE INVESTMENT CALCULATION

OGDEN NELSON

1. Examine the sale and purchase market and estimate the current charter-free price for the vessel.

   -- A 1973-built 330,000 DWT tanker just sold for $23 million, about $70 per ton. The OGDEN NELSON would therefore be worth about: $70 x 266,000 = $18.6 million. Adjust this down for her extra year of age but up for inert gas equipment, therefore assume $18.0 million.

2. Subtract the scrap value from that price to determine the present investment in the vessel as an operating entity.

   -- Current scrap value for the OGDEN NELSON is $4.05 million, therefore, $18.0 - $4.05 = $13.95 million.

3. Calculate the annual revenue required to recover this investment during half the vessel's remaining economic life.

   -- The OGDEN NELSON is 8 years old and should have 17 years of remaining economic life. To recover $13.95 million in 8.5 years using a discount rate of 11.5%, annual payments must equal $2,658,000.

4. Add the annual operating cost of the vessel to the required revenue.

   -- The OGDEN NELSON's annual operating cost is $1,550,000. Assuming that future escalation flows through to the charterer, the required annual revenue is $2,658,000 + $1,550,000 = $4,208,000.

5. Basis the vessel's deadweight and estimated operational days/year, derive the required time chartered rate.

Fleet Investment Analysis

Exhibit 7.2 Continued

--   The OGDEN NELSON's deadweight is 266,120
      tons and she routinely operates about 11
      1/2 months of the year. Therefore, the
      required time charter is:

$$\frac{\$4,208,000}{266,120 \times 11.5} = \$1.38/DWT/month$$

Exhibit 7.3

ROLE OF SPECULATIVE CONTRACTING AND PURCHASING

A long-term commitment to bulk shipping requires the ownership of a modern, well-maintained, diversified fleet of ships with profitable period charters. The capital cost of the vessels must be matched by charters at satisfactory levels. As charters expire and the ships become exposed to the market, it is important that these ships be of a relatively low capital cost, i.e., either paid off or purchased at low cost. Since most operators face roughly equal operating costs, to be competitive one must have relatively low vessel capital costs.

Long-term charters from strong charterers, if done back-to-back with construction contracting, are relatively thin, that is, the charterer will make a "lease vs. buy" analysis and not allow the owner a rapid payout. Otherwise, it would pay for him to own the ship and not charter it. Such charters, when available, are done under the pressure of competition from other owners, many of whom have lower return on equity goals. The relatively thin margins in these deals can be eradicated by unpredictable events such as currency changes, escalation, interest rate, and off-hire. A fleet cannot be built entirely with back-to-back charters. (From time to time, certain back-to-back deals are attractive for other specific reasons.)

A company must take advantage of depressed markets to purchase selectively quality tonnage and then take advantage of strong markets to obtain period charters from first-class companies. This separation of the act of obtaining a vessel from chartering that vessel permits the owner to obtain a market rate, not a present financial rate.

Therefore, a careful market analysis must be done, a speculative purchase or contract made, and at a later date, a timely charter fixed.

Due to the inherent uncertainty of the timing of the market, a company can only tolerate a certain amount of speculative risk. The number of speculative contracts/purchases is therefore financially limited by a "worst case" approach.

When satisfactory characters are obtained, more risks can then be entertained.

Chapter 8

OGDEN MARINE, INC.

In September 1978, Richard T. du Moulin, Assistant to
the President of Ogden Marine, Inc. (OMI), was
preparing a recommendation relative to the potential
purchase of tankers for the U.S. domestic trade. OMI
was part of the Ogden Corporation that was involved
in transportation, metals, and food. (Exhibit 8.1
shows the consolidated balance sheets for the Ogden
Corporation and subsidiaries. Exhibit 8.2 presents
revenues and operating profits for each business
segment.)

Ogden Transportation Corporation comprises OMI;
Avondale Shipyards, Inc.; and International Terminal
Operating Co., Inc. (ITO). OMI owns and operates a
diverse fleet of oceangoing vessels that it charters
to various customers. Avondale designs, builds,
modernizes, and repairs major oceangoing vessels, and
builds and repairs various types of non-oceangoing
craft and offshore structures. ITO provides
stevedoring and terminal services in major East Coast
ports.

BACKGROUND

OMI's fleet operated in three distinct trades: U.S.-
flag tanker, U.S.-flag dry cargo, and foreign-flag

This case study was prepared by Richard T. du Moulin
and Henry S. Marcus as a basis for discussion rather
than to illustrate either effective or ineffective
handling of administrative problems.

Copyright (c) 1980 by the President and Fellows of
Harvard College. Reprinted by permission of the
Harvard Business School.

(both tanker and dry cargo). Exhibit 8.3 shows a summary of the OMI fleet.

All OMI's U.S.-flag tankers were "Jones Act" vessels, that is, they were unsubsidized, U.S.-built, U.S.-crewed, and U.S.-flag. They therefore qualified to carry cargoes between U.S. ports, a protected trade. The dominant movements included Alaskan crude oil to California and the U.S. Gulf (via Panama), refined oil products from the U.S. Gulf to the East Coast, and crude oil and refined products between the East and West Coasts.

OMI's seven tankers were all about 38,000 deadweight tons (DWT) and therefore competed against 171 other Jones Act tankers between 19,000 and 51,000 DWT.* The average age of this fleet was quite old-- over 25 years--and virtually the entire fleet was steam-powered.

There also was a Jones Act chemical trade. The major marine participants were Dow, Union Carbide, Diamond Shamrock, Exxon, Monsanto, Shell, Phillips, and Union Oil. Only about ten chemical tankers operated in the open charter market; the remainder were all locked into proprietary trades. Almost all these ships were overage.

OMI's U.S.-flag dry cargo fleet operated in the U.S. government-financed food/fertilizer give-away programs. Fifty percent of these cargoes must move on U.S.-flag vessels, if available. The extra cost of the U.S.-flag ships was paid by the U.S. government. Since this program was budgeted on a year-to-year basis, it was difficult to project future demand. OMI's competition in this trade included a small fleet of similar old bulkers, occasional oil tankers, and several large U.S.-flag liner companies.

OMI's foreign-flag fleet, both dry cargo and tankers, operated in the international bulk market, which was where the most substantial segment of the world fleet served. OMI's foreign-flag fleet included two 270,000 DWT VLCC's (Very Large Crude Carriers), two product tankers, one OBO (Ore-Bulk-Oil), two LPG (Liquefied Petroleum Gas) tankers, and ten dry bulk carriers ranging from 26,700 to 60,000 DWT.

As a result of the oil embargo of October 1973, the world bulk shipping market had generally been depressed. Consequently, world shipbuilding was also

----

* Jones Act Tankers over 51,000 DWT typically operated in the Alaska/U.S. West Coast trade.

generally depressed. Mr. du Moulin was analyzing
tankers for the U.S. domestic trade, which was
protected from both foreign-flag vessels and U.S.-
flag subsidized ships. Therefore, the freight rates
in this trade were not directly affected by the
depressed rates in international trades.

In a similar manner, U.S. shipyards such as
Avondale were protected from foreign competition in
building vessels for domestic trades. Exhibit 8.4
presents ship construction under contract in U.S.
yards on September 1, 1978. Although 50 vessels were
under contract, all but two were scheduled to be
delivered before 1981. It could take more than two
years from the time of final contract negotiations
until shipyard labor became heavily involved in the
building of a new vessel. This time was necessary to
take care of such tasks as signing the contract,
arranging for financing, arranging any government
subsidies or financing aids, completion of
engineering drawings, obtaining bids from suppliers,
placing orders for steel and equipment, and taking
delivery of purchases. Because of this time lag,
shipyards that did not have vessel construction
contracts on the books for 1981 delivery by the end
of 1978 could face lay-offs of workers in 1981.
Exhibit 8.5 shows the pessimistic outlook for U.S.
shipyards as expressed by the President of the
Shipbuilders Council of America.

JONES ACT TANKERS

Mr. du Moulin looked at the results of the analysis
he had performed. His analysis included the
following segments: supply of Jones Act fleet
tankers, potential impact of the Tanker Safety Law on
product tankers, demand for Jones Act tankers,
Avondale designs for tankers, and economic
considerations.

The Jones Act tanker fleet from 15,000 to 51,999
DWT is shown in Exhibit 8.6, while Exhibit 8.7
presents a breakdown of those vessels that oil
companies owned or long-term chartered. The new
tanker safety law could require additional equipment
on tankers. Exhibit 8.8 provides further details on
the requirements and their impact.

While there was no doubt that vessel supply
would decrease, vessel demand was more difficult to
predict. Exhibit 8.9 shows historical data available
from the Maritime Administration (MarAd). The
decrease in the movement of oil from the USG (U.S.

Gulf) to the USNH (U.S. North of Hatteras, North Carolina) was due to the opening of the Colonial Pipeline. It is possible that this movement will shrink further with future expansion of the Colonial Pipeline. Nevertheless, Alaska oil movement to the mainland had dramatically increased and should continue at high levels for a long time. A proposed Cal.-Tex. pipeline could be in operation by 1982, but an expansion of the Alaska Pipeline should offset this. Consequently, large movements through the Panama Canal (restricted to shipments of approximately 60,000 tons or less) should continue. Export of Alaskan oil was probably the single largest threat to the American tanker market. However, the Export Administration Act required Congressional action to permit such exports, which was unlikely.

The Strategic Petroleum Reserve program might be extended to 1984, with half of this reserved for U.S.-flag tankers. Similarly, PL-480 and Soviet grain were potential markets, but these would only be fallbacks to coastwise oil.

Exhibit 8.10 shows the principal characteristics of a vessel design by Avondale. This vessel could be used either as a product or chemical tanker due to the tank segregations and coatings. Exhibit 8.11 presents the potential manning level for this diesel-powered vessel.

Exhibit 8.12 illustrates the advantage in operating cost of the Avondale design over existing Jones Act vessels on a round trip voyage between Corpus Christi, Texas, and New York City. Exhibit 8.13 expresses this operating cost advantage in terms of a time charter rate.

If OMI were to purchase new motor tankers, it appeared that the minimum order quantity was two. In this way the engineering cost would be spread over two vessels and the yard would experience some benefits of the "learning curve". While OMI had talked with potential charterers of such vessels, no commitments had been obtained to date.

The cost of each vessel would be approximately $50 million. Under the Title XI insurance program, the U.S. government would guarantee a vessel mortgage for up to 87.5% of the investment cost. Under the government program, the vessel owner could acquire a 20-year to 25-year mortgage at AAA bond rates (i.e., approximately 9.5% at this time) for an additional cost of only 0.5%. Under Internal Revenue Service regulations, a shipowner could take a 10% investment tax credit on the vessel purchase and use accelerated depreciation over a 14.5-year vessel life.

Ogden Marine, Inc.

In the event that a potential vessel owner could not take advantage of all the tax shelters available, he could arrange a leveraged lease from a firm who wished to hold the title of the vessel and gain the accompanying tax shelters involved. In September 1978, a vessel operator could obtain a 20-year lease at an annual rate equal to approximately 6% of the purchase price of the vessel.

160

Exhibit 8.1

CONSOLIDATED BALANCE SHEETS

Assets

	Estimated 1978	1977
Current Assets:		
Cash	$ 37,217,000	$ 44,859,000
Marketable Securities – at cost, which approximates market . . .	69,266,000	22,627,000
Receivables (less allowances: 1978, $4,297,000; 1977, $4,837,000	222,889,000	136,126,000
Inventories.	183,314,000	197,651,000
Prepaid expenses, etc.	8,973,000	8,732,000
Total Current Assets	521,659,000	409,995,000
Property, Plant, and Equipment (at cost):		
Land	20,553,000	19,555,000
Buildings and improvements	132,735,000	119,993,000
Machinery and equipment.	279,274,000	269,901,000
Vessels.	355,277,000	338,393,000
Capitalized lease.	11,928,000	11,686,000
Total.	803,767,000	759,528,000
Less accumulated depreciation and amortization. . . .	284,751,000	261,584,000
Property, Plant, and Equipment – net.	519,016,000	497,944,000
Other Assets:		
Investment in unconsolidated subsidiaries.	2,719,000	29,853,000
Goodwill and other intangible assets	41,038,000	23,293,000
Miscellaneous.	80,705,000	60,602,000
Total other assets	124,462,000	113,748,000
Total.	$1,165,137,000	$1,021,687,000

Ogden Marine, Inc.

Exhibit 8.1 Continued

Liabilities and Shareholders' Equity	Estimated 1978	1977
Current Liabilities:		
Current portion of long-term debt	$ 50,320,000	$ 33,667,000
Accounts payable	179,630,000	148,525,000
Federal and foreign taxes on income	62,044,000	18,345,000
Accrued expenses, etc.	81,467,000	63,713,000
Total current liabilities	373,461,000	264,250,000
Long-Term Debt (exclusive of amounts due within one year)	331,996,000	332,875,000
Deferred Taxes, Reserves, etc.	76,140,000	66,531,000
5% Convertible Subordinated Debentures Due 1993	32,528,000	32,528,000
Shareholders' Equity:		
Serial preferred stock, par value $1 per share; authorized, 4,000,000 shares;		
$1.875 cumulative convertible shares; outstanding: 1978, 615,000; 1977, 706,000	615,000	706,000
$2.00 cumulative convertible shares; outstanding: 1978 and 1977, 321,000	321,000	321,000
Common stock, par value $.50 per share; authorized, 20,000,000 shares; outstanding: 1978, 8,488,000; 1977, 8,790,000	4,244,000	4,395,000
Capital surplus		10,988,000
Earned surplus	315,832,000	309,093,000
Total shareholders' equity	351,012,000	325,503,000
Total	1,165,137,000	$1,021,687,000

Exhibit 8.2

NET SALES AND SERVICE REVENUES AND OPERATING PROFIT OF BUSINESS SEGMENTS
(ESTIMATED)

(Expressed in thousands of dollars)

	1978	1977	1976	1975	1974
Net Sales and Service Revenues					
Transportation					
Marine construction	$ 456,881	$ 426,774	$ 359,057	$ 366,402	$ 267,865
Shipping	104,002	98,226	97,812	90,471	85,692
Marine Terminals	136,930	116,679	102,225	89,232	98,398
Total Transportation	697,813	641,679	559,094	546,105	451,955
Metals	709,750	584,934	640,116	586,042	1,037,523
Food and Leisure Services	224,058	200,086	191,691	185,349	184,666
Food Products	159,973	138,328	142,250	145,093	156,979
Other	43,021	27,245	24,322	28,675	26,996
Total Net Sales and Service Revenues	$1,834,615	$1,592,271	$1,557,473	$1,491,264	$1,858,119
Operating Profit					
Transportation					
Marine Construction	$ 55,704	$ 46,432	$ 34,646	$ 24,931	$ 18,574
Shipping	27,332	29,464	25,137	21,285	15,944
Marine Terminals	5,897	1,261	1,315	173	2,824
Total Transportation	88,993	77,157	61,098	46,389	37,342
Metals	26,529	16,564	31,689	35,608	66,218
Food and Leisure Services	(8,940)	4,885	6,816	6,566	373
Food Products	8,960	7,566	2,003	344	16,543
Other	8,569	1,811	876	258	(12,364)
Total Operating Profit	124,111	107,983	102,482	89,165	108,112
Unallocated other income, and corporate expenses - net	(2,225)	(1,688)	754	(1,307)	(4,489)
Interest - net	(25,423)	(26,790)	(25,560)	(20,211)	(21,401)
Income Before Taxes	$ 96,463	$ 79,505	$ 77,676	$ 67,647	$ 82,222

Ogden Marine, Inc.

Exhibit 8.3

OGDEN FLEET STATISTICS

A.   AVERAGE OF OMI FLEET (years)

	1970	1972	1974	1976	1978
Foreign Tanker*		0(new)	1.5	1.5	3
Foreign Dry**	5	4	3	4.5	6.5
U.S. Tanker	9	11	12	14	13
U.S. Dry ***	25.5	25	27	31	29

B.. TOTAL NUMBER OF VESSELS

	1970	1972	1974	1976	1978
Foreign Tanker	0	1	2	6	7
Foreign Dry	3	5	10	13	13
U.S. Tanker	4	4	6	6	5
U.S. Dry	12	10	10	7	6
Total number of Vessels	19	20	28	32	31

C.   TONNAGE OF VESSELS (000 DWT)

	1970	1972	1974	1976	1978
Foreign Tanker		266	315	714	784
Foreign Dry	80	201	408	505	505
U.S. Tanker	142	142	215	215	187
U.S. Dry	231	203	203	138	131
Total Tonnage of Vessels	453	812	1,141	1,572	1,607

*LPG, OBO, Tankers
**Bulkers, Car/Bulkers, excludes transfer from U.S. fleet.
***Includes vessels transferred foreign.

164

Exhibit 8.4

SHIP CONSTRUCTION UNDER CONTRACT
SEPTEMBER 1, 1978

No.	Type	Total DWT	Cost##	Government Participation	Owner	Scheduled Delivery Date
THE AMERICAN SHIPBUILDING COMPANY, Lorain, Ohio						
1*	Ore Carrier	59,000	35.0	CCF	National Steel	1978
1*	Ore Carrier	59,000	45.0	None	United States Steel	1979
1*	Ore Carrier	61,000	45.0	None	Interlake Steamship	1980
AVONDALE SHIPYARDS, Inc., New Orleans, Louisiana						
1*	LNG##	63,170	106.0	CS(16.5%),MI,CCF	El Paso Columbia	1979
1*	LNG##	63,170	103.0	CS(16.5%),MI,CCF	El Paso Savannah	1979
1	LNG##	63,170	100.0	CS(16.5%),MI,CCF	El Paso Cove	1979
2*	T	328,000	133.4	None	Exxon	1978/79
2	L	83,042	139.5	CS(40.08%),MI	Waterman	1980
BATH IRON WORKS Corp., Bath, Maine						
1*	Cn	16,300	43.2	CS(49.64%),MI	American Export	1979
1*	Cn	16,300	43.2	CS(49.64%),MI	American Export	1980
BAY SHIPBUILDING Corp., Sturgeon Bay, Wisconsin						
1	Ore Carrier	62,000	32.5	CCF,MI	American Steamship	1979
1	Ore Carrier	23,300	18.0	None	American Steamship	1978
1	Ore Carrier	62,000	32.5	CCF	Bethlehem Steel	1980
1*	Ore Carrier	62,000	45.0	None	United States Steel	1978
1	Ore Carrier	23,300	20.0	None	Oglebay Norton	1979
1	Ore Carrier	32,600	35.0	None	Cooper SS Co.	1980
BETHLEHEM STEEL Corp., Sparrows Point, Maryland						
2*	Cn	54,680	156.6	CS(49.64%),MI	Farrell	1979
EQUITABLE SHIPYARDS, Inc., New Orleans, Louisiana						
3*	Cargo	6,600	28.5	CS(48.52%)	American Atlantic	1979
GENERAL DYNAMICS Corp., QUINCY SHIPBUILDING DIVISION, Quincy, Massachusetts						
5*	LNG##	318,000	475.0	MI	Patriot	1978/79
2	LNG##	125,000	310.0	CS(25.48%)	LACHMAR, Inc.	1979/80
NATIONAL STEEL & SHIPBUILDING Co., San Diego, California						
2(1*)	T	300,000	123.8	CCF	ARCO	1979/80
1*	T	188,500	67.0	None	Shell	1978

Exhibit 8.4 Continued

No.	Type	Total DWT	Cost##	Government Participation	Owner	Scheduled Delivery Date
NEWPORT NEWS SHIPBUILDING & DRYDOCK Co., Newport News, Virginia						
1*	LNG###	63,460	96.8	CS(25.74%),MI,CCF	El Paso Arzew	1978
1*	LNG###	63,460	94.2	CS(25.74%),MI,CCF	El Paso Gamma	1979
1*	CT	390,770	139.7	CS(38.75%)	VLCC I	1979
PETERSON BUILDERS, Inc., Sturgeon Bay, Wisconsin						
2*	Ro-Ro'''	6,000	33.5	CS(42.15%)	American Heavy Lift	1978/79
SEATRAIN SHIPBUILDING Corp., Brooklyn, New York						
1*	CT	125,000	70.6	CS(40.83%),MI	Fillmore Tanker Corp.	1978
2*	Tug Barge'	12,900	42.5	CS(38.05%),MI	Coordinated Caribbean	1978
1	Ro-Ro	4,700	12.7	CS(41.34%)	Cumberland	1978
SUN SHIPBUILDING Corp., Chester, Pennsylvania						
2	LNG''	137,660	205.0	CCF,MI	Pacific Lighting Marine	1982
1*	T	118,300	25.0	MI	Shipco 669 Inc.	1978
2*	T	62,000	72.0	None	Sun Trading	1979
1	Cn	26,600	75.5	None	Matson Navigation Co.	1980
TODD SHIPBUILDING Corp., Galveston, Texas						
1*	Pipe Barge	N.A.	34.0	None	Santa Fe	1978
TOTAL						
50(35*)		3,571,812	3,716.9			

* Keel has been laid.
* In commercial shipyards having facilities to build vessels 475 by 68 feet.
Millions of dollars estimated.
125,000 cubic meters.
' Artubar (articulated Tug/Barge). Tugs being built by Marinette Marine Corp.
'' 130,000 cubic meters.
''' Heavy-lift Ro-Ro cargo ships.

Key: B-Bulk; C-Cargo; c-Conversion; CCF-Capital Construction Fund; Ch-Chemical Carriers; Cn-Containership; CP-Cargo Passenger; CS-Construction Subsidy; CT-Crude Tanker; DS-Deep Sea Mining Ship; F-Freighter; L-Lighter-Aboard Ship; LNG-Liquefied Natural Gas Tanker; MI-Title XI Vessel; PT-Product Tanker; Ro-Ro-Roll-on/Roll-off; SB-Sea Barge; T-Tanker; TB-Tug Barge; Cn-p-Partial Containership; O-Ore Carriers; OBO-oil-bulk-ore.

Exhibit 8.5

COMMENTS OF ED HOOD, PRESIDENT,
SHIPBUILDERS COUNCIL OF AMERICA

Historically, the shipbuilding industry of the United
States has gone through recurring periods of high,
then low, activity. The absence of stability has
been caused by various influences: among them,
changing demands for new ships, changing domestic and
international economic conditions, and changing
governmental policies.

In 1978, production activity in U.S. private
shipyards was generally high. Total employment
averaged close to 174,000, down slightly from 1977.
But the illusion of relative stability has quickly
evaporated. A downward movement in shipbuilding has
commenced and is accelerating in this country as well
as abroad. Ocean shipping worldwide, by reason of
adverse economic repercussions following the 1973
Middle East oil embargo, has been in a state of
oversupply and depression. This condition is
expected to persist into the early 1980's and perhaps
longer.

The demand for new merchant ships has
accordingly dropped substantially. More than 35
million DWT of tankers and about 13 million DWT of
dry cargo vessels are currently idle throughout the
world. Some recently delivered ships have gone
immediately into lay-up. The result has been a
global surplus of shipbuilding capacity, and an
increasing number of shipbuilders are thereby chasing
a decreasing number of ship construction
opportunities. Amid international discussions of
ways to reduce over-capacity multilaterally, below-
cost prices are being offered by many foreign
shipbuilders, in most cases, with the approval and
financial support of their governments. A
devastating subsidy war could readily develop.
Nationalism to maintain shipyard and shipping assets,
rather than economic doctrine, is the motivation.

**To date, the United States has been less
affected and less motivated than other
countries.**

Tonnage in lay-up has been minimal, but the
overall volume of U.S. exports and imports carried by
U.S.-flag shipping has continued to decline and is
now less than 5%. Competition from foreign-flag
shipping has intensified. Soviet shipping has

Ogden Marine, Inc.

Exhibit8.5 Continued

engaged in predatory rate cutting, and the Soviet
Navy is moving toward supremacy on the seas. Several
U.S.-flag shipping lines face insolvency. Inflation
and domestic regulatory requirements have steadily
escalated U.S. shipbuilding prices. Shipowners
generally have thus not been enthusiastic about
ordering new ships or replacing older vessels.

As a consequence, the backlog of merchant
shipbuilding contracts in U.S. shipyards, placed
earlier in this decade, is rapidly diminishing, and
the present unpromising outlook for new business will
not support a stable workforce. Over the next four
years, 45,000 to 50,000 skilled shipyard workers are
expected to lose their jobs. More than 150,000
employees in supporting industries face the same
prospect of unemployment.

> **Some U.S. shipbuilders, of course, will be less
> affected than others. Six or seven yards will
> perform better than 80% of the foreseeable
> workload.**

Contrary to general surmise, newbuilding
requirements for the U.S. Navy will not offset the
downturn to merchant ship construction. The five-
year naval shipbuilding program has already been
reduced from 157 to 70 ships, and there have been
reliable indications of a further reduction in 1979.
In this difficult period, those yards building guided
missile frigates, submarines, and destroyers will
probably fare better than certain of their
counterparts.

Repair and conversion work, though believed to
be spotty in the near-term, will also sustain only a
part of the industry. The specter of idle production
capacity, however, is unavoidable. Supply and
demand, rather than multilateral agreements reached
arbitrarily to reduce capacity, will, in the end,
determine which yards, if any, in this country are
destined to close their gates.

Meantime, vacillations concerning U.S. naval
ship construction are reflective of the perfidy of
governmental indecision which continues to surround
the formulation and implementation of an effective
and coordinated naval/maritime/shipbuilding policy.
The future size and missions of the Navy have yet to
be settled. Programs anticipating the construction
of liquefied natural gas (LNG) carriers have been
inhibited by the incoherence of Administration

Exhibit 8.5 Continued

intentions. Unlike other governments, the United States has not pragmatically addressed the need for preservation of shipping and shipbuilding capabilities under sovereign control.

Shipbuilding, despite its proven importance to national security and economic growth, has not received priority attention over the past 12 months. In this void, a Congressional Shipyard Coalition, composed of 42 representatives from 19 states, was established in the fall of 1978, and with Federal departments and agencies clearly operating at cross purposes, this broadly-based bi-partisan group could well compose the "court of last resort" with respect to the direction of national shipbuilding policy in both the near-term and the long-term.

In sum, the outlook for shipbuilding will improve only as the world economy recovers. With overall economic improvement, the demand for oceanborne commerce will surely increase and the need for shipbuilding production will be stimulated.

The state of the world economy, however, is beyond the control of shipbuilders--individually or collectively. This is a matter for governments, and so it should be. It might therefore not be improvident to suggest that the sense of nationalism motivating the present shipping and shipbuilding policies of many individual governments could contribute to a recovery of the world economy.

Most industrialized countries and all developing countries cannot survive without imports and exports. In volume movements, ships are the practical mode of transportation. In the United States, for example, 69 strategic materials must be imported, in part or totally--by oceangoing vessels-- to sustain essential national endeavors. U.S. dependency on nearly half of these critical items ranges from 50% to 100% of total needs. Many come from developing countries. At the same time, the United States is a major exporter of agricultural, and finished and semi-finished products, including items of critical importance to other nations.

But there is little orchestration of these exports and imports in a manner which will assure an optimum enhancement of the world economy as well as a more rational utilization of domestic shipping/ shipbuilding resources. With the so-called 40-40-20

Ogden Marine, Inc.

Exhibit 8.5 Continued

UNCTAD formula for the sharing of seatrade still not
ratified by most countries, including the United
States, the alternative of bi-lateral agreements for
the coordinated movement of exports and imports has
an attractive ring. On a selective, though
organized, basis, it would seem that involved
countries could effectively pursue this alternative
as a step toward more worldly order in shipping and
shipbuilding. This approach, rather than arbitrary
reductions in capacity or wishful hopes, might
provide a needed framework for an orderly return to
normalcy and stability.

Exhibit 8.6

JONES ACT FLEET INDEPENDENT AND OIL COMPANY

DWT Range	# of Vessels	Total DWT	AGE PROFILE (Number of Ships)								Year Built	Average Age as of 1/81
			1941 -45	1946 -50	1951 -55	1956 -60	1961 -65	1966 -70	1971 -75	1976 -80		
5,000-19,999	25	448,000	16	0	8	0	1	0	0	0	1947.8	33.3
20,000-24,999	17	392,000	16	0	1	0	0	0	0	0	1944.4	36.7
25,000-29,999	52	1,421,000	23	4	11	9	5	0	0	0	1950.0	30.1
30,000-34,999	38	1,235,000	3	0	7	23	2	0	1	2	1957.6	23.5
35,000-39,999	26	988,000	0	0	1	6	0	11	4	5	1967.4	13.7
40,000-44,999	5	208,000	0	0	1	4	0	0	0	0	1957.0	24.1
45,000-51,999	15	742,000	0	0	0	6	9	0	0	0	1961.1	20.0
TOTAL 5,000-51,999	178	5,434,000	58	4	29	48	17	11	5	7	1954.5	26.6

#1 Excludes MSC vessels; includes all
contracted newbuildings.

171

Ogden Marine, Inc.

Exhibit 8.7

OIL COMPANY JONES ACT FLEET
19,000-51,000 DWT
OWNED AND LONG-TERM CHARTER

Company	# of Vessels	Total DWT	Average DWT	Average Age as of Jan. 1981
Amoco	3	68,800	22,900	38
Arco	5	172,200	34,400	22
Chevron	5	199,000	39,800	5
Cities	6	176,900	29,500	33
Coastal	3	89,700	29,900	30
Exxon	10	382,800	38,300	27
Getty	4	106,500	26,600	32
Gulf	14	396,900	28,350	26
Hess	3	97,000	33,000	31
Mobil	9	283,200	31,500	24
Phillips	2	54,000	27,000	20
Shell	12	354,000	29,500	27
Sohio	0	0	0	--
Sun**	8	288,200	36,000	21
Texaco	13	363,700	28,000	30
Union	2	59,200	29,600	31
Total	99	3,092,500	31,240	26.5

*Chartered for more than three years.

**Includes 2 x 31,000 DWT modern tankers to be delivered in 1978-79.

172

Exhibit 8.8

JONES ACT TANKER SUPPLY
POTENTIAL IMPACT OF TANKER SAFETY LAW
ON PRODUCT TANKERS

A. Key Requirements for Existing Product Tankers

   1. Tankers 20,000-40,000 DWT must have segregated or clean ballast by January 1986 or when they are fifteen years old, whichever is later.

   2. Tankers over 40,000 DWT must have segregated or clean ballast by June 1981.

   3. Tankers over 20,000 DWT must have inert gas by June 1983.

B. Analysis: The tables below indicated that as of January 1986 only twelve vessels will be less than fifteen years old. The twelve tankers include

   1. Five Chevron gas turbine segregated ballast tankers built in 1976.

   2. Two Sun segregated ballast motor tankers to be delivered in 1980.

   3. Five non-segregated turbine tankers that will reach fifteen years of age between 1986 and 1988.

Because of their old age, almost all vessels must convert to segregated or clean ballast at the stipulated dates. About 30% of the fleet capacity will be lost to segregated or clean ballast. A substantial amount will be scrapped due to the cost of inert gas installation, loss of cargo capacity, and steel deterioration. Given the Tanker Safety Law and assuming scrapping at age 40, the present coastwise fleet of 178 tankers (15,000-52,000 DWT) totaling 5,434,000 will decrease to 120 tankers totaling 2,962,000 DWT by 1986. Only forty of these tankers will be less than 25 years old.

C. Tables:

   1. Unregulated Tankers: Below 20,000 DWT

Size Category	# of Vessels & Total DWT	Average Age Jan. 1986	# of Vessels older than 15 years	# of Vessels & DWT after compliance	# of Vessels & DWT after compliance & scrapping
15,000-19,999	25 448,000	38.3	25	25 448,000	9 161,000

*assuming scrapping at age 40, regardless of regulation.

173

Ogden Marine, Inc.

Exhibit 8.8 Continued

Size Category	# of Vessels & Total DWT	Average Age Jan. 1986	# of Vessels older than 15 years	# of Vessels & DWT after compliance	# of Vessels & DWT after compliance & scrapping*
2. Regulated Tankers: 20,000-39,999 DWT					
20,000-24,999	17 / 392,000	41.7	17	17 / 274,000	1 / 16,000
25,000-29,999	52 / 1,421,000	35.1	52	52 / 995,000	29 / 555,000
30,000-34,999	38 / 1,235,000	28.5	35	38 / 883,000	35 / 815,000
35,000-39,999	26 / 988,000	18.7	17	26 / 750,000	26 / 750,000
3. Regulated Tankers: Over 40,000 DWT (up to 52,000)					
40,000-44,999	5 / 208,000	24.6	5	5 / 146,000	5 / 146,000
45,000-51,999	15 / 742,000	20.6	15	15 / 519,000	15 / 519,000
4. All Tankers: 15,000-52,000					
15,000-52,000	178 / 5,434,000	31.6	166	178 / 4,015,000	120 / 2,962,000

*assuming scrapping at age 40, regardless of regulation.

Exhibit 8.9

DOMESTIC SEABORNE CHEMICAL & PETROLEUM MOVEMENTS
1972-1976: SHIP ONLY
MARAD DATA
(MM. LT)

Voyage	1972	1973	1974	1975	1976
USNH to USNH	13.0	13.4	14.7	14.2	14.8
USG to USNH	55.5#2	40.6#2	39.0	40.1	38.5
USG to USSH	10.3	11.2	10.8	10.9	11.1
USG to USG	7.6	10.9	10.7	10.0	6.7
Cal. to Cal.	14.0	14.6	13.3	14.7	15.7
Cal. to Pacific NW	5.7	5.7	4.7	4.3	5.3
Cal. to Hawaii	1.6	1.3	1.5	1.2	1.2
Pacific NW to Cal.	2.4	2.5	2.0	2.2	2.1
Alaska to Cal. & NW	8.5	8.3	7.9	7.5	7.0
PR & VI to USNH	20.8	21.2	20.2	19.2	20.3
PR & VI to USSH	0.8]4.1#3	1.4]4.5	2.3]4.6	2.4]4.2	3.9]4.7
PR & VI to USG	1.1	2.4	2.8	1.6	1.7
Total Ship (incl. VI)	141.3	133.5	129.9	128.3	128.3
Total Ship (excl. VI)	122.7	113.0	109.2	109.3	107.1
Total Ship & Barge for all movements (incl. VI)	184.2	177.8	174.6	176.1	184.7
% Ship vs. Barge	76.7%	75.1%	74.4%	72.9%	69.5%

#1 Ignores all movements less than 1.0 mil./yr.
#2 Breakdown for 1972 and 1973 USG to USNH:

	Crude	Resid.	Distil.	Gas
1972	14.5	4.0	17.8	11.8
1973	8.5	2.4	12.5	9.9

#3 1976 St. Croix = 21.2; P.R. = 4.7
Therefore assume for all years 82% St. Croix & 18% P.R.

ALL THE ABOVE DATA EXCLUDES ALASKA NORTH SLOPE CRUDE WHICH BEGAN MOVING
IN 1977.

Key: USNH   - United States North of Cape Hatteras, North Carolina;
     USSH   - United States South of Cape Hatteras, North Carolina;
     USG   - United States Gulf; Cal.-California;
     Pacific NW - United States Pacific North West; P.R. - Puerto Rico;
     VI   - Virgin Islands

Ogden Marine, Inc.

Exhibit 8.10

PRINCIPAL CHARACTERISTICS

LENGTH OVERALL, ft.	629'-3 1/2"	TOTAL CARGO CAP., bbls., 100%	367,799
LENGTH BETWEEN PERP., ft.	610'-0"	WING TANK CAP., bbls., 100%	220,416
BREADTH, ft.	105'-10"	CENTERLINE TANK CAP., bbls., 100%	147,383
DEPTH, ft.	60'-0"	CAUSTIC SODA CAP., bbls., 100%	110,070
DESIGN DRAFT, ft.	38'-0"	BALLAST CAPACITY, L.T., 100%	16,257
SCANTLING DRAFT, ft.	43'-6"	FUEL OIL CAPACITY, L.T., 98%	2,630
DEADWEIGHT @ 38'-0"	42,466	DIESEL OIL CAPACITY, L.T., 98%	410
DEADWEIGHT @ 43'-6"	51,287	LUBE OIL CAPACITY, L.T., 100%	308
HORSEPOWER, BHP, MCR	14,100	FRESH WATER CAPACITY, L.T., 100%	383

Exhibit 8.11

OGDEN JONES ACT MOTOR TANKER
MANNING LEVEL

<u>Deck Officers</u> - Masters, Mates & Pilots Union

1 Master
1 Chief Mate
1 Second Mate
1 Third Mate

<u>Radio Officer</u> - American Radio Association

1 Radio Officer

<u>Engineering Officers</u> - Marine Engineers Beneficial
Association - Dist. 2

1 Chief Engineer
1 First Assistant
1 Second Assistant
1 Third Assistant

<u>Unlicensed Personnel</u> - Seafarers International Union

1 Bosun
6 A/B Seamen
1 QMED*/Pumpman
3 QMED
1 Steward/Cook
1 Chief Cook
2 Utilitymen

<u>Total Crew</u> = 24

----

* "QMED" Stands for Qualified Member of the Engine
Department.

Ogden Marine, Inc.

Exhibit 8.12

EXISTING FLEET VS. OGDEN MOTOR TANKER

Assumptions
- i) Corpus Christi/New York, round voyage, 4002 n.m.
- ii) 1978 vessel operating costs/day including crew, insurance, M&R, etc.
- iii) full no-heat cargo on 38' draft
- iv) $78/LT IFO, $75/LT Bunker C (for all steam tankers) $110/LT Diesel
- v) Steam tankers consumption – waiting = 30% steaming
  - pumping = 50% steaming
- vi) Motor tankers consumption – waiting = 4 LT diesel
  - total discharge = 12 LT diesel
- vii) 300 LT constant for water, stores, crew
- viii) Carry round voyage bunkers plus 20% margin

SAMPLES OF EXISTING FLEET OF STEAM TURBINE VESSELS

								NEW VESSEL
Full DWT	17,000	23,000	27,300	32,500	38,000	41,600	49,500	51,300
DWT on 38'	17,900	23,000	27,300	32,500	38,000	41,600	49,500	42,355
Speed/Consumption*	13 on 50	13 on 50	13 on 55	15.5/76	16 on 82	16/105	16/110	16/46+4
Op. Cost/Day	$7,500	$7,600	$7,700	$7,800	$8,000	$8,500	$9,000	$6,500
No. of Days Steaming	12.83	12.83	12.83	10.76	10.42	10.42	10.42	10.42
5% Delay	.64	.64	.64	.54	.52	.52	.52	.52
No. of Days Load	1.50	1.50	1.50	1.50	1.50	1.50	1.50	1.50
No. of Days Discharge	1.50	1.50	1.50	1.50	1.50	1.50	1.50	1.50
Port Delay	.50	.50	.50	.50	.50	.50	.50	.50
Total Days	16.97	16.97	16.97	14.80	14.44	14.44	14.44	14.44
Vessel Cost	$127,275	$128,972	$130,669	$115,440	$115,520	$122,740	$129,960	$93,860
Consumption	746 LT	746 LT	821 LT	962 LT	1,008 LT	1,290 LT	1,452 LT	479FO/70I
Bunker Cost	$ 55,950	$ 55,950	$ 61,545	$ 72,105	$ 75,584	$ 96,784	$101,393	$ 45,062
Port Charges 18,000	$ 14,000	$ 14,500	$ 15,000	$ 15,500	$ 16,000	$ 16,500	$ 18,000	$ 16,500
Total Cost	$197,225	$199,422	$207,214	$203,045	$207,104	$236,024	$249,353	$155,422
Cargo DWT	16,705	21,805	26,015	31,046	36,490	39,752	44,578	41,382
$/LT Delivered	$11.81	$ 9.15	$ 7.97	$ 6.54	$ 5.68	$ 5.94	$ 5.59	$ 3.76
$/BBL @7.5 BBL/LT –	$ 1.57	$ 1.22	$ 1.06	$ .87	$ .76	$ .79	$ .75	$ .50

*"Speed/Consumption" refers to the number of tons per day of fuel to produce a particular speed. For an existing steam tanker, "13 to 50" or "13/50" means a speed of 13 knots requires a daily consumption of 50 tons of Bunker C. The new vessel has a main engine that uses intermediate fuel oil (IFO or FO) in the exhibit (although it could use Bunker C) and a separate auxiliary ship services engine that uses diesel fuel (D). For the new ship, "16/46 + 4" means a 16 knot speed requires a daily consumption of 46 tons of IFO and 4 tons of diesel.

Exhibit 8.13

OGDEN JONES ACT MOTOR TANKER

Analysis

1. Time Charter Advantage vs. Existing Fleet
Weighted Average Cost/ton for all existing vessels
greater than 30,000 DWT:

30-35,000	1,235,000 DWT =	39%	x	$6.54	
35-40,000	988,000 DWT =	31%	x	5.68	
40-45,000	208,000 DWT =	6.5%	x	5.94	= $6.01
45-52,000	742,000 DWT =	23.5%	x	5.59	
	3,173,000	100%			

Advantage of New Vessel Per Voyage:
    41,382 LT x (6.01-3.76) = $ 93,110

Advantage Per Day:
    $93,110 / 14.44 days   = $ 6,448

Time Charter Equivalent Advantage:
$6,448 x 30.4   = $4.63/DWT/month
  42,355

2. Time Charter Advantage if Bunker Prices Double
New Vessel vs. existing 41,600 DWT vessel:

	Existing Vessel	New Vessel
Vessel Cost	$122,740	$ 93,860
Bunkers	193,568	90,124
Port Charges	16,500	16,500
	$332,808	$200,484
Tons	39,752	41,382
Per Ton	$8.37	$4.84

Advantage of New Vessel Per Voyage:
    41,382 x (8.37-4.84)   = $146,078

Advantage Per Day:
    $146,078 / 14.44 days   = $ 10,116

Time Charter Equivalent Advantage:
$10,116 x 30.4   = $7.26/DWT/month
  42,355

Chapter 9

TRITON OIL COMPANY

In October 1979, James Lund, Marine Vice-President of Triton Oil Company, was preparing to contract for construction of the largest vessel in the company's fleet. For two years he had directed studies which included analyses of supply and demand considerations, present and future port facilities, historical weather conditions by trade route, power plant design, and a variety of significantly different vessel concepts. The final decision on vessel type and parameters would be made shortly.

COMPANY BACKGROUND

Triton supplied a variety of fuel oils, both distillants and residuals, to utilities and industries in the southern United States. (Exhibits 9.1 and 9.2 show recent balance sheets and income statements.) From its beginnings in Florida, it had expanded to serve Georgia, the Carolinas, Tennessee, Arkansas, Alabama, Louisiana, and Texas. The company also provided vessel bunkering service in Port Everglades, the Port of Miami, Palm Beach, Canaveral, Mobile, Memphis, Corpus Christi, Pensacola, Tampa, Manatee, Savannah, and New Orleans.

Triton owned and operated a fleet of 16 tugs ranging from 450 to 4,200 horsepower. In addition, the firm owned and operated 25 barges with a total capacity nearing 500,000 barrels. (The number of barrels per ton varies with the substance, but there are approximately 6.67 barrels per ton for #6 oil, 7.5 barrels per ton for #2 oil, and 8.5 barrels per ton for gasoline.) Triton's barges ranged from a 2,500 barrel barge for specialty shipside service to a 96,000 barrel unit for travel across the Gulf of Mexico. Triton tows encompassed waters from Corpus Christi, Texas; New Orleans, Louisiana; Memphis, Tennessee; Mobile, Alabama; and all major Florida ports on the Gulf Coast, to the East Coast in South and Central Florida and north to Savannah, Georgia; Charlestown, South Carolina; New York; and Boston.

VESSEL CONCEPTS

Lund considered the four following different vessel concepts:

1. Conventional tankers.
2. Tug boat pushing and hauling a barge, dependent on weather, using a conventional hawser pushing system.
3. Tug boat pushing a barge but combining the conventional hawser pushing system with a sophisticated pad system to increase pushing time.
4. Integrated tug-barge (ITB) system similar to Ingram and/or Port Everglades towing units.

Because of the vessel size and weather conditions being considered by Triton, the tug-barge concepts they were studying fell into the category of ocean-going tug-barge (OGTB) systems. Exhibit 9.3 provides background information on OGTB's.

All vessel concepts above exhibited economies of scale; that is, the cost per ton of oil moved decreased as vessel size increased. Factors which could limit the maximum size vessel that Triton could effectively utilize included: cargo volume, water depth at port terminals, channel depth and width, docking facilities, and storage tank volume. For Triton, water depth was the most constraining factor. Exhibit 9.4 shows information on vessel draft at port facilities Triton wished to serve with its new vessel.

Triton Oil Company

Triton decided on a maximum vessel draft of 39 feet, which placed the maximum deadweight tonnage between 55,000 and 60,000. When using tugs and barges, it is a lot more efficient, in terms of propulsive force, to push a barge rather than haul it behind a tug. Lund estimated from model test data that with a 55,000 DWT barge and a 13,000 horsepower tug, pushing rather than towing would account for an increase in speed of 2.5 to 3.0 knots loaded, and 1.5 to 2.0 knots in light condition. When a tug and barge were designed for push operations, the stern of the barge would contain a shallow notch into which the tug would fit. Based on historical weather conditions in the Gulf of Mexico, Lund estimated that a tug-barge combination conventionally designed for push operation (Vessel Concept #2) would be able to operate in a push condition 60% of the time and would be required to tow 40% of the time.

With the supplemental pad system that Triton was considering (Vessel Concept #3), the units could operate in a push condition approximately 99% of the time. For this system, the notch would be considerably deeper (115 feet) and wider (53 feet) than the conventional push system. With the linkage system chosen by Triton, which uses no hard connection between the tug and the barge, the tug's bow is not restricted against heave. Instead, the tug bow is fitted with rubber rollers mounted on a horizontal axis to facilitate relative vertical movement between tug and barge. Additionally, the tug is secured to the barge notch laterally by four hydraulically operated laminated steel/plastic pads, two located on either side of the tug, fore and aft of amidships, which mate with steel guides mounted on the barge. Tensioning nylon hawsers are led from the barge wings via rollers on each of the tug's quarters to hydraulic tensioning rams. These serve the dual purpose of holding the tug in position longitudinally and providing the means for transmission of astern power. It should be mentioned that the tug is equipped with a towing winch and 2 3/4" steel wire to operate in the towing mode, if necessary.

COAST GUARD REGULATIONS

One factor affecting the vessel cost is the impact of United States Coast Guard (USCG) regulations, in particular, whether the vessel involved would require a Certificate of Inspection. There were three elements of importance connected with a Certificate of Inspection. First, the vessel must be constructed to strict USCG standards. Second, the vessel must undergo scheduled periodic USCG inspections as well as arbitrary additional inspections held at the discretion of the USCG. Every two years the vessel must be drydocked and udergo an extensive examination. Every other year, the USCG performs a mid-term inspection that is less extensive and typically does not involve drydocking. Third, an inspected vessel must operate in accordance with the minimum manning scales mandated by the USCG. In addition, the number of personnel who must hold USCG licenses and the type of licenses they must hold are specified as a condition of certification.

Lund was not concerned with the first requirement, construction standards. Triton would build to USCG standards whether or not the vessel required a Certificate of Inspection. Triton would also arrange for periodic inspections of the new vessel by the American Bureau of Shipping (ABS) if the vessel were not USCG-inspected. However, Lund was concerned with some "horror stories" he had heard in the industry of unqualified USCG reservists performing inspections and the inexperience of even the regular inspectors assigned to Officer in Charge of Marine Inspection (OCMI) duties.

The manning standards dictated by the USCG were of particular concern to Lund. If the vessel was over 300 gross registered tons (GRT), it would require a Certificate of Inspection and be subject to relatively strict manning standards. A diesel-powered vessel between 200 and 300 GRT would not require certification and would be subject to considerably less stringent manning standards. When analyzing the types of written examinations that officers had to pass to be licensed for each of the categories, Lund discovered that for either size of vessel, officers would be asked identical questions relative to operation of coastal tankers. The examination for the unlimited licensed officers of the inspected vessel would include a few theoretically oriented questions on deep sea operations not asked of those getting a Master Freight and Towers license, but Lund felt they were irrelevant to Triton's activities. Lund concluded that there would be no difference in terms of safety between the two categories of manning standards as far as the Triton operations were concerned, except that the lower licensed operators would actually have grown up in the tug and barge business, the exact business in which Triton was engaged.

Triton Oil Company

Any tanker or barge considered by Triton would require a USCG Certificate of Inspection. However, by designing a tug between 200 and 300 GRT, rather than over 300 GRT, Triton would avoid certification of the tug and be subject to less stringent manning standards.

COST ANALYSIS

In early 1978, a consultant report compared the costs of a 15-knot, 60,000 DWT tanker with a 12-knot, 55,772 DWT tug/barge unit. In 1978 dollars, the extreme minimum price of the tanker was estimated at $35 million; a price of $45 million was felt to be more probable. The ITB (Vessel Concept #4) systems examined were indicated to require almost the same investment as a regular tanker. The tug/barge unit (Vessel Concept #2) investment was estimated at $24.2 million. Vessel Concept #3 was estimated to cost approximately $1 million more, or $25.2 million.

Intuitively, one might have expected that the tug/barge unit would cost the same or more than an equal-sized tanker. After all, it would take more steel to build the two separate units than the tanker. The lower tug-barge unit cost is attributed to the following three factors:

1. Tugs and barges are constructed by yards that specialize in such vessels. This degree of specialty results in lower costs.
2. The tanker would typically be built by a large shipyard, which is staffed to compete for U.S. government work and would have a much higher overhead rate than the small yards building tugs or barges.
3. The unmanned barge can obtain a 25% reduction in accordance with the 1966 International Load Line Convention.

Triton planned to use a tug between 200 and 300 GRT that would not require USCG certification; consequently, an 11-man crew was assumed. In contrast, the tanker would require certification. A 30-man crew was assumed (although this was higher than the USCG minimum manning scale which deals only with operating functions).

Assuming a 15% return on equity after tax, when operating on the Corpus Christi/Port Everglades trade, the $45 million tanker moves oil at a cost of $6.27 per ton, the $35 million tanker at $5.22 per ton, and the $24.2 million tug-barge unit at $4.10 per ton. Exhibit 9.5 gives a breakdown of the $1.12 per ton difference between the $35 million tanker and the $24.2 million Vessel Concept #2 tug-barge unit. Even when the tanker was evaluated on a foreign-flag construction and operation basis, the tug and barge under U.S. flag compared favorably with the tanker for short haul foreign trades. Exhibit 9.6 presents a cash flow projection using the tug-barge unit at estimated market rates.

Exhibit 9.7 shows the incremental costs associated with USCG inspection of the tug. If the tug were over 300 GRT, it would require certification. The USCG could also require inspection if it determined the tug was "mechanically linked" to the barge. Lund felt that the linkage system he had chosen could not be interpreted to be "mechanically linked". Consequently, unless the USCG changed their regulations, their tug design between 200 and 300 GRT would not require certification. However, the USCG had already stated that they were in the process of re-evaluating the relevant regulations.

Triton used non-union crews on its vessels. It was rumored in the industry, however, that if he accepted a particular union on his new vessel, the union would "guarantee" that the USCG would not attempt to inspect the proposed tug, if built.

Lund attempted to bring together and evaluate all the relevant data as he prepared to make his decision for a new addition to the Triton fleet.

Triton Oil Company

Exhibit 9.1

BALANCE SHEET

	December 31	
	1978	1977
ASSETS		
CURRENT ASSETS		
Cash	$ 807,636	$ 576,239
Accounts and Notes Receivable (less allowance for uncollectible amounts: 1978-$625,000; 1977-$500,156).	43,232,254	48,892,167
Inventories		
Oils	23,719,714	35,120,370
Other Products and Supplies.	2,251,662	1,692,968
Other Current Assets	65,903	614,883
TOTAL CURRENT ASSETS	70,077,169	86,896,627
PROPERTY AND EQUIPMENT-NET	50,221,674	27,594,370
INVESTMENTS.	502,543	3,612,975
OTHER ASSETS	1,737,410	1,513,648
TOTAL.	$122,538,796	$119,617,620

LIABILITIES AND STOCKHOLDERS' EQUITY

	1978	1977
CURRENT LIABILITIES		
Accounts Payable--Trade.	$ 28,822,747	$ 41,130,286
Accounts Payable--Affiliates	6,669,422	1,457,161
Banks Loans--Prime Rate (1978-11 3/4%; 1977-7 3/4%)	9,000,000	8,000,000
Income Taxes Payable	(1,996,340)	7,824,075
Other Current Liabilities.	2,307,281	2,567,590
TOTAL CURRENT LIABILITIES	44,803,110	60,679,112
LONG-TERM LIABILITIES (less Current Portion: 1978-$161,027; 1977-$669,779).	17,054,416	842,431
STOCKHOLDERS' EQUITY		
Capital Stock-$10 Par Value, Authorized 600,000 shares. Outstanding: 300,874	3,008,740	3,008,740
Capital Surplus.	4,120,000	4,120,000
Retained Earnings.	53,552,530	50,667,337
TOTAL STOCKHOLDERS' EQUITY	60,681,270	57,796,077
TOTAL.	$122,538,796	$119,617,620

Exhibit 9.2

STATEMENT OF CONSOLIDATED INCOME
AND RETAINED EARNINGS

	12 Months Ended December 31 1978	12 Months Ended December 31 1977
INCOME		
Sales of Products and Services	$600,354,131	$616,220,170
Interest and Other Income.	1,079,003	2,139,023
TOTAL	601,433,134	618,359,193
EXPENSES		
Cost of Products and Services Sold	544,556,084	570,851,355
Operating, Selling & Admin. Expenses . . .	38,282,402	27,568,543
Depreciation	2,709,448	2,402,361
TOTAL	585,547,934	600,822,259
INCOME FROM OPERATIONS	15,885,200	17,536,934
PROVISION FOR INCOME TAXES	6,000,000	8,100,000
NET INCOME	9,885,200	9,436,934
RETAINED EARNINGS		
Beginning of Period.	50,667,330	41,230,403
Dividends Paid	7,000,000	——————————
RETAINED EARNINGS-END OF YEAR.	$ 53,552,530	$ 50,667,337

STATEMENT OF CHANGES IN
CONSOLIDATED FINANCIAL POSITION

SOURCE OF WORKING CAPITAL		
From Operations:		
Net Income	$ 9,885,200	$ 9,436,934
Expenses Not Requiring Outlay of Working		
Capital - Depreciation	2,709,448	2,402,361
Working Capital Provided		
from Operations.	12,594,648	11,839,295
Issuance of Long-Term Debt	16,500,000	
Decrease in Investments.	3,110,432	161,588
TOTAL	32,205,080	12,000,883
USE OF WORKING CAPITAL		
Additions to Property & Equipment - Net. .	25,336,759	9,286,828
Reduction of Long-Term Debt.	288,015	711,574
Increase in Other Assets	223,762	29,478
Dividends.	7,000,000	——————————
TOTAL	32,848,536	10,027,880
INCREASE (DECREASE) IN WORKING CAPITAL . . .	$ (643,456)	$ 1,973,000

187

Triton Oil Company

Exhibit 9.3

BACKGROUND ON
OCEAN-GOING TUG-BARGE (OGTB) SYSTEMS

INTRODUCTION

Historically, OGTB's have been used as low-value bulk
cargo coastal carriers with slow, sometimes unsafe,
obsolete, and/or surplus equipment. However, in the
last two decades, OGTB's have developed into ship-
sized, trans-ocean capable, medium-speed carriers of
low- and high-value cargoes with safe, modern, and
economical equipment. How such a rapid metamorphosis
occurred is explained in the following sections.

HISTORICAL DEVELOPMENT OF OGTB'S

In this country, tugs and barges first began to
appear on the East Coast during the late nineteenth
century. This was the time when steam ships and the
developing railroads began displacing the slower and
less reliable sailing vessels in the coastal trades.
Rather than scrapping all of these sailing ships, the
enterprising shipping operators of the day decided to
take advantage of their sound hulls and the new steam
technology by converting the ships into barges and
towing as many as four to six of them behind steam
tugs. These tug-barge systems were very successful
in low-value bulk cargo trades, especially in the
carriage of coal between Virginia and New England.
Similarly, large ocean sailing vessels were
occasionally converted into barges and successfully
towed across the Atlantic. However, since such tug-
barge systems depended on obsolete hulls, these
trades began to fade out as the hulls deteriorated.
So by 1950, tug-barges became practically extinct on
the East Coast, most coastal trades.being served by
WWII surplus Victory ships and T-2 tankers.
     However,on the West Coast, tug-barge operations
began really to take off at this time. This was

With minor modification, this exhibit has been taken
verbatim from "Applications of Ocean-Going Tug-Barges
to Military Operations", by Jonathan D. Kaskin,
prepared for the Office of Naval Research/Military
Sealift Command, Massachusetts Institute of
Technology, July 1979.

Exhibit 9.3 Continued

because the WWII surplus BCL's (barge-converted LST's), 1200 HP Miki class tugs, and 1500 HP Navy ATA tugs were readily available at very low cost, to carry expanding West Coast and Alaskan bulk trades in cement, lumber, and other building materials. These tug-barge systems, using converted military equipment, continued in operation through the 1950's.

By 1960, the tug-barge operators on the West Coast, and the coastal ship operators on the East Coast, had to consider how to replace their aging WWII surplus equipment. There were several incentives for these operators to invest in new tug-barge systems rather than ships, particularly in non-liner trades where speed was relatively unimportant. The primary incentive was in the much lower crewing expenses resulting from tug operation. This was because ship manning scales, due to aggressive union pressures and Coast Guard regulations, were more than four times* that of tugs, and the average crewman's wage was significantly more than that of the average tugboat sailor.** As this was a time when fuel costs were low, crewing costs were the major operating expense, so such savings were significant.

----

* Ocean-going tugs under 200 GRT can under U.S. law be manned with approximately seven men on voyages of less than 600 miles. Longer voyages require crews of approximately 11 men. In comparison, in 1977, U.S.-flag tankers had an average crew size of 33 men, with new tankers crewed with approximately 26 men.

** It has often been argued that the ship unions were able to achieve such high manning and wage scales because liner shipping operators with vessels in foreign trades could pass their crewing expenses back to the government, who was subsidizing their operational costs via the MarAd Operating Differential Subsidy (ODS) program. Unfortunately, the ship operators operating in domestic trades had to pay for similar union manning and wage scales, but without the benefit of subsidy due to the cabotage provisions of the "Jones Act". Tugboat crewmen, who are not required to be licensed by the Coast Guard and who are trained on fishing or inland waterway vessels, have traditionally not been members of these ship unions, so the higher manning and wage scales did not pertain to them.

Triton Oil Company

Exhibit 9.3 Continued

Another important incentive for the operators to choose tug-barge systems was that they typically cost less to build, compared to ships of equal capacity. This was because tugs, if under 300 GRT, were free from expensive governmental inspection procedures. Also, barges which were designed for slow speeds could be built with simple inexpensive hull lines. Thus, in the early 1960's, several shipping operators built large barges for bulk trades, especially for oil, cement, and lumber. Practically all of these tug-barge systems were operated in the hawser pull-tow mode. But, as described in the next section, push-towing was beginning to be seriously considered as an alternative operating method.

DEVELOPMENT OF PUSH-TOWED OGTB'S

The idea of a towboat or tugboat pushing a barge or integrated group of barges is not a new one. For several decades, the river tugboat operators have been taking advantage of the better control and lower drag resistance provided by push-towing over pull-towing a barge on a hawser.

The reason why push-towing allows the tug captain to have better control over the barge is obvious. Pulling a large barge at the end of a long wire provides little control over its direction, except in the calmest seas, or unless an active rudder or high resistance skegs* are installed on the barge hull. Additionally, maneuvering the barge in congested areas requires shortening the wire to allow better control. However, this can lead to a dangerous situation if the tug loses power or is underpowered, so that the tug is run over or dragged off course by the barge. Due to these factors, hawser towing of barges greater than 20,000 DWT is considered unusual.

The reason why push-towing results in significantly less drag than pull-towing is because, when a barge is towed, both hulls develop their own wave-making resistance. In push-towing only one hull form generates waves. Additionally, in pull-towing, the hawser which forms a catenary in the water

----

* Skegs are fins that are added near the stern of the barge's underwater hull, which by their lateral drag increase the barge's steerability and stability.

Exhibit 9.3 Continued

develops its own frictional resistance, and skegs that are used to prevent the barge from yawing too severely also can increase the barge frictional resistance by more than 30%. This additional drag usually limits ocean-going barges towed on a hawser to speeds of 6 to 8 knots, although average speeds of up to twelve knots have been achieved by light displacement shipshape roll-on/roll-off (Ro-Ro) barges towed by 9,000 HP tugs. On the other hand, push-towed OGTB systems have achieved speeds in excess of 15 knots with tugs of less than 15,000 HP, and higher speeds can be achieved if desired.

Given these reasons why push-towing is superior to pull-towing, it would be expected that push-towing on the oceans would have developed long ago. However, the simple pin and wire/chain lashings used on the rivers to link the tugs and barges together were not capable of withstanding the forces generated by ocean winds and seas. Nevertheless, the advantages of push-towing were so compelling that in the 1950's, tug and barge operators began experimenting with push-tow operation.

The first push-tow tug-barge design was by George G. Sharp, Inc., for Cargill Grain Co.'s trade on the Great Lakes and the New York Barge Canal. This system, the Car-Port/G1, had a wedge-notch type linkage which was the prototype for the Breit/Ingram linkage design. This rather small system (less than 5,000 DWT) ran into serious difficulty with the USCG manning authorities, which eventually demanded that the tug be manned the same as a ship since it was not capable of safe independent operation. This forced the system into foreign-flag service where the tug-barge unit, and later an additonal tug and two barges, operated successfully with standard tug crews in a drop-and-swap* mode for many years. Although not successful in U.S. trade, the Car-Port system did prove the feasibility of push-tow operation.

Seeing the advantages and the feasibility of push-tow operation, the tug and barge operators began to seek some means of pushing their barges without being levied with increased manning scales similar to those imposed on the Car-Port. So, in the 1960's, they began constructing new large barges (some over

----

* In a "drop-and-swap" mode, the tug separates from one barge and connects with another during its normal activities.

Exhibit 9.3 Continued

10,000 DWT) with stern notches for their tugs to push in. The notches in these first-generation ocean-going barges were rather shallow, so that push-tow operation could only be conducted in the calm waters of river estuaries, bays, harbors, and calm seas. However, since standard tugs were used for pushing these barges, no manning penalty was incurred. Later, the tug and barge operators wanted to increase the percentage of time that they could push the barges. This would allow them to take advantage of the increased speed as well as the better maneuverability available with push-towing. Thus they began deepening the notches and using sophisticated cable/chain linking and chafing gear so that push-tow operation of these second-generation OGTB's could be extended to all but severe seas.

The ultimate goal of the tug and barge operators, however, was 100% or all-weather push operation, with standard tugs with normal tug manning. This was first attempted in 1963 by L.R. Glosten & Associates, Inc., with the Sea-Link articulated tug-barge linkage. The linkage was prototype-tested with only partial success in 1964 and 1965. However, it was shown that push-towing with standard tugs was a viable concept, so that experimentation continued in the development of improved linkages.

In the early 1970's, the technology was developed for high horsepower diesel engines that could drive large barges (greater than 20,000 DWT) at moderate speeds, and for linkages that would allow the tug and barge to remain linked together in all types of weather and seas. Three third-generation linkages were developed in the U.S., two rigid (the Breit/Ingram and CATUG designs) and one semi-rigid (the ARTUBAR design). These linkages have been built for OGTB's of up to 55,000 DWT and have been designed for barges of up to 80-100,000 DWT. The Coast Guard determined that these tug-barge units were "mechanically linked"* ships so that ship manning scales would pertain to them. However, since the tugs were very highly automated and had unattended enginerooms, they were certificated for the smallest manning possible--about 13 men throughout, including

----

* Triton's Vessel Concept #4 falls in the category of a "mechanically linked" third-generation OGTB or integrated tug-barge (ITB) system.

Exhibit 9.3 Continued

stewards and cooks.* This meant that these tug-barge units could be manned with approximately 14 to 16 men, substantially less than ships of the same capacity.

These low manning scales were very attractive to operators who needed to build new ships. They saw these mechanically linked third-generation OGTB's as a way of reducing ship crewing costs substantially. Also, they found that they sometimes could obtain a tug-barge system at lower capital cost than the equivalently sized ship, even if the tug was built under Coast Guard inspection. For these reasons, several of these mechanically linked units were built to operate as pseudo-ships in coastal and foreign trades.

On the other hand, tug and barge companies operating with standard tugs and notched barges did not like these mechanically linked tug-barge systems. The linkages were expensive** and caused the tug to be modified so much that it usually could not be used for anything except pushing its own barge. But the primary reason why operators did not accept these mechanically linked systems was because it would allow the Coast Guard inspection of their tugs. This would substantially increase the size and the licensing standards of their crews. This would in turn increase their operating and capital costs significantly, probably making their push-towed units uncompetitive in comparison with pull-towed units with tugs manned with standard crews and built without inspection.

Nevertheless, the tug and barge operators wanted to take advantage of push-towing 100% of the time. The better barge control and fuel savings available, particularly in the longer distance coastal trades,

----

* A typical manning certificate would require a licensed Master, three Mates, Chief and Assistant Engineer, a Qualified Member of the Engine Department, and six Able Bodied Seamen (AB's).

** Third-generation OGTB mechanical linkages require special reinforcement of the barge notch and tug bow to absorb the stresses resulting from the linkage. In addition to sophisticated coupling and decoupling gear, the rigid linkage systems require heavier scantlings overall, increasing the hull steel weight and cost even further.

Exhibit 9.3 Continued

with push-towing could not be denied. But since
mechanical linkages would result in increasing
manning and capital costs, they instead began to
develop improved cable/chain linkages (with some
additional hardware) that allowed push-towing in
practically all types of sea conditions but would not
force their tugs to come under Coast Guard
inspection. Recently, several of these "loosely
linked" third-generation OGTB's* have been built for
coastal liquid bulk trades, replacing the overaged
WWII jumboized T-2 tankers. Additionally, other
linkage designs are being developed.

So today, we have two different forces
stimulating OGTB development. One is exerted by ship
operators who are investing in the "mechanically
linked" OGTB designs. They see these pseudo-ship
OGTB's as a means of reducing the crewing and
construction costs of their domestic and foreign
fleets. The other force is exerted by tug and barge
operators who are investing in the "loosely linked"
OGTB designs. They see these OGTB's as a means of
taking advantage of push-tow operation without any
manning penalties for their domestic coastal trades.

----

* Triton's Vessel Concept #3 falls into the category
of a "loosely linked" third-generation OGTB.

Exhibit 9.4

DRAFT AND TIMING ESTIMATES

Tampa (Manatee)	39'	1980 and beyond
Tampa (Bartow)	32'	Unchanged (two port with Manatee)
Pensacola	32'	39' 1982 and beyond
Miami	36'	1980 and beyond
Port Everglades	37'	39' 1981 and beyond
Port Canaveral	39'	1980 and beyond
Savannah	34'	39' 1982 and beyond (assumes relocation)
Boston	40'	1980 and beyond
New York	32'	Lightering

Triton Oil Company

Exhibit 9.5

COMPARISON BETWEEN
60 M. DWT TANKER COSTING $35.0 MILLION AND
55,772 DWT TUG/BARGE UNIT* COSTING $24.2 MILLION
IN CORPUS CHRISTI/PORT EVERGLADES TRADE**

Cost + 15% Return on Full Equity, $/Ton

60 M. DWT Tanker	5.22
55,772 DWT Tug/Barge	4.10
Δ =	1.12/Ton

Reconciliation

1.	Salaries, Wages & Benefits	0.479
2.	Subsistence	0.016
3.	Maintenance and Repair @ 2.5% of Inventory	0.045
4.	Insurance @ 1.5%	0.042
5.	Stores & Supplies	-
6.	Overhead	0.001
7.	Fuel	0.216
8.	Return on Investment	0.348
9.	Other	(0.027)
	TOTAL:	1.120

---

* Vessel Concept #2 being pushed at 12 knots 60% of the time and pulled at less than 10 knots 40% of the time for an average speed of 10.7 knots.

** For each round trip of 2440 nautical miles, approximately 2.5 days would be spent in port.

196

Exhibit 9.6

ECONOMICS OF 372 M. BARREL UNIT WITH MARAD FINANCING

Year	12.5% Equity	Depre- ciation	87.5% Prin- cipal	8.5% Interest	Annual Operations Cost	Estimated Annual Revenues	Taxable Income	48% Taxes	Inv. Tax Credit	Net Cash
1980	3044	3044	1065	1811	2675	8507	977	469	2679	5166
1981		2664	1065	1720	2675	8700	1641	788		2452
1982		2330	1065	1630	2675	9080	2445	1174		2536
1983		2038	1065	1539	2675	9109	2857	1371		2459
1984		1785	1065	1449	2675	9134	3225	1548		2397
1985		1561	1065	1358	2675	9147	3553	1705		2344
1986		1366	1065	1268	2675	9147	3838	1842		2297
1987		1196	1066	1177	2675	9147	4099	1968		2261
1988		1047	1066	1087	2675	9147	4338	2082		2237
1989		1045	1066	996	2675	9147	4431	2127		2283
1990		1045	1066	905	2675	9147	4522	2170		2331
1991		1045	1066	815	2675	9147	4612	2214		2377
1992		1045	1066	724	2675	9147	4703	2257		2425
1993		1045	1065	634	2675	9147	4793	2301		2472
1994		872	1065	543	2675	9147	5057	2427		2437
1995			1065	453	2675	9147	6019	2889		2065
1996			1065	362	2675	9147	6110	2933		2112
1997			1065	272	2675	9147	6200	2976		2159
1998			1065	181	2675	9147	6291	3020		2206
1999			1065	91	2675	9147	6381	3063		2253
	(1218)	1218								

Avg Revenue = 9087   Net Present Value @ 20% = 10,908

*This exhibit reflects vessel concept #2 operating at an average speed of 10.7 knots.

Triton Oil Company

Exhibit 9.7

Estimate that crew increases from 11 to 16 men:

1	Engineer
2	Ordinary Seamen
1	Able Bodied Seaman
__1__	Messman/Utility Man

TOTAL: 5

Wages change from uninspected tug to ship orientation:

	Monthly Wages
Captain	$4,170
Mate	2,257
Mate	2,257
Assistant Engineer	2,519
Assistant Engineer	2,519
Chief Engineer	3,707
Able Bodied Seaman	1,066
Able Bodied Seaman	1,066
Able Bodied Seaman	1,066
Able Bodied Seaman	1,066
Ordinary Seaman	851
Ordinary Seaman	851
Cook	1,264
Utility Man	795

Exhibit 9.7 Continued

Utility Man		795
Utility Man		___795_
	TOTAL:	$27,044

Since crew members work 30 days, then take 30 days of vacation,two sets of crew are needed, so crew cost doubles to $54,088 per month, or $649,056 per year.

Annual benefits at 30% add $194,717, and an estimated overtime cost of 15% adds another $126,566; therefore, total annual crew-related costs equal $970,339.

Annual operating costs excluding fuel and port charges of uninspected base unit being planned (in thousands):

Salaries & Benefits		$391
Provisions		23
Spares & Supplies		177
Maintenance & Repair		443
Insurance		266
Overhead Allocation		____45_
	TOTAL:	$1,345

Annual cost differential between uninspected base unit and inspected tug (in thousands):

Salaries & Benefits		$579
Provisions		__11_
	TOTAL:	$590

Chapter 10

TECHNICAL NOTE ON THE USE OF AVERAGE
FREIGHT RATE ASSESSMENT BY OIL COMPANIES

Tankers engaged in spot market transportation are
compensated on a WORLDSCALE basis, a "dollars per
cargo long ton delivered from Port A to Port B".
WORLDSCALE rates are indices above or below a
"WORLDSCALE 100" base rate which has been computed
for several thousand port pairs and is reviewed and
updated twice annually. The WORLDSCALE rate for a
port pair reflects fuel prices, exchange rates, and
port fees. Exhibit 10.1 gives background information
as well as details of the hypothetical vessel for
which the WORLDSCALE rate is calculated.

Exhibit 10.2 presents a comparison of spot rates
and time charter rates for Very Large Crude Carriers
(VLCC's).

For intra-company oil movements, the Internal
Revenue Service has allowed the use of Average
Freight Rate Assessment (AFRA) to arrive at a cost
for tax purposes. AFRA consists of a weighted
average of all period and voyage charters. Exhibit
10.3 provides background information on AFRA and
presents a set of calculations. Exhibit 10.4
graphically shows AFRA values over a multi-year
period.

Oil companies use AFRA in three ways in terms of
their tax accounting on intra-company movements.

————————————————

This note was prepared by Henry S. Marcus for class
discussion. This technical note describes the U.S.
tax law as it existed at the time of the Venture Oil,
Marine Department case study. Revisions in the tax
laws have since occurred.

200

First, when a fully loaded tanker delivers a cargo, the oil company determines which size range the vessel is within; then the AFRA rate is applied to the cost of the cargo movement for tax purposes.

Second, if part of a vessel is unloaded at a port, the AFRA rate for the cargo parcel is used. For example, if 40,000 tons of oil are unloaded from a VLCC, the cost for tax purposes is the same as if the oil was delivered in a "medium range" vessel as defined in the AFRA system.

Third, the AFRA rate is used in determining the legal maximum price of gasoline sold by the oil company. The legal maximum is determined based on the various costs used in producing the gasoline. Where imported oil is used, the AFRA rate is used in determining the "cost" of the oil movement.

Average Freight Rate Assessment

Exhibit 10.1

WORLDWIDE TANKER NOMINAL FREIGHT SCALE
APPLYING TO TANKERS CARRYING OIL IN BULK

GENERAL PURPOSE

This Schedule of nominal freight rates is intended solely as a standard of reference, by means of which rates for all voyages and market levels can be compared and readily judged. It is the custom to express market levels of freight in terms of a percentage of the WORLDSCALE nominal freight rate. Thus WORLDSCALE 100 (or WORLDSCALE FLAT which is sometimes used) means the rate as calculated and published by the Associations, while WORLDSCALE 175, for example, means 175 percent of the published rate and WORLDSCALE 75 means 75 percent of that rate.

The schedule was originally issued, effective 15th September 1969, in replacement of the International Tanker Nominal Freight Scale issued in London and the American Tanker Rate Schedule issued in New York.

For the original Edition bunker prices as at 1st January 1969 were used, but for subsequent Editions weighted average bunker prices over a stated period have been used. On the 16th June 1976 it was announced that the Schedule would in future be issued twice a year with rates effective as from 1st January and 1st July, respectively. The 1st January issue will contain revised rates reflecting changes in both bunker prices and port charges, as has applied for previous 1st January revisions, while the 1st July issue will be updated only in respect of changes in port charges.

As originally introduced the Schedule was a dual currency one, separate rates being shown in both U.K. Sterling and in U.S. Dollars, but on the 26th November 1971 it was announced that it had been decided to discontinue the concept of a dual currency schedule and, for business concluded on or after 1st January 1972, only the WORLDSCALE U.S. Dollar rates would have validity, also that thereafter WORLDSCALE rates would be calculated and quoted only in terms of U.S. Dollars. Parties to a contract should specify clearly the currency of payment, should this be other than U.S. Dollars, and the rate of exchange to be used.

Exhibit 10.1 Continued

All rate calculations are per ton of 2240 lbs.
for a full cargo based on a round voyage from loading
port or ports to discharging port or ports and back
to first loading port using the following factors:

1. Standard Vessel
    Summer deadweight: 19,500 long tons
    Summer draught
        laden in salt water: 30'6"
    Average service speed: 14 knots
    Bunker Consumption
        at sea: 28 tons High Viscosity
                                Fuel Oil (180 cSt)
                                per day

    Bunker Consumption
        in port: 5 tons High Viscosity
                                Fuel Oil (180 cSt)
                                per day

2. Fixed Hire element: $1,800 per day

3. Bunker Prices/Port Costs

    For this Edition weighted average contract
    bunker prices applicable during the period 1st
    October 1979/31st March 1980 and port charges as
    known to the Associations at the end of March
    1980 have been taken into account.

4. Brokerage: 2 1/2%

5. Laytime allowance: 72 hours for loading
                                and discharging

6. Port Time (for rate calculations only):

    In addition to Laytime, 12 hours is allowed for
    each port involved in the voyage.

7. Canal Transit Time (for rate calculation
    purposes only):

    36 hours is allowed for each transit of the
        Suez Canal.
    24 hours is allowed for each transit of the
        Panama Canal.
    Mileage is not taken into account in either
        case.

Average Freight Rate Assessment

Exhibit 10.1 Continued

The fixed hire element of $1,800 per day is not intended to represent an actual level of operating costs, nor to produce rates providing a particular level of income or margin of profit, either for the standard tanker or for any other tanker under any flag. This figure is purely nominal and for calculation purposes only.

In calculating WORLDSCALE rates no allowance is made for any Tax on Freight or Income Tax which may be incurred by Owners when trading to or from certain countries. Neither is any provision made as to whether these taxes are for Owners' or for Charters' Account.

Source: "Worldwide Tanker Nominal Freight Scale, Code Name WORLDSCALE, As Revised Effective 1st July 1980", The International Tanker Freight Tank Association Limited and the Association of Ship Brokers and Agents (Worldwide) Inc., 1980.

Note: In the 1st July 1985 Edition of WORLDSCALE ASSOCIATION (NYC), INC., the brokerage fee was excluded (in accordance with U.S. anti-trust laws), and transit times for the Suez and Panama Canals were changed to 30 hours.

Exhibit 10.2

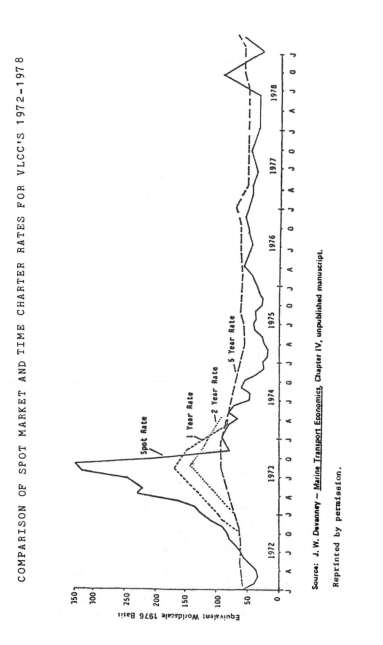

COMPARISON OF SPOT MARKET AND TIME CHARTER RATES FOR VLCC'S 1972-1978

Source: J. W. Devanney – Marine Transport Economics, Chapter IV, unpublished manuscript.

Reprinted by permission.

Average Freight Rate Assessment

Exhibit 10.3

LONDON TANKER BROKERS' PANEL
AVERAGE FREIGHT RATE ASSESSMENTS (AFRA)

The results of the Average Freight Rate Assessments,
or AFRA as these are more generally known, are now
published on the first business day of each month and
appear in publications such as "Lloyd's List",
"Platt's Oilgram", and similar periodicals circulated
in the Oil and Shipping trades. Results are provided
for five different deadweight groups as follows:

```
GENERAL PURPOSE  -   16,500/ 24,999 DWT
MEDIUM RANGE     -   25,000/ 44,999 DWT
LARGE RANGE 1    -   45,000/ 79,999 DWT
LARGE RANGE 2    -   80,000/159,999 DWT
VLCC             -  160,000/319,999 DWT
ULCC             -  320,000/549,999 DWT
```

The calculations are made over a monthly period
running from the 16th of one month to the 15th of the
following month, and the assessments represent the
weighted average cost of commercially chartered
tonnage as employed in the international transport of
oil during the calculation period. For example, the
results published on 1st December 1976 represent the
average cost during the period 16th October/15th
November 1976. Certain categories of vessels are
excluded from the assessments, e.g., vessels owned by
governments (except those operating on commercial
charter), and vessels employed in specialized trades
such as the carriage of clean oils, petro-chemicals,
lube oils, and bitumen, etc. Vessels engaged in
protected coastwise trades (for example, American-
flag vessels trading between American ports) are also
excluded.
    In each size group, tonnage is divided into the
following four categories:

```
1.   Company Vessels
2.   Vessels engaged on Long Term Charters
3.   Vessels engaged on Short Term Charters
4.   Vessels engaged on Single Voyage Charters.
```

For results published up to and including 1st
December 1976, "Long Term" meant charters originally
concluded for a period of 12 months or more, while
"Short Term" meant charters originally concluded for

Exhibit 10.3 Continued

a period of less than 12 months. For subsequent results, the period of "Long Term" is more than 18 months, while the period for "Short Term" is 18 months or less. Naturally, this change has no effect upon the result (the overall weighted average).

The carrying capacity of each vessel operating during the assessment period in each of these categories is calculated on the basis of a standard voyage, taking into account the various characteristics of each vessel, e.g., size, type of propulsion, speed, and bunker consumption. Then the weighted average rate in U.S. Dollars per ton for carrying a ton of oil on the basis of that standard voyage is obtained for each of these four categories, time charters being converted to a voyage cost per ton. The result for each size group is the overall weighted average obtained by multiplying the total carrying capacity for each of the charter categories by the weighted average rate for that charter category, the rate applicable to company vessels being the weighted average rate applicable to all chartered vessels. The answer thus arrived at in U.S. Dollars per ton is converted to a WORLDSCALE equivalent on the basis of the standard voyage and this is the published result.

Table 10.1 shows a set of AFRA calculations.

TABLE 10.1

LONDON TANKER BROKERS PANEL

Details of Breakdown of AFRA Monthly Assessment
for Vessels of 16,500/549,999 DWT
Covering Period March 16, 1980 to April 15, 1980

	DWT	Percent	WORLDSCALE Points
General Purpose (16,500-24,999)			
Company	1,241,243	64.5	255.9
Long Term	347,699	18.1	239.9
Short Term	178,377	9.3	249.0
Single Voyage	156,425	8.1	299.5
	1,923,744	100.0	255.9

Average Freight Rate Assessment

Exhibit 10.3 Continued

	DWT	Percent	WORLDSCALE Points
Medium Range (25,000-44,999)			
Company	3,826,509	52.1	198.0
Long Term	939,298	12.8	154.4
Short Term	786,146	10.7	215.0
Single Voyage	1,793,940	24.4	213.3
	7,345,893	100.0	198.0
Large Range 1 (45,000-79,999)			
Company	6,797,014	31.6	121.3
Long Term	4,865,287	22.6	98.5
Short Term	2,319,462	10.8	137.7
Single Voyage	7,525,203	35.0	130.9
	21,506,966	100.0	121.3
Large Range 2 (80,000-159,999)			
Company	12,670,980	32.4	79.6
Long Term	10,688,785	27.3	79.3
Short Term	3,691,763	9.4	78.5
Single Voyage	12,075,067	30.9	80.2
	39,126,595	100.0	79.6
VLCC (160,000-319,999)			
Company	49,431,900	49.1	49.8
Long Term	34,249,724	32.7	57.2
Short Term	3,896,613	3.7	46.2
Single Voyage	17,311,547	16.5	35.9
	104,889,784	100.0	49.8
ULCC (320,000-549,999)			
Company	7,658,942	46.9	42.4
Long Term	4,373,295	26.8	54.1
Short Term	1,230,890	7.5	38.5
Single Voyage	3,078,187	18.8	27.4
	16,341,314	100.0	42.4

Exhibit 10.3 Continued

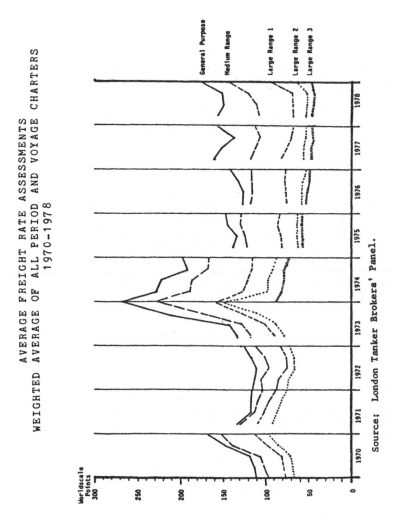

AVERAGE FREIGHT RATE ASSESSMENTS
WEIGHTED AVERAGE OF ALL PERIOD AND VOYAGE CHARTERS
1970-1978

Source: London Tanker Brokers' Panel.

Chapter 11

VENTURE OIL, MARINE DEPARTMENT

In March 1980, Will MacKay had recently received two
interoffice communications requiring his attention.
One dealt with the future operations of the LONE
STAR, a tanker now being used in the Gulf of Mexico.
The other involved the future of overall cargo
handling activities in the Gulf of Mexico. The
potential interrelationship between these issues
meant that he could not deal with them independently.

BACKGROUND

Will MacKay was Vice President-Marine of Venture Oil.
In addition, he was President of the Venture Oil
shipowning company. From his office in Houston,
Texas, he headed up the Marine Department, which was
responsible for providing the most economical marine
transportation for Venture Oil and its affiliates,
and for increasing marine profits by an aggressive
program of marine transportation contracts with third
parties. The marine transportation movements
included all crude oil and clean product cargoes as
required by Venture Oil and its affiliates that
necessitated movement in an ocean-going vessel. The

This case study was prepared by Henry S. Marcus and
Raphael L. Vermeir as a basis for discussion rather
than to illustrate either effective or ineffective
handling of an administrative situation. Names and
some other information used in this case study have
been disguised.

Marine Department provided the necessary vessels to move the cargoes. (Exhibit 11.1 contains more information on the organization and activities of the Marine Department.)

In March 1980, Venture Oil owned or time chartered 16 vessels as shown in Exhibit 11.2*. The Marine Department moved on the order of 300 thousand barrels per day (M. BD) in its worldwide operations. The largest single movement was the importation of crude oil from Northern Africa to the U.S. Gulf of Mexico. This movement made up roughly half of all company shipments in terms of volume and was expected to increase in the future.

LIGHTENING

The Venture Oil lightening operations** evolved because of the need to develop low-cost, competitive transportation into draft-limited ports in the U.S. Gulf. The system provides for the use of Venture Oil's VLCC's and LR2-type ships for the longest leg of the voyage, yet provides for delivery of cargo into the shallow U.S. Gulf ports using Venture Oil's dedicated lightening fleet. Not only does Venture Oil lighten its own cargo for import, Venture Oil's lightening operation is distinctive, to the extent that it is marketed to third party interests as a service. More information on lightening procedures is included in Exhibit 11.3.

----

* Venture Oil used the following descriptions for vessel size categories:

```
General Purpose (GP):      16,500 to  24,999 DWT
Medium Range (MR):         25,000 to  44,999 DWT
Large Range 1 (LR1):       45,000 to  79,999 DWT
Large Range 2 (LR2):       80,000 to 159,999 DWT
Very Large Crude Carrier (VLCC):
                          160,000 DWT and above
```

** The terms "lightering" and "lightening" are used interchangeably, although some people refer to lightering to mean complete unloading of a large vessel onto smaller vessels, and lightening to mean partial unloading into one or more smaller ships, where the large vessel subsequently proceeds to a dock for final unloading.

LONE STAR

The first interoffice communication Mr. MacKay
received described economic calculations for future
use of the LONE STAR, a Venture Oil steam turbine-
powered vessel used in the Gulf lightening
operations. Federal legislation promulgated in
accordance with an international agreement on Tanker
Safety and Pollution Prevention (TSPP) would require
tankers over 40,000 DWT operating in U.S. waters to
meet certain requirements (e.g., involving
combinations of crude oil washing, inert gas systems,
segregated ballast, etc.) in 1981. The LONE STAR,
with a deadweight of 44,328 tons would need $1
million worth of work (to be performed in 1981) to
meet these requirements.

In 1983, the LONE STAR would have her five-year
hull survey. In order to pass such a survey and be
able to operate until her next survey in 1988, a
total of $9.906--$1 million in 1981 and $8.905
million in 1983--would need to be spent to renovate
the vessel (including the additional TSPP
requirements). Exhibit 11.4 shows the cash flows for
repairing and operating the LONE STAR through 1988.
The exhibit assumes that lightening operation costs
will escalate at 10% per year between 1981 and 1988.
If the LONE STAR were only operated through 1983, the
costs of operations for years 1981, 1982, and 1983
would be identical to Exhibit 11.4 (but the capital
cost would only be $1 million). Port charges, which
make up a small proportion of the total costs, are
not included in this exhibit.

It was assumed that the LONE STAR would have a
scrap value of $3 million at the end of either 1981,
1983, or 1988.

An alternative to operating the LONE STAR was to
time charter a new medium-speed diesel-powered tanker
of 59,999 DWT. It was estimated that this larger
vessel could be time chartered for the three-year
period 1981-1983 at a rate of $10.25/DWT/month
($7,060,718 per year) or for the eight-year period
1981-1988 for $8.35/DWT/month ($5,751,897 per year).
In either case this would be a fixed rate with no
escalation.

Being a relatively shallow draft design, this
vessel could serve Freeport, Texas, fully loaded
carrying 15,900 tons more cargo than the LONE STAR.
While the LONE STAR carries 36,000 tons per trip and
makes approximately 57.4 trips per year (at 6.1 days
per trip), the larger vessel could carry 51,900 tons
per trip and make 50.7 trips per year (at 6.9 days

per trip). Consequently, the larger vessel could move 2,631,330 tons per year, an excess capacity of 564,930 tons more than the 2,066,400 tons carried by the LONE STAR. At a third party lightening rate of $0.50 per barrel (BBL), the excess capacity is worth $2,155,208 per year (assuming 7.63 BBL/ton).

Viewed in terms of time rather than capacity, the larger vessel needs only 39.8 trips per year to match the capacity of the LONE STAR. At 6.9 days per trip, the time chartered vessel could lift the necessary cargo in 275 days, leaving an additional 75 operating days per year. At her time chartered cost of $20,185 or $16,444 per day (depending on the length of the charter), this excess time is worth $1,513,875 or $1,233,300 per year, respectively.

Because the time chartered vessel is diesel-powered, it burns less fuel than the steam-powered LONE STAR. The LONE STAR burns an average of 30 tons per day (TPD) of Bunker C, while the time chartered vessel would consume an average of 20 TPD of Intermediate Fuel Oil (IFO) and 3.2 TPD of diesel fuel. While a ton of Bunker C costs less than a ton of diesel fuel, this disadvantage is more than outweighed by the lower consumption rate of the diesel engine. This cost differential is shown by comparing the fuel cost of the time chartered vessel in Exhibit 11.5 with the fuel cost of the LONE STAR in Exhibit 11.4.

FUTURE CARGO HANDLING IN THE GULF

The second interoffice communication Mr. MacKay looked at contained an economic comparison of alternative means of moving oil from North Africa to Lake Charles, Louisiana, and Freeport, Texas, the two major Venture Oil marine terminals in the Gulf of Mexico. In 1980, the percentage of tonnage received at Lake Charles vs. Freeport would be 63% vs. 37%.

Exhibit 11.6 shows the costs of the present system of lightening. Demurrage is charged when a vessel exceeds its allotted time (i.e., laytime) in a port. For the purposes of the calculations in the interoffice communication, laytime was taken to be 84 hours for a round-trip voyage. Because of inefficient loading facilities in North Africa, demurrage was a normal cost for vessels serving this port. Inclement weather conditions at the lightening area, as well as the pumping operations, made average demurrage costs in the Gulf even greater than in North Africa. Demurrage rates were based on Average

Freight Rate Assessment (AFRA), the commonly accepted basis of intra-company freight billings within the oil industry. AFRA represents the current average cost of moving oil by tankers in worldwide trade, including time charters and spot charters.

An alternative to lightening was transshipping, through the use of shoreside storage facilities in the Bahamas. Exhibit 11.7 shows the costs of transshipment under current conditions. Exhibit 11.8 represents the costs of moving oil through the Louisiana Offshore Oil Port (LOOP), a system using single-point moorings several miles offshore. LOOP was expected to become operational in 1981.

Exhibit 11.9 considers the installation of a single-point mooring (SPM) system off Freeport, Texas. No contracts for such a system had yet been signed, and it was expected such a facility (on a much smaller scale than LOOP) could be operational not sooner than 1983. Exhibit 11.9 assumes that Freeport would receive its cargo through the single-point mooring, while lightening would still be used at Lake Charles.

Exhibit 11.1

MARINE ORGANIZATION

1. <u>Houston</u>

   The Houston office is the center of Marine Department activities within Venture Oil. The Vice President in charge of Marine and most department heads are located in Houston. In addition, all other Marine offices are functionally responsible to the Vice President-Marine.

   There are three main departments in Houston. (For ease in understanding, the Controllers Department has been included below as a fourth Department due to the degree of interface with Marine, although technically it is not a part of Marine).

   <u>Operations and Technical</u>

   Basic Functions:

   a. Operations, personnel, safety, and repair policy for Venture Oil vessels
   b. Port information and port limitations
   c. Vessel newbuilding
   d. Local, national, and international rules and regulations.

   <u>Project Development</u>

   Basic Functions:

   a. Capital budget/profit objective
   b. Economic analyses

      1. Vessel acquisition
      2. New trade alternatives
      3. Special marine projects.

   c. Computer projects.

   <u>Marine Controllers</u>
   (Technically not within the Marine Department)

Venture Oil, Marine Department

Exhibit 11.1 Continued

Basic Functions:

a. Marine Department accounting
b. Profit objective
c. Monthly income forecasting
d. Authorization for expenditure and limits of authority.

Vessel Trading and Traffic

Basic Functions:

a. Scheduling vessel movements
b. Monitoring daily tanker charter market
c. Chartering term and spot coverage for Venture Oil's marine transportation requirements
d. Ship sales and purchases
e. Trafficking in all-owned, time chartered, and single-voyage chartered vessels in the worldwide trades
f. Contract administration.

2. London
The London Marine office is concerned with the owner-oriented operational aspects of the Venture Oil fleet.

Basic Functions:

a. Supervisor of deck operations and navigation
b. Engineering and related services
c. Safety
d. Manning
e. Training
f. Vessel inspection, ship repair and maintenance
g. Vessel storing.

3. Galveston
The primary function of the Galveston office is to provide on-site operational supervision for the U.S. Gulf lightening operation. Mooring masters, workboat, and engineering support personnel are headquartered in Galveston.
The Senior Marine Superintendent in charge of the Galveston office reports directly to the Manager of Operations and Personnel in London.

Exhibit 11.1 Continued

4.   <u>Bilbao</u>
     The Venture Oil Shipping Company's manning agent
     is located in Bilbao, Spain. The company,
     besides supplying merchant seamen, acts as
     liaison between the Spanish crews, and Spanish
     immigration and labor authorities. They also
     administer payroll, allotments, employee
     benefits, medical checkups, etc. Venture Oil
     maintains one full-time representative in the
     agent's office in Bilbao.

5.   <u>Venture Oil Shipping Company</u>
     Venture Oil's owned, bareboat, and time
     chartered vessels are owned or chartered by one
     offshore corporation. Venture Oil Shipping
     Company is the operator of the fleet and is
     incorporated in Liberia. Separate contracts of
     affreightment exist between Venture Oil Shipping
     Company and other Venture Oil affiliates,
     forming the contractual basis for the supply of
     transportation to cover Venture Oil's many
     shipping requirements.

     <u>Marine Relationship within Venture Oil</u>
     The Vice President-Marine of Venture Oil reports
     to the Executive Vice President of Supply and
     Transportation. Also reporting along the same
     lines is the Vice President of Transportation
     and Natural Gas Products, the Vice President of
     Supply and Trading, and the Manager of Aviation.
     The Executive Vice President of Supply and
     Transportation reports to the Group Executive
     Vice President of Petroleum Products. This area
     is commonly referred to as "Downstream
     Operations", which also includes Petroleum
     Marketing and Petroleum Refining.

Venture Oil, Marine Department

Exhibit 11.1 Continued

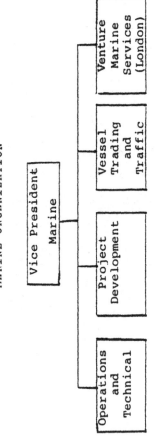

MARINE ORGANIZATION

Vice President Marine

Operations and Technical

Project Development

Vessel Trading and Traffic

Venture Marine Services (London)

Exhibit 11.2

VENTURE OIL VESSELS: OWNED AND TIME CHARTERED FLEET

Owned	Flag	DWT (Summer)	Draft (Summer)	Power Plant*	Year Built	T/C Expiration Date
AMERICAN SPIRIT	Liberian	271,857	69'1"	S	1973	
CANADIAN LIBERTY	Liberian	272,426	69'2"	S	1083	
IBERIA	Liberian	115,851	49'9"	D	1973	
EUROPEAN CHALLENGER	Liberian	271,685	69'1"	S	1975	
WASHINGTON	Liberian	270,435	69'1"	S	1976	
NEPTUNE	Liberian	75,670	45'2"	D	1967	
SEA EXPLORER	Liberian	71,443	41'8"	S	1964	
LONE STAR	Liberian	44,328	38'0"	S	1959	
NEW ORLEANS	Liberian	52,548	40'4"	S	1964	
Time Chartered						
GOOD HOPE	Liberian	61,928	43'3"	D	1964	8/81
SEA GUARDIAN	Liberian	37,410	36'5"	D	1975	2/82
CHAMPAGNE	French	115,425	49'6"	D	1968	10/80
PACIFIC MARU	Japanese	36,452	36'2"	D	1976	2/84
RED SKY	Italian	20,622	31'9"	D	1959	5/81
BEAUFORT	Italian	20,610	31'10"	D	1958	10/80
ODIN 2	Norwegian	53,740	41'6"	D	1979	12/80

* S = Steam Turbine, D = Diesel

Venture Oil, Marine Department

Exhibit 11.3

LIGHTENING OPERATIONS

Lightening provides the mother vessel (or ship to be lightened) and the shuttle vessel (or service ship) to meet at a rendezvous point and transfer a full cargo into a smaller vessel. For the Venture Oil Lightening Program, the rendezvous point is about 60 miles off the Texas coast. The light-cargoes are moved to either Venture Oil's Lake Charles Refinery; Freeport, Texas, for the Seaway Pipeline; or Beaumont for the Texoma Pipeline. Third party business involves calls at other U.S. Gulf discharge ports including St. James, New Orleans, Port Arthur, Houston, Texas City, and Corpus Christi. The point is strategically well-placed, not only for company discharge ports, but also for other disharge ports as well.

The two ships are maneuvered together at low speed, usually not exceeding four knots, and are kept apart by heavy-duty fenders. Fenders are arranged along the side of the mother ship, and she steams at a predetermined course and speed. A total of four fenders in two strings are positioned on the mother ship by the offshore workboat. The fenders are pulled off the transom as the boat moves ahead. The fenders remain in place alongside the mother vessel throughout the lightening operation.

After the ships have been safely moored, both vessels stop engines and drift, or one anchors. Hoses and gangways are passed across as quickly as possible with the ship's crane. Access between the vessels is restricted to ship's business. If weather conditions are poor, the mother ship manuevers to act as a shelter for the shuttle vessel.

The two transfer hoses are 10 inches in diameter. Rigging time for the hoses is less than one hour. Personnel from each vessel make their own connections. The time required to transfer all cargo for one lightening is roughly 12-14 hours. It should be pointed out that generally the entire process of mooring and connecting hoses on third-party vessels may take longer due to the unfamiliarity of the third-party vessel officers and crew to lightening procedures. In general, a Very Large Crude Carrier or VLCC (over 160,000 DWT) requires five or six lightenings, depending on the size of each offtaken cargo. The hoses and fenders remain on the VLCC

Exhibit 11.3 Continued

throughout the lightening operation. At the
completion of lightening, the workboat collects the
equipment and holds it for the next operation. Of
course, the number of lightenings depends not only on
the vessel's size, but also in cases of third-party
deals, the contracted terms and conditions.

There are four vessels dedicated to the
lightening service. Three of the vessels, the LONE
STAR, SEA EXPLORER, and NEW ORLEANS, are company-
owned vessels; and the fourth, GOOD HOPE, is under
term charter. The principle dimensions of these
vessels reflect the severe draft and length
restrictions at all Gulf Coast discharge ports.

The workboat is 171 feet long and is capable of
carrying two complete sets of lightening equipment.
The boat is fully equipped with radio equipment and
supplies for long-term offshore operation and with
a stern ramp for off-loading and re-loading fenders.
Her winch is used to pull the fenders over the
transom when loading the vessel at sea. She carries
two hundred gallons of chemical dispersant, which can
be used in case of an oil spill, as well as an 1800-
foot oil boom for spill containment. There are two
full sets of lightening equipment in service, with
additional fenders and hoses, which are maintained as
spares, allowing simultaneous lightening of two
mother vessels. A set of equipment consists of four
large fenders, two strings of 10-inch cargo hose, and
assorted auxiliary equipment.

The cornerstone of the lightening operation is
the Lightening Master. He is the on-scene decision-
maker and provides assurance to Venture Oil of the
continuing exercise of good judgment. All lightening
masters have served as masters aboard tankers in the
Venture Oil fleet and have undergone extensive
training before they are considered qualified
lightening masters.

Venture Oil, Marine Department

Exhibit 11.4

CASH FLOW COSTS OF REPAIRING
AND OPERATING THE LONE STAR
(FROM 1981 TO 1988)

Year	Capital Cost	Fuel Price Per Ton ($/ton)	Fuel(2) Cost ($,000)	Total(3) Vessel Expenses ($,000)
			Operating Cost	
1981	$1,000,000 (1)	195	2,047.5	3,151.2
1982	---	225	2,362.5	3,466.3
1983	$8,905,000 (1)	258	2,709.0	3,812.9
1984	---	294	3,087.0	4,194.2
1985	---	334	3,507.0	4,613.7
1986	---	368	3,846.0	5,075.0
1987	---	406	4,263.0	5,582.5
1988	---	445	4,672.5	6,140.8

(1) Assume entire capital expenditure is dade in 1981 and 1983.

(2) Fuel consumption 30 TPD at design speed for 350 days per year of operating time.

(3) Operating cost for lightening escalated at 15% per year to 1980 and 10% per year.

Exhibit 11.5

TIME CHARTERED VESSEL
POTENTIAL FUEL CONSUMPTION/COSTS

	IFO Consumption/Cost		MDO Consumption/Cost		Total Fuel
	Cost Per Ton	Annual IFO(1) Costs ($,000)	Cost Per Ton	Annual MDO(2) Cost ($,000)	Cost ($,000)
1981	205	1,435.0	332	371.84	1,806.84
1982	235	1,645.0	383	428.96	2,073.96
1983	268	1,876.0	440	492.8	2,368.80
1984	304	2,128.0	500	560.0	2,688.0
1985	344	2,408.0	569	637.28	3,045.28
1986	378	2,646.0	628	703.36	3,349.36
1987	416	2,912.0	692	775.04	3,687.04
1988	455	3,185.0	759	850.08	4,035.08

(1) IFO consumption: 20 TPD at design speed for 350 days/year of operating time.

(2) MDO consumption: 3.2 TPD at design speed for 350 days/year of operating time.

Venture Oil, Marine Department

Exhibit 11.6

LIGHTENING
($/BBL-1980)

	To Lake Charles	To Freeport
VLCC - North Africa/ Lightering Position	$.76	$.76
VLCC - Demurrage (15 days)	.28	.28
Lightening	.36	.36
SUBTOTAL:	$1.40	$1.40
% Volume	.63	.37
SUBTOTAL:	.88	.52
TOTAL COST:	$1.40	

Exhibit 11.7

TRANSSHIPPING
($/BBL-1980)

	To Lake Charles	To Freeport
VLCC - North Africa/ Bahamas	$.67	$.67
VLCC - Demurrage (4 days)	.07	.07
Throughput	.20	.20
LR1 to Lake Charles	.56	.58
SUBTOTAL:	$1.50	$1.52
% Volume	.63	.37
SUBTOTAL:	.95	.56
TOTAL COST:	$1.51	

ALTERNATE:

LR2 to Lake Charles	.51
* Demurrage	-
SUBTOTAL:	1.45
% Volume	.63
SUBTOTAL:	.91
TOTAL COST:	$1.47

----

* 1 day's demurrage on LR2 = $ .07
        or total cost = $1.52

Venture Oil, Marine Department

Exhibit 11.8

GULF COAST DEEPWATER TERMINAL
($/BBL-1980)

	To Lake Charles	To Freeport
VLCC - North Africa/ LOOP	$.77	$.77
VLCC - Demurrage (6 days)	.12	.12
Throughput	.35	.35
Pipeline to Lake Charles (est.)	.26	.26
Pipeline to Freeport (est.)	-	.26
SUBTOTAL:	$1.50	$1.76
% Volume	.63	.37
SUBTOTAL:	.95	.65
TOTAL COST:		$1.60

Exhibit 11.9

FREEPORT SPM & LIGHTERING
($/BBL-1980)

	To Lake Charles	To Freeport
VLCC - North Africa/ U.S. Gulf	$.77	$.77
VLCC - Demurrage (10 days)	.20	.20
Lightening	.36	-
SPM Throughput	-	.20
SUBTOTAL:	$1.33	$1.17
% Volume	.63	.37
SUBTOTAL:	.84	.43
TOTAL COST:	$1.27	

Chapter 12

LAVAL MARITIME INC.

The founder of Laval Maritime Inc. (LMI), Pierre
Laval, enjoyed great respectability and admiration
in the shipping world. After 35 years of intensive
involvement in the maritime industry, Pierre passed
away in the middle of 1981. When his son Jean Laval,
who had joined the company 16 years before, took
charge of the family interest, he was left with a
strong and well-known shipping company. However, in
the previous two years, the combination of
unsuccessful investments and high interest rates had
been hurting LMI's cash flows, though not to the
extent of threatening the company's existence.
     With the recent death of its founder, LMI's life
had been perturbed and its activities slowed. The
time had come to take a more circumspect look at the
market and to consolidate LMI's structure. In
addition to handling current problems, some thought
had to be given to LMI's future.
     LMI was structured as a management company,
acting on behalf of foreign shipowners representing
the offshore interest of the Laval family. It
offered centralized asset management and chartering
services. Of the 25 vessels under its management,
nine were controlled by the firm through nine wholly
owned Canadian subsidiaries. For the other 16
vessels, LMI acted as the representative of owners
and received management and agency fees. In the last
few years, LMI had been involved mostly in ship
finance; it was structured more as a leasing company
than a shipping company.
     Through the years, LMI had enjoyed good returns
on its investments, thanks to wise management mixing
speculation with long-term contracts. The company's
reputation has always been that of a first-class
shipping company, and LMI has been and still is
regarded by its peers as an outstanding company fully

devoted to its commitments.

In 1973, LMI began to develop a more cautious approach toward the shipping industry. Speculative deals were not in the strategy. The prime objective was to build a constant and regular flow of revenue to allow the company to ride out the downward cycle of the shipping industry.

The strong point of LMI's management team was flexibility. LMI's history had shown its great versatility and a willingness to accommodate its customers by adapting to new situations. This willingness and open-minded attitude matched LMI's goal of establishing good and strong relationships with its charterers.

COMPANY HISTORY

The Beginning

In 1946, just after the war, Pierre Laval took advantage of the liquidation of the war-built Canadian merchant marine. In the space of two years he acquired nine Liberty-type ships. The company entered worldwide tramping activities and continued until the end of the Korean War. At that time, freight rates were good and the ships were amortized quickly. Feeling the end of the war, Pierre Laval began to dispose of his fleet at the peak of the market. The vessels were sold six months before the end of the war. By May 1954, having made substantial gains, Pierre Laval decided to move towards the tanker business.

The Tanker Market

In 1955, the tanker market was in a slump, and by June 1955 the market was at its lowest since 1949. Pierre Laval took his chances and ordered two 20,000 DWT tankers. In late 1955 and during 1956, the impact of the closing of the Suez Canal was dramatically felt. From October 1955 to December 1955 rates jumped 280%! By the end of December 1956, rates had jumped another 55%. Pierre Laval "caught the ball" at its very height by selling the contract of one of his new orders not yet delivered. The profits from the sale were such that the second tanker was almost paid off before delivery. The vessel was delivered in 1958 in the middle of a new slump, but being almost paid for, she enjoyed profitable trading under short to medium time charter with major oil companies until 1972, when she went out of the fleet.

Laval Maritime Inc.

   In 1957, Pierre Laval concluded his first long-
term bareboat charter with an oil major, Atlantic
Oil, and simultaneously ordered a 40,000 DWT tanker,
the LAVAL I.   The vessel was financed through a
private placement with American institutions, and
this was the first step towards the development of
financing skills which today are the strength of the
management team.
   During this same period, the company was still
active in the tramping market. Good relations with
Orco, a large international steel company, were built
in the 1950's as a consequence of an interesting set
of circumstances. In the 1950's, Orco was to import
iron ore from the Orinoco River in Venezuela.   In
1955, it chartered from Pierre Laval two 10,000 DWT
vessels for five years.   In the late 1950's, the
famous Greek owner, Nastopoulos, introduced the two
largest bulk carriers ever built up to that time: two
60,000 DWT ships. Nastopoulos offered the vessels to
Orco on a time charter based on the amount of cargo
carried instead of the usual deadweight capacity.
Because of their draft, the vessels could only load
30,000 tons, and Orco was able to enjoy a good
contract.   After the signing of the contract,
Nastopoulos dredged the Orinoco river to accommodate
his vessels fully laden. Confronted with sudden
overcapacity, Orco turned to the owners of the
smaller vessels it had chartered. Pierre Laval was
the only one who agreed to lay up his vessels and to
reduce the charter hire to a level just high enough
to cover the debt service of the vessels.   Since
then, LMI has constantly had vessels on long-term
charter with Orco, and today four of its vessels are
time chartered to Orco for its worldwide needs.

The Great Lakes
In 1962, with his typical versatility, Pierre Laval
made a new move. Sensing an opportunity with the
opening of the St. Lawrence Seaway, six lakers of
26,000 DWT were ordered from Canadian shipyards.
Using the large tax capacity of one of the major
Canadian distillers, Pierre Laval structured a
leveraged tax lease and was able to pay effectively
only 60% of the quoted price. He then undercut the
rates with his modern and efficient vessels.
   During the Great Lake years, Pierre Laval built
up a good relationship with the major international
trading houses and the Canadian Wheat Board. But in
the late 1960's, the future of lake operations
appeared bleak because of deteriorating volume and
the constant threat of strikes by a number of unions.

Again, Pierre Laval felt it was time to move, and by 1972 he had sold all his laker fleet for $25 million, keeping only three vessels: a mid-fifties' 20,000 DWT tanker trading short-term time charter (T/C); a 40,000 DWT tanker on bareboat to Atlantic Oil; and a 31,000 DWT self-unloader bulk carrier chartered to Orco.

The Japanese Deals

In the late 1960's and early 1970's, Japan started its formidable export trade expansion. The fleet requirements were enormous, and Japanese owners contacted foreign owners to obtain bareboat charter agreements, the "Shikumi Deals". Since Pierre Laval, who was 71 years old at the time, felt that the future of international shipping was shaky, he decided to move towards long-term contracts with first-class charterers supported by bank guarantees. Until 1979, most of LMI's revenues came from bareboat agreements concluded in the early 1970's. Only one vessel, the self-unloader bulk carrier SERENIA, was on a time charter.

Events in 1973 and thereafter proved that Pierre Laval, once again, had the farsighted judgment which had marked his shipping career.

Since 1979, ten vessels had been added to the fleet and one sold, the largest, a 1974-built VLCC sold back to its charterers in 1980 for $30 million. In 1979, LMI purchased "en bloc" for US$ 35 million, three Panamax bulk carriers and time chartered them for ten-year periods to Orco.

1980 saw the acquisition of four vessels, of which one was the 95,650 DWT tanker ASTRAPI, built in Japan in 1976. ASTRAPI was acquired from one of LMI's charterers; she is currently trading in the spot market. The largest vessel currently owned, a 224,336 DWT VLCC built in late 1973, was also acquired in 1980 and chartered back, as were two small tankers of 20,507 and 26,468 DWT. The last three vessels were acquired at an inflated price and subsequently chartered back to their previous owners. For the first time, LMI made an exception to its rules not to charter vessels to other shipowners if they were not backed by an industrial concern.

In 1981, three second-hand vessels were acquired and chartered out under long-term contract to Japanese customers, one 116,000 DWT tanker built in 1973 and two combined carriers. This was the last deal made by Pierre Laval. In a period of three years, 10 vessels were purchased, corresponding to a total capital commitment of about US$ 122 million.

Laval Maritime Inc.

Because all but one vessel had a long charter commitment, the investment program was financed mainly through commercial loans.

The Fleet

As of August 1981, LMI's fleet consisted of 25 ocean-going vessels totalling 1.8 million DWT. As shown in Exhibit 12.1, the vessels range in size from 20,500 to 224,336 DWT. (Exhibits 12.2 and 12.3 show the balance sheet and consolidated earnings statement, respectively.)

Among the vessels are:

1. Fourteen tankers, of which three are product tankers
2. Eight bulkcarriers, three of them of a more specialized type:

   a. Two combined oil/ore carriers
   b. One liquefied petroleum gas (LPG) carrier, 75,000 cubic meters.

The fleet consists of large vessels, with average deadweight of 72,000 DWT. However, its average tanker fleet tonnage is 85,605 DWT while the world average tanker deadweight is 102,684 DWT. LMI is not very involved in the VLCC segment of the tanker fleet. The future trend is towards smaller vessels, and taking into account the existing and on-order fleet, the future average tanker size will be 97,674 DWT, according to H.P. Drewry (Shipping Consultants) Ltd. On the bulk carrier side, all the vessels are either handy-sized bulk carriers or small Panamax.

Although a large number of the vessels were acquired second-hand, the average fleet is 8.5 years old. All the vessels are employed under long-term contracts, varying from 8 to 18 years, with one exception: ASTRAPI.

CHARTERING POLICY AND CHARTERERS

The company is engaged under contracts which allow a substantial recovery of the capital costs of each vessel. The logic behind such a philosophy is to limit LMI's exposure to market cycles.

LMI's policy has always been to ask a bank guarantee to back up the charterer's commitments. The effect of this strategy has been to limit LMI's dependence on their charterers. On the other hand,

LMI has always been willing to pass on to these charterers the financial advantage it enjoyed in its financing packages, with various devices like purchase options, equity participation, or grace period on principal repayment.

The fleet is on charter to seven international industrial and shipping concerns. The charter plan is shown in Exhibit 12.2. Only four vessels will come out of charter before 1985. Two of these are small old tankers acquired in 1980, one used as a bunker vessel in the Persian Gulf, and the other as a coastal tanker in Indonesia. The other two are fairly old bulk carriers. Fourteen out of the 25 vessels have their employment terminating after 1989.

COMPANY FINANCES

Like most shipping companies, LMI has had to support high interest rates over the last two years. The bulk of its fleet, being second-hand, has had to be financed through commercial loans. The loans were secured as "LIBOR plus" type loans. Because of the extreme financial gearing of its fleet and the structure of its income (i.e., more than 50% of the charter income is fixed), the company profits have been limited by the increasing charge of its debt services. Nevertheless, LMI has enjoyed a secure position.

In line with its cautious approach, almost all the loans were contracted in charter-hire currency, thus protecting LMI against violent exchange rate fluctuations. Despite the availability of low interest rates at Japanese shipyards--80% credit at 8.75% over 8.5 years--the firm has been reluctant to pursue any deals which do not offer a full protection against currency fluctuations.

Among the financial practices used by LMI is the vessel-refinancing strategy. Basically, the firm tries to refinance the original floating rate loans at fixed rates through private placements, usually guaranteed by the bank which manages the placement. The bank then manages the sinking funds incurred by the private placement. This strategy implies a careful reading of money market trends. Three product tankers owned by LMI were financed using this strategy and enjoyed a healthy 9.75% fixed interest rate on loans issued over the charter duration. Usually, when financing a ship as a security for a loan, the shipowning company mortgages the vessel and assigns all freight, earnings, and insurance policies to the bank. The owner is sometimes asked to give a personal guarantee.

In line with its financial philosophy, LMI is currently contemplating fleet refinancing, the objective being to develop a more amenable cash flow stream, able to withstand sustained high interest rate periods. (Exhibits 12.3 and 12.4 show LMI's recent financial history.)

CAPITAL BUDGETING PROCEDURE

When evaluating an investment, the firm uses the net present value criterion. To blend different interest rates payable under parallel financing schemes (some of which are available under subsidized ship export programs), LMI discounts the cash outlays under the various debt service streams at its cost of capital. The resulting implicit amortization rate underlying the quoted charter-hire gives full recognition to any subsidized ship credit facility. No other measure of financial performance is used by LMI.

Despite its small size, LMI is gifted with a very sophisticated computerized financial planning system. Among the documentation produced by the information system, two types can be differentiated:

1. The financial planning system: consisting of cash flow analysis, loan retirement schedule, interest rate statistics, and a variety of other programs.
2. The project evaluation system: consisting of a capital cost analysis of accounting for different financing options, time charter evaluation, and bareboat charter analysis. (Exhibit 12.5 shows a sample computerized charter calculation.) Finally, a voyage-hire calculation and its WORLDSCALE equivalent have been developed for the purpose of trading in the spot market.

Later in 1981 LMI will be connected to an international maritime data bank which can give detailed information on the world fleet, including:

1. The fleet on order, per type of vessel
2. A vessel's characteristics
3. Time and voyage charter fixtures since 1976 in the dry cargo and tanker market
4. Ship casualties.

For a company of its size, LMI has been far in advance of its competitors in realizing the benefits of a good information system.

OPERATIONS

In the last ten years, operating ships has not been a major activity of LMI. Before 1979, only SERENIA was operated on time charter. Moreover, Jean Laval had always been very keen on the financial and chartering aspects but was never very interested in operations.

Recently, however, Jean Laval had realized the importance of developing a strong in-house operating capability. In a depressed market, such as he now confronted, monitoring the operating costs had become an absolute necessity.

The operations are divided into two functions, one in charge of the day-to-day management of the vessel, and the other, controlling and evaluating the operating costs of the project. However, this separation is only theoretical.

There are some communications difficulties between the chartering and the operations departments. Operating costs studies are not yet produced in a systematic and efficient way, but new people have been hired and improvement is underway. Jean Laval is fully aware that his future role as a ship operator relies very much on LMI's ability to cope with this problem.

Of the five vessels it operates, LMI has encountered some difficulties due to very high overtime costs in the case of the 96,550 DWT tanker ASTRAPI, and high maintenance and repair costs for PRIMA, SECUNDA, and TERZIA, three sisterships time chartered to Orco. Operating expenses for the three bulk carriers are given in Exhibit 12.6. Figures for 1981 are based on first-quarter results. These time charters include an escalation clause which covers LMI fully for crew and insurance increases.

The three vessels are sisterships bought from three different owners. PRIMA was acquired from a Greek owner who did little or no maintenance on her during her first four years and sold her before her first special survey. SECUNDA was bought from a Swiss owner. TERZIA was bought from an American owner. Even though the ships incurred some start-up costs the first year of operations, SECUNDA and PRIMA saw their operating expenses ("OPEX") increased 48.3% and 45%, respectively, where TERZIA's OPEX remained

Laval Maritime Inc.

constant (see Exhibit 12.6). The main expenses
responsible were maintenance, stores and lubes, and
miscellaneous. Even though currency exchange may
have amplified the phenomenon of some special
incident that may have occurred, clearly, two of the
three vessels present an operating problem.

THE CURRENT DILEMMA

LMI has only one vessel on the "spot market",
ASTRAPI. She was bought in August 1980, for US$ 17.8
million. Until the end of May 1981, she was fixed on
a profitable time charter to Exxon. Since then, the
market has continued to deteriorate with no recovery
in sight. Recently, some charterers have been
looking for vessels of her size, and although she has
inert gas systems (IGS) and crude oil washing (COW),
she is not fitted with segregated ballast tanks. She
can only take two grades of crude oil. Despite good
maintenance and young age, she is not in a good
competitive position.

With other changes in the world oil market, even
her size appears to be a disadvantage: she is either
too big or too small. Her current scrap value is
about US$ 2.3 million.

Most recently, ASTRAPI has been trading in the
Caribbean area, where the market has been slightly
better. Over the last six months, she has been
covering, on average, about 54% of her operating and
voyage costs with no contribution towards capital.
Typical voyage details are given in Exhibit 12.7.
Alternatively, the lay-up cost based on an extensive
lay-up (one-year or more) in Greece is about US$
1,130 per day.

Today LMI is confronted with the following
alternatives:

> Alternative 1: Keep ASTRAPI in either lay-up or
>   trade, depending on the least costly
>   solution.
> Alternative 2: Keep ASTRAPI and retrofit her
>   with segregated ballast tanks; this would
>   require an additional expense of about US$
>   2 million. This solution would present the
>   advantage of transforming ASTRAPI into an
>   SBT Aframax tanker (i.e., 79,999 DWT) at a
>   relatively low cost in comparison with the
>   competition. Newbuilding Aframax tankers
>   were priced at $28 million in 1979 and at
> $38 million in 1980. On the other hand,

she will be too large to trade effectively
because of her dimensions.

Alternative 3:   Sell ASTRAPI and write off the
debt. Hopefully, the market value of
ASTRAPI is about $14 million.

Alternative 4:   Sell ASTRAPI and buy a ULCC and
finally reorient the company strategy in
the market. A 1978-built 330,000 DWT
tanker, fully IMCO, has been offered for
sale at about US$ 17-18 million, with an
export credit attached (80% over 5 years at
8.5%).   Such a tanker, in the current
market, may not perform much worse than
ASTRAPI. Exhibit 12.8 presents a typical
voyage calculation for a ULCC.   On the
other hand, a small recovery could produce
a much larger return.   Exhibit 12.9
compares a ULCC with a 150,000 DWT vessel.
The current scrap value of a ULCC is about
US$ 6 million, thereby limiting the
financial exposure, to US$ 11 million.

Despite the tremendous increase in the price of
oil, it is still cheaper to carry oil in large
vessels, and therefore they will be needed. Large
numbers of VLCC's of the first generation are not
IMCO-fitted. Their owners will eventually prefer to
scrap them rather than invest anything to upgrade
them.

In addition to the refitting expenses, most of
the old VLCC's have to have their second or third
special survey (occuring in five-year intervals),
which is expensive. It is likely that they will be
scrapped.

The world's fleet of medium-size tankers (i.e.,
70-99,999 DWT) comprises 422 tankers, of which only
78 are known to be "IMCO tankers," representing about
18% in total deadweight. However, in the world of
the ULCC fleet (i.e., above 300,000 DWT), out of the
115 existing tankers, only 59 are fully IMCO,
representing 51% of the fleet capacity. Most of the
ULCC fleet was built after 1975, where the medium-
size tanker fleet is composed of a two-tier
distribution (i.e., vessels are either built mid-
1970's or mid-1960's).

Another marketing factor to consider is that
only a handful of oil companies have such lifting
needs that they can use a ULCC.   In the previous
year, only Texaco had taken a ULCC on charter for 12
months.

Laval Maritime Inc.

 International shipping was in a completely new stage of evolution, and Jean Laval felt that new opportunities would come. Aware of his current management problem, he had arrived at a point where a direction had to be decided for the years ahead. Because of his strong educational background, he would like to conduct the change in a more rational and systematic way, without departing from his father's philosophy and attitude.

GROUP FLEET AS AT AUGUST 3, 1981

(OWNED VESSELS)

#		Name	Type	Year	Tonnage	Flag
1	S.S.	SERENICA	Self Unloader	1956	30946	Panama
2	M.T.	DUPONT II	Product Carrier	1975	25500	New Zealand
3	M.T.	DUPONT III	Product Carrier	1976	25500	" "
4	M.T.	DUPONT IV	Product Carrier	1976	32289	" "
5	M.V.	PRIMA	Bulk Carrier	1974	54681	Greece
6	M.V.	SECONDA	Bulk Carrier	1975	55009	Greece
7	M.V.	TERSIA	Bulk Carrier	1973	55057	Greece
8	M.T.	DUPONT VI	Tanker	1974	96550	Liberia
9	M.T.	ASTRAPI	Tanker	1976	96550	Greece
			SUB-TOTAL		472082	

(REPRESENTED VESSELS)

#		Name	Type	Year	Tonnage	Flag
1	M.S.	AJACCIO	Ore/Oil Carrier	1968	94346	Liberia
2	M.T.	BASTIA	LPG Carrier	1974	50606	"
3	M.S.	BONIFACCIO	Scrap/bulk Carrier	1965	22174	"
4	M.S.	ST. LAURENT	Log/Bulk Carrier	1973	34574	"
5	M.T.	SARTENE	Tanker	1975	123863	"
6	M.T.	PORTO	Tanker	1975	89736	"
7	M.S.	BASTEL	Bulk Carrier	1970	26588	"
8	M.S.	PORTICCIO	Bulk Carrier	1976	43112	"
9	M.T.	ST. LUCIE	Tanker	1976	141179	"
10	M.T.	OSPEDALE	Tanker	1974	96493	"
11	M.T.	PORTO YECCHIO	Tanker	1958	26468	Singapore
12	M.T.	MAGDALENA	Tanker	1959	20507	"
13	S.T.	SARDENA	Tanker	1973	224336	Liberia
14	S.S.	TLEMCEN	Ore/Oil Carrier	1972	164545	"
15	M.T.	BORAN	Tanker	1973	113900	"
16	M.S.	BOUGIE	Ore/Oil Carrier	1972	78010	"
			SUB-TOTAL		1350437	
			TOTAL		1822519	

Laval Maritime Inc.

Exhibit 12.2

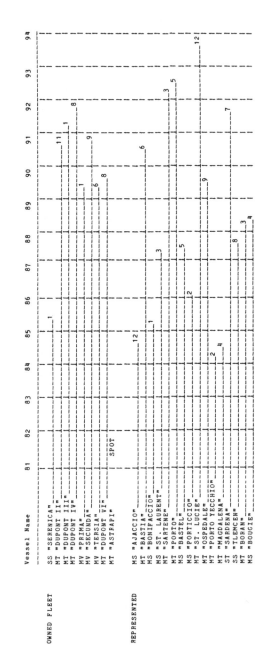

FLEET CHARTERING SCHEDULE

Exhibit 12.3

BALANCE SHEET
December 1980
Assets

CURRENT	1980	1979	1978
Cash	276,272	381,658	341,999
Term Deposit			1,316,585
Accounts Receivable	2,439,219	1,019,808	55,809
Income Taxes Recoverable	2,745	7,627	162,330
Inventories at Cost	363,371	76,812	
Prepaid Expenses	203,632	75,525	5,376
	3,285,234	1,571,430	1,382,099
Advances Receivable	356,456	171,193	342,532
Fixed Assets	122,618,847	105,038,575	45,898,363
Other Assets	7,454,613	4,962,865	5,464,687
Total Assets	134,065,905	111,744,863	53,587,861

Liabilities and Shareholders' Equity

	1980	1979	1978
Bank Loan	3,122,603	2,751,054	10,079
Accounts Payable	1,471,784	1,518,891	125,994
Interest Accrued Payable	706,009	679,100	428,248
Income Received in Advance	1,212,620	683,565	377,048
Current Portion of Long Term	3,449,247	4,345,449	2,589,186
	9,962,263	9,978,061	3,530,550
Proportion for Special Quadrennial Survey	480,000	225,000	225,000
Advances Payable	4,948,473		6,274
Unrealized Exchange Gains		35,401	
Long Term Debt	108,365,202	89,186,883	41,556,952
Deferred Income Taxes	2,660,907	2,418,816	95,142
Shareholders' Equity			
Capital Stock	1,611,051	1,611,051	1,611,051
Retained Earnings	6,036,729	8,238,351	6,562,712
	7,647,780	9,849,902	8,173,763
Total	134,065,905	111,744,063	53,587,681

Laval Maritime Inc.

Exhibit 12.4

CONSOLIDATED EARNINGS
YEAR ENDED DECEMBER 31, 1980

GROSS INCOME	1980	1979
Hire of Vessels	$17,852,247	$11,747,350
Off-Hire.	57,418	132,660
	17,794,829	11,614,690
Operating Expenses.	6,803,386	3,261,000
	10,991,443	8,353,690
Agency Fees	571,158	646,600
Commissions	682,139	212,774
Management fees, Associated Companies	155,000	150,000
Interest on Loans	8,500	17,903
Interest on Term Deposits	48,667	129,435
Rental Income	7,940	6,856
Gain on Sale of Fixed Asset		785
Insurance Claims.	211,373	
	12,676,220	9,518,043
GENERAL AND ADMINISTRATIVE EXPENSES .	1,381,599	1,087,802
FINANCIAL EXPENSES.	10,288,112	7,160,036
	11,669,711	8,247,838
EARNINGS BEFORE DEPRECIATION AND SURVEY.	1,006,509	1,270,205
DEPRECIATION AND SURVEY	3,176,191	289,488
EARNINGS (LOSS) BEFORE INCOME TAXES AND EXTRAORDINARY ITEM.	(2,169,682)	980,717
INCOME TAXES		
Current		28,701
Deferred.	136,933	932,559
	136,933	961,260
EARNINGS (LOSS) BEFORE EXTRAORDINARY ITEM.	(2,306,615)	19,457
Extraordinary Item.		28,701
NET EARNINGS (LOSS)	$(2,306,615)	$ 48,158
BALANCE AT BEGINNING.	$ 6,418,485	$ 6,370,327
NET EARNINGS (LOSS)	(2,306,615)	48,158
BALANCE AT END.	$ 4,111,870	$ 6,418,485

Exhibit 12.5

CHARTER CALCULATION

```
Case 1:     Newbuilding                  95,000 DWT Tanker
    (1)     Capital Cost                 USD 20,000,000
            Shipyard Credit              80% at 9% over 8 years
            Company Cost of Capital      17.5%

            First Step:  Determination of the amount of capital  to
                         be charged to the charterer.
            Outstanding Debt:   USD 16,000,000
            Debt Amortization:
                - monthly lumpsum:  USD 234,403.25
                - present value of the monthly lump sum  discounted
                  at 17.5%:  USD 12,069,446.22
                - discount in price of vessel stemming from
                  lower interest rate on debt service:
    (2)             USD 3,930,553.78
                - price of vessel for bareboat hire determination
                  (1) - (2):  USD 16,069,446.22
            Duration of the charter: 10 years
```

Bareboat Charter (B/C)   Capital cost basis: USD 16,069,446.22
                              over 10 years at 17.5% discount rate

```
B/C Monthly Lumpsum  Adjustment for Off-hire  Adjustment for Brokerage
USD 284,395.07              None                  USD 291,687.25
      Flat Rate:  USD 3.070/DWT/month
```

Time Charter (T/C)   Capital cost basis: USD 16,069,446.22
                              over 10 years at 17.5% discount rate
                              350 operating days

```
T/C Monthly Lumpsum  Adjustment for Off-Hire  Adjustment for Brokerage(2 1/2%)
USD 284,395.07       USD 296,583.43           USD 304,188.13
```

(a)   Flat rate for capital cost recovery purpose: USD 3,202/DWT/month

                              Operating Cost: Greek crew, 32 men
                                               USD 1,825,000/year

No Escalation Clause

```
Monthly Lumpsum       Adjustment for Off-hire  Adjustment for Brokerage
USD 152,083.33        USD 184,584.46           USD 189,317.40
```

(b)   Flat rate for opex purpose: USD 1,712/DWT/month
      T/C flat rate (a) and (b)   USD 4,914/DWT/month

With 10% Yearly Escalation Clause

Monthly Lumpsum   Adjustment for Off-hire Adjustment for Brokerage

Laval Maritime Inc.

Exhibit 12.6

MONTHLY/YEARLY EQUIVALENT ON A DWT BASIS
($/DWT/MO)

PRIMA OPEX	1979		1980		1981
Manning	1.221	17.2%	1.431	26.6%	1.812
Insurances	0.270	24.8	0.337	9.8	0.370
Stores & Lubes	0.438	27.2	0.557	86.0	1.036
Maintenance	0.505	(30.7)	0.350	34.9	0.472
Miscellaneous	0.079	77.2	0.140	183.0	0.397
	2.513		2.816		4.087
		12.1%		45.0%	

SECUNDA OPEX					
Manning	1.095	15.2	1.261	17.7	1.484
Insurances	0.275	29.1	0.355	9.0	0.387
Stores & Lubes	0.252	(4.0)	0.242	114.5	0.519
Maintenance	0.117	53.0	0.179	210.0	0.556
Miscellaneous	0.081	92.6	0.156	96.8	0.307
	1.820		2.193		3.253
		20.5		48.3%	

TERSIA OPEX					
Manning	1.162	15.2	1.261	17.7	1.484
Insurances	0.275	29.1	0.333	9.0	0.387
Stores & Lubes	0.750	7.79	0.248	28.6	0.177
Maintenance	0.061	78.4	0.282	(48.6)	0.145
Miscellaneous	0.262	(41.6)	0.153	54.2	0.334
	2.568		2.356		2.201
		(8.3)		(6.6)	

Average change in Opex from year to year

	2.300	(6.7%)	2.465	(22.5%)	3.180

Exhibit 12.7

"ASTRAPI": VESSEL SHEET
(ON A TYPICAL VOYAGE)

Aruba/New York/Bonaire

Capital Cost   US$ 17.8 million

Daily Operating Cost   US$ 5,700
        Operating Year   350 days

DWT   95,025
        at 98% Capacity: (about) 93,000 Tons

Consumption at sea on 12.50 Kn:
                                  (about) 40 Tons/Day HVF
                                          3.8 Tons/Day MDO

                    in port: 50 Tons/Day HVF
                                          3.0 Tons/Day MDO

HVF Price: $177.50/Ton
MDO Price: $277.50/Ton

Bonaire/New York: Load Leg   1,768 NM
                  Ballasting   1,855 NM

Lay Time as per WORLDSCALE: 72 hours to load
                                                 and unload

Port Charges: Bonaire $20,000
                  New York $17,000

Brokerage as per WORLDSCALE: 1.25%

Bunker Safety Margin: 20%

WS 100: $6.34/T (as of
                                                 July 1981)

Laval Maritime Inc.

Exhibit 12.8

ULCC: VESSEL SHEET
(ON A TYPICAL VOYAGE)

Capital Cost	US$ 17 million
Daily Operating Cost	US$ 8,500
Operating Year	350 days
DWT	332,600
at 98% Capacity: (about)	326,000 Tons
Consumption at sea on 12 Kn: (about)	100 Tons/Day Bunker C
on 15 Kn: (about)	146 Tons/Day Bunker C
BC Price:	$185/T - $175/T
Ras Tanura/Rotterdam via Cape:	11,465 NM
Rotterdam/Ras Tanura via Suez:	6,436 NM
Lay Time:	48 hours at each port
Port Charges: Rastanura	$33,000
Rotterdam	$160,000
Canal Charges: Suez	$243,000
Brokerage as per WORLDSCALE:	1.25%
Bunker Safety Margin:	20%
WS 100:	$25.79/Ton (as of July 1981)

Exhibit 12.9

COMPARATIVE VOYAGE COSTS 150,000 VS. 300,000 DWT SHIPS

	RasTanura-Marseille		RasTanura-Freeport		RasTanura-Rotterdam	
DWT	150,000	330,000	150,000	330,000	150,000	330,000
Route	2 x Suez	Cape-Suez	2 x Suez	Cape-Suez	2 x Suez	Cape-Suez
Voyage Cost :Bunker ($/T)	3.92	4.39	6.96	6.00	5.28	5.10
:Canal	2.06	0.82	2.06	0.82	2.06	0.82
	5.98	5.21	9.02	6.82	7.34	5.92
Cargo Inventory ($/T)	2.79	4.19	5.03	5.66	3.79	4.89
Total Cost ($/T)	8.77	9.40	14.05	12.48	10.12	10.81

Calculation based on
- Vessel 150,000 DWT - 15Kn - 90 Tons HVO
  3 Tons DO/35 Tons HVO - 1.5 Tons DO
- Vessels 330,000 - 15Kn - 170 Tons
  BC/85 Tons BC
- Suez fees as per Intertanko Info
  Letter No. 11A/1980
- HVO: $185/T; BC: $170/T; DO: $300/T
  as per Sept. 81
- Interest Rate: 15%
- 7.3 bbl/T - $32/bbl
- No adjustment for off hire and brokerage fees
- Calculation based on one voyage only
- 10% deadfreight

By definition, the voyage costs are the costs incured when the vessel is sailing, i.e., fuel expenses, port charges, canal fees and other minor expenses.

247

Laval Maritime Inc.

Exhibit 12.9 Continued

	Yenbo-Marseille		Yenbo-Freeport		Yenbo-Rotterdam	
DWT	150,000	330,000	150,000	330,000	150,000	330,000
Route	Suez/Suez	Cape/Suez	Suez/Suez	Cape/Suez	Suez/Suez	Cape/Suez
Voyage Cost: B/C	2.03	3.63	5.07	5.07	3.39	4.34
Canal Total (S/T)	2.06 / 4.09	0.82 / 4.45	2.06 / 7.13	0.82 / 5.88	2.06 / 5.45	0.82 / 5.15
Cargo Inventory (S/T)	1.39	3.43	3.64	4.86	2.39	4.13
Total (S/T)	5.48	7.88	10.77	10.72	7.84	9.28

Assumptions as in previous case.

248

Chapter 13

LEGRAND SHIPPING COMPANY

As Pierre Legrand stared at the stained glass windows
of his posh Paris office, his thoughts drifted
towards the future of Legrand Shipping, the firm he
controlled and managed. On that sunny morning of
June 1979, he wondered what actions he should take to
improve the company's financial situation. 1977 had
been a barely profitable year, and 1978 showed a
substantial loss. (Exhibits 13.1 and 13.2 show
balance sheets and income statements, respectively.)
The outlook for 1979 seemed also unfavorable.

In the various ocean shipping markets in which
the firm was involved, freight rates were low, and
the company's costs were high. (Exhibit 13.3
presents an organizational chart, while Exhibits 13.4
and 13.5 illustrate characteristics of the tramping
and liner segments of the company fleet,
respectively.) Beyond this immediate but pressing
concern, other problems came to his mind as he
reviewed the evolution of Legrand Shipping during the
previous sixty years. (Exhibits 13.6 and 13.7 show a
historical overview of company performance and fleet
ownership, respectively.) He felt that the time had
come not only to solve current problems, as the
company had always done in the past, but also, and

This case was written by Jean-Marc Cangardel in
conjunction with Henry S. Marcus for discussion
rather than to illustrate either effective or
ineffective handling of an administrative situation.
The name of the company, and some other information,
has been disguised.

maybe for the first time, to forge a long-term strategy for the company.

BACKGROUND

Legrand Shipping was created in 1919, when Henri Legrand was asked by the British and French governments to manage 13 ships received as war damage compensation. Six of these ships were built of steel, and seven of wood; they had an average deadweight tonnage of 3,000 tonnes.* Henri Legrand was then a public servant and knew little about shipping. It was very difficult to find qualified personnel to run the company. In 1919, the freight rate market was very unstable and very often too low to exploit economically the vessels. Henri Legrand managed to overcome this problem with a long-term charter agreement with the City of Paris, France, for the transport of coal. This agreement lasted only two years, but the company had had in the meantime the opportunity to learn the ropes of the international shipping market. At the expiration of the agreement, the ships found employment in a then very unusual trade: tramping.

By 1922, Legrand Shipping had become a full-fledged ocean shipping company. It was bidding, along with other firms, for part of France's state-owned fleet, much of which was acquired as reparations after World War I. It also purchased tugboats, including the famous tug, L'IROISE, which was later the topic of a book by Roger Vercel and of a film. It also managed a 3,200-tonne, four-masted sailing vessel. By the end of 1922, the company owned and managed 46 ships, totalling 118,700 deadweight tonnes, of three principle types: the "Gharb" type, with a deadweight tonnage of 1,450 tonnes and a speed of seven to nine knots; the "Marie Louise" type, of 3,100 tonnes, with initially a very major stability problem; and the "War" type, of 3,400 DWT, a very basic and rustic vessel. The wooden ships, because of the poor quality of the woods used for their construction, were rapidly scrapped. Many others were also scrapped rapidly because of either age or condition. By 1925, total deadweight tonnage was down to 75,000 tonnes, for 28 ships. Average unit DWT increased from 2,580 DWT in 1922 to 2,678 in 1925.

————————————

* A tonne is a metric ton (2,204.6 pounds).

In 1930, the older, less efficient ships were sold off also. The company still owned 19 ships, with an average tonnage of 3,110 DWT. Most of these ships specialized in coal trades. By 1930, personnel had been trained and operations were running smoothly. In 1931, the world depression caused many shipping companies to go through difficult times. The devaluation of the British pound caused revenue earned from the transportation of coal and ore to drop considerably, because freight rates had been set in British currency. Costs could not be decreased, and as a consequence, about half the fleet was laid up.

By 1933, the rates had inched up and the company put the ships back in trading. However, by then, Henri Legrand, the founder of Legrand Shipping, was asked by the government of France, once again, to solve a major problem: the national fleet, Compagnie Generale Transatlantique, could no longer meet its debt obligations. Henri Legrand accepted the job of President of that company. He continued, however, to oversee the operations of Legrand Shipping in the meantime. By then, Legrand Shipping was operating most of its ships in the coal trades. It was, however, facing severe competition from other French shipowners; because the world crisis was not yet over, demand for coal transport was low in relation to supply. To avoid this cutthroat competition, a conference of coal carriers was created. It provided for fixed rates and pooling of revenue. By 1934, revenue had increased considerably.

The replacement of the fleet continued steadily. Old ships were sold off, and new ones ordered. By 1938, the fleet's largest ship had a deadweight tonnage of 5,040 tonnes. Four ships were smaller than 3,600 tonnes. The fleet was composed of 13 ships, and their average age was 16 years. Eighty percent of the revenues came from the coal trades, and 15% from the ore trades. All ships served the coastal trade along the European and North African coasts.

In September 1939, war was declared. Legrand Shipping's fleet was taken over by the French government, but operations of the vessels were left in the hands of the company. Moreover, 22 ships were chartered by the government and handed over to the company. The French Navy also requested that Legrand purchase for its account tugboats, patrol boats, and minesweepers, since it lacked both the time and the expertise to do so. Heavy tugs and fishing boats were also purchased. War took its toll on Legrand

Shipping. Many employees were killed or died in prison camps. Eight ships were sunk, either by German or British ships.

As the war drew to its end, a major strategic plan was elaborated by the government of France in cooperation with shipowners. Its purpose was to renew the French fleet in an orderly manner. In the coal trades, where Legrand Shipping was active, an elaborate plan was designed to determine with accuracy the requirements for ships in that trade, both in economic terms and in technical terms. In economic terms, the total tonnage requirements, as well as required freight rate break-even calculations, were carried out. In technical terms, optimal ship size, hold size, harbor specifications, and other technical details were elaborated. Older ships were redesigned, and new ones ordered.

In 1945, the French government gave Legrand Shipping four ships of 5,000 DWT each. Henri Legrand, however, felt that the time had come to change the company's past policies and to move away from the traditional coastal trade orientation. He requested that the French government allocate to the company some larger vessels in order to get involved in deep sea trades. The company received in 1946 a 10,300 DWT Liberty ship, and in 1948 a twin-deck 9,400 DWT break-bulk cargo vessel.

By then, Henri Legrand had returned from the French line to Legrand Shipping. His son, Pierre Legrand, who had fought the Pacific War on a French destroyer, joined him at Legrand Shipping. Henri's other son, Maurice, also joined the company, but concentrated on the tugboat side of the operation. On the technical side, most vessel power plants were converted from coal-burning steam boilers to fuel oil-burning boilers. The new ships which were ordered then were designed with diesel engines. Average power per ship increased considerably, and therefore, so did average speed.

By 1948, Legrand Shipping's operations were composed of two distinct trades: tramp trades and liner trades. This split came from the war, when the company was asked to operate a general cargo line in the Mediterranean zone. Tramping had always been the company's main line of business.

1.   Tramping

In tramping, the company was still a major factor in French coal trades. It participated in the conference described earlier, the scope of which was increased to include all high-density bulk cargoes, coal, phosphates, and various ores. This conference contracted with France's major importers to carry their cargoes at a rate which took into account both shipping market conditions and operating costs. It insured a minimum return on ship investment and thus gave a boost to new buildings within the members of the conference, of which Legrand Shipping was one. As a consequence, Legrand ordered new ships. A 20,000 DWT bulk carrier was ordered in 1955 for the Conakry (Guinea) to Dunkirk (France) ore trade. The following year, a 17,000 DWT coal vessel was also ordered for the U.S.A./France coal trade. The company sold off its older ships. The fleet was then very small. The company owned eight tramp vessels, but most were new and efficient by 1957.

At that point in time, the major problem faced by the company was to find financing to meet its capital investment needs. In the past, ships had been obtained inexpensively, but now the company had to pay a much higher price for these new ships than it had ever thought possible. Also, because the company was privately held by Henri Legrand and a few friends, the issuance of stock to raise additional capital would have diluted the ownership. Henri Legrand wanted to maintain control. On the other hand, the sale of debt was limited, because it added financial leverage to an already high-fixed/low-variable cost operation--in other words, to a firm with high operating leverage. In the event of a downturn in rates, both of these leverages would accentuate the problem and could push the firm into bankruptcy.

Henri Legrand devised a financing method which avoided both the sale of equity and the sale of debt: it came from the ancient Greek notion of a ship co-ownership, the "quirat," in which persons or firms accept to buy shares of a ship. They benefit from the ship's gross income and depreciation. A number of investors became co-owners, usually of about 10%, of Legrand ships. Legrand Shipping maintained an 80% to 90% stake in each ship and continued operating it.

At the same period, long-term contracts for the carriage of coal were devised. Two ships were placed on ten-year charters for the transportation of U.S. coal to France. The French coal importers' association, the ATIC, took a substantial share in the co-ownership of these coal-carriers.

In 1957, the Conakry to Dunkirk trade became seriously jeopardized by the political strife occurring in Guinea. The 10,000 DWT vessel placed on that trade was shifted to the U.S./France coal trade. This, in turn, forced the cancellation of a 16,500 DWT vessel which had been ordered for that specific trade. Legrand Shipping, because of its agreement with the shipbuilders, had to design another vessel to be built to compensate the builders for the cancellation. A trade niche was sought. After some research, it was found that the harbor of Bayonne in France badly needed a medium-sized bulk carrier to export solid sulphur from Lacq. The Port of Bayonne imposed very strict draft, width, and length dimensions, while the economics of the trade required a large vessel. The company's engineering department designed an 11,000 DWT bulk carrier to suit these requirements. However, because of the risks involved in tying a ship to a single port in a single trade, the bulk carrier was designed both for the carriage of coal, which required a large hold volume, and for the carriage of ore, which required a much smaller hold for stability reasons. Thus, the ship was designed for holds of different sizes. The engineering department also had the foresight to allow for the transportation of grain, which required maximum volume; lateral ballasts (wing tanks) could be used for grain, together with the holds.

The 1960's. Legrand Shipping in the early 1960's had refocused its policies. Its major tramping orientation was now towards deep sea carriage of bulk cargoes. Coastal trades were no longer economical: the conferences had broken up, and foreign competition was undercutting the high cost of French vessels. The French vessels no longer had a monopoly over French coastal trades as a result of a change in regulations. But international trade to and from France remained economical for French vessels because of the cartel agreement between French shipowners and French importers. Also, Legrand Shipping now operated modern ships. Fuel-powered diesels, larger ships, designed for specific trades allowed Legrand to compete effectively. A typical trading pattern in 1962 for an 11,000 DWT vessel was loading iron ore in Brazil for Louisiana, then grain for North Africa, then ore to France, and then general cargo units, such as pipes and tubes back to Brazil. Many ships were still on regular trades, such as Hampton Roads, U.S.A. to Dunkirk, France, and return on ballast.

Henri Legrand wrote in 1962 that Legrand Shipping's niche was to be ahead of technology and never to be satisfied with vessels of the past. He felt that technological innovation was increasingly rapid and that maintaining the status quo was impossible. Legrand Shipping's major strength, he felt, was to adapt itself to changes in bulk cargoes and trades very rapidly, but to have always the best-designed ship for each trade. The double goal of flexibility and specialization is hard to reach without elaborate engineering and design, which was and still is one of the company's major strengths.

Most of the strategic decisions regarding the entry in new markets were made by Henri Legrand, initially. By the early 1960's, input from Henri's son Pierre was gradually becoming increasingly important in the decision process. Pierre had been the head of a French diplomatic mission in Canada from 1945 to 1947. During that time, he realized the potential of the Saint Lawrence's newly conceived seaway. A few Legrand ships of the 12,000 to 15,000 DWT range had been placed on the Great Lakes to Europe trades during the early 1960's. The commodities carried on the Eastbound leg of the voyage were almost always grain, and on the Westbound leg, specialty steels. The lateral ballasts of the Legrand ships allowed them to load different kinds of grain such as wheat, barley, oats, and corn for the same trip. Thus their ships became increasingly popular with charterers, and this type of traffic increasingly rewarding for Legrand Shipping. As a consequence, the company decided to intensify its efforts on the North America/Europe trade.

This decision was also justified by the perception that average ship size was increasing rapidly on a worldwide basis, in order to reap the economies of scale. Although construction costs per ton were declining as size increased, total cost increased, albeit less than proportionately. The company had to increase the size of its vessels to remain competitive, which meant constant renewal of the fleet and unamortized ships.

Henri and Pierre Legrand felt that in view of their limited resources, both human and financial, they could not effectively compete in worldwide trades without specializing in a trade. They felt that large bulk carriers, over 40,000 DWT, at that time were not perfectly suited to the company's background and field expertise. They felt that newer entrants in the shipping industry, with strong financial backing, would be better equipped to undertake to specialize in large bulk carriers. For the Great Lakes trades, however, maximum size was limited by the size of the locks. Therefore, a decision was taken to design a ship which could use

the St. Lawrence Seaway to its full capacity. A new
type of ship was designed in cooperation with a
French shipyard. In 1965, an approximately 30,000
DWT "Seaway-Max" ship was ordered, and another in
early 1966. These ships had segregated ballasts.
The first 30,000 DWT ship made its first trip to
Duluth in June 1967, breaking the port's record with
31,135 tonnes of grain loaded for an overseas
destination. Other Legrand ships were lengthened to
optimal size, and many were taken off other trades to
enter the Great Lakes/Europe route. On average,
lengthening increased deadweight tonnage by 4,000
tonnes. Average speed was increased from 13.5 to 15
knots.

The 1970's. In 1970, to increase flexibility,
Legrand ordered from a Norwegian shipyard a geared
bulk carrier of 30,000 tonnes, which could use either
port discharging facilities or its own gear, 5 to 10-
ton cranes.

A buoyant freight market in 1970 gave Pierre
Legrand optimistic thoughts about the future, after
having taken over from his father the management of
the company. However, in 1971, freight rates became
rapidly depressed. On a trade route typical for
Legrand ships, such as Great Lakes to Rotterdam, the
rate dropped from an average of $8 per tonne in 1970
to an average of $3 per tonne in 1971 for a 30,000
DWT vessel. Thus in 1971, revenues dropped by 35%.
The result could have been worse had a few ships not
been on long-term charter at favorable rates. The
devaluation of the dollar in December 1971 worsened
the situation, since most of the company's costs had
been and still were incurred in French francs. The
rise of freight rates in 1970 led to numerous new
building orders. These ships came for the most part
into the market in late 1971 and early 1972. This
further depressed the previously high rates,
particularly in Legrand's usual trades.

Pierre Legrand decided to form a consortium with
another, similar firm of the Worms group operating
similar vessels along similar routes. GIE was
created in early 1973 to operate a fleet of 12 bulk
carriers with a total tonnage of 30,000 DWT. GIE
also chartered three ships for the Great Lakes
region. GIE allowed Legrand Shipping to spread
risks, to spread fixed headquarters cost, and to have
more ships with which to satisfy its strong and loyal
customer base. It allowed Legrand ships to enter new
trades such as cement from Great Britain and Spain to
the United States, as well as fertilizer from Belgium

to the Great Lakes.

As freight rates inched up in 1973 to exceed 1970 levels, GIE let its ships out on long-term charters. In early 1973, two 27,000 DWT vessels were ordered for 1974 delivery. The other GIE partner ordered two similar ships. All four were geared and were designed for Great Lakes service. In spite of the recession which hit the tanker market badly, the dry bulk market in 1974, especially in the trades where Legrand Shipping was involved, remained particularly strong. The company continued to position its ships on long-term charters, fearing a descent in freight rates similar to that of the tanker market. Also, because of its specialization, however, the company was untouched by the drop in freight rates which occurred in late 1974 for the dry bulk markets. Most of the GIE ships were then long-term charters at 1973 rates. On average, the duration of the charters was two to three years.

As a consequence, in spite of the very low 1975 freight rates, the company managed to obtain a satisfactory profit in 1975. It was felt that the 1975 recession in rates would not continue much beyond 1977, and Pierre Legrand ordered three ships for delivery in 1977, including a 38,000 DWT bulk carrier from Japanese shipyards (obtaining favorable conditions from the yard because of low demand for new buildings at the time). The 38,000 tonne vessel, which was to become the flagship of GIE and Legrand Shipping, was too wide to enter the St. Lawrence Seaway. It was hoped that GIE could find long-term employment for this ship.

In 1976, freight rates remained low. Legrand, however, remained unaffected because of its long-term charters contracted either directly or through GIE. Thus 1976 returns exceeded average market returns considerably. The company felt that its ships had succeeded in finding niches suited to their characteristics: difficult conditions where a first-rate vessel and a top-quality crew are required. This would compensate for the vessel's high cost. However, by the end of 1976, many of the company's long-term charter agreements came to an end and renewals had to be considered at a less favorable rate. Therefore, 1976 financial performance remained good, but the future looked bleak unless freight rates were to pick up in 1977. Thus, the company did not let out its ship under two-year or more contracts but maintained a short-term chartering strategy.

When 1977 started, the general shipping outlook was unfavorable. There were numerous deliveries of new buildings in the 15,000 to 35,000 DWT range, and also very few lay-ups in that category. Because demand for ships of that category was generally expected to be 10% to 20% lower in 1977, the supply/demand equilibrium seemed to indicate much lower rates. However, Legrand's revenue did not drop as expected. Pierre Legrand attributed this to two factors. First, because Legrand Shipping's principle trade was grain, it was felt to be less sensitive to fluctuations in economic activity. Second, the characteristics of the company's ships allowed them to find employment in trades somehow protected from the freight rate depression.

The company's annual report noted that a bulk carrier of 25,000 DWT had a total daily revenue far in excess of that of a 75,000 or 125,000 DWT bulk in 1977. The company felt it succeeded in maintaining its niche in difficult trades because of its high level of technology and high-quality crews. Some events, however, marred 1977. The 38,000 DWT vessel's financing, which had been done in Japanese yen, had to replaced by U.S.-dollar financing because of the rise of the yen in relation to the U.S. dollar. The switchover took many months and led to a substantial increase in the ship's costs.

Pierre Legrand felt that the banks, for the first time in Legrand Shipping's history, had not been very cooperative in arranging the switchover financing. He felt that, in general, the banking industry, the major supplier of funds to the shipping industry, was starting to have serious qualms about financing shipowners. Worse than the immediate problems of rates, he felt that the company's access to financing could be jeopardized in the long run. Pierre Legrand, however, hoped that this attitude could be only temporary, stemming largely from the current rate depression.

Current Dilemma. In 1978, Legrand's shipping revenue had dropped 23% from 191 million French francs in 1977 to 147 million. Net losses before depreciation reached 2.5 million francs, and after including depreciation, 17.5 million francs. It was estimated that 15 to 18 million francs would be required in 1979 to meet current debt obligations. The market showed, in early 1979, few signs of picking up from the very low 1978 levels. The company's common stock, traded at the Paris stock exchange, seemed to have reached an all-time low of 45 French francs, about one-half to one-third of the average price. This situation made the issuance of additional common stock a costly alternative to debt financing. Also, the Legrand family controlled 60% of the stock. The sale of additional stock would reduce that share to very little. In early 1979, there were 260,000 outstanding shares. The company would have to sell 500,000 shares at 40 French francs to receive the 20 million French francs it required. The 156,000 shares held by the family would represent 20.5% of the stock. Investment bankers felt that if stock was to be sold by Legrand Shipping, and they doubted this could be done even at a 40 French franc price, the company had to sell at least 250,000 shares. Pierre Legrand feared that with an issue of that size, he might have to relinquish control of the company to outsiders, a thought he could not accept.

Another alternative was to issue debt. However, Legrand Shipping's debt-to-equity ratio was almost two to one. This ratio seemed much higher than that of similar companies. Because of the company's high operating and financial leverage, and because of the poor environment the company was to operate in the future, Legrand's bankers refused to provide additional debt financing without the provision of additional equity, either through the sale of additional stock or through the sale of a subsidiary. The Legrand family did not have the financial resources to purchase 50% of the stock to be issued, and as mentioned earlier, because of the costs involved in selling the stock, at least 200,000 shares had to be sold.

The tugboat company seemed to be the only successful subsidiary. Its sale could well bring in 50 million French francs, if Pierre's brother Maurice were to accept that course of action. Pierre felt that Maurice would be adamantly opposed to the sale of the company he managed. Other subsidiaries could be sold, but as a whole, their total value would not exceed 5 million French francs.

Lastly, Pierre Legrand considered selling ships. A 30,000 DWT bulk carrier with five years of age would bring in about 25 million French francs at current market rates. He felt that this was the easiest course of action to take, but by no means the best. He thought that Legrand Shipping could afford to sell a ship or two because there were few economies of scale derived from owning more than one ship. He listed in his mind headquarters cost, training and staffing, and purchasing power for supplies, and could find few other economies derived from scale. But could the company continue to sell off its assets forever?

259

The emotional reaction to selling a ship was too strong for him to consider this alternative further. However, he wondered whether his company was either going to have to 1) grow and diversify itself into shipping alone or in other areas, or 2) reduce its size, strip down its operations to the bare minimum, and weather the storm. Considering the first alternative, he wondered what the company's strengths and weaknesses were in tramping. The company owned high-quality ships, had expert crews, and had found niches which were often in the past protected from the inroads of competition.

The company's weakness was that it could no longer compete in the world tramping market. Legrand Shipping had to find new markets. Some observers of the bulk shipping market had expressed the thought that the supply of transportation was becoming more and more commodity-like, and that product differentiation was impossible to achieve. The emphasis, the observers noted, should be on competitive pricing, therefore cost control instead of relying on the high-quality/high-cost policies of companies such as Legrand. If the market were to evolve along these lines, Legrand should consider initiating drastic cost reductions.

Personnel costs, amounting to about 30% of direct costs in 1979, seemed to be the expense that Legrand should attempt to reduce first. An able seaman on a Legrand ship cost the company 65,000 FF, about $14,000 per year, while a crew member from Hong Kong or the Phillipines would cost about 4,000 FF, about $1100 a year, a thirteen-fold reduction in costs. If staffing per ship was to remain constant, a conservative hypothesis because in all likelihood it would be reduced, direct costs would drop by 25%, possibly from 18,500 FF per day for a 14,000 DWT vessel to 13,500 FF per day with re-crewing.

French law, however, expressly prohibited the hiring of foreign crews on French ships. The solution would be to register the ships under a convenience flag, such as Panama or Liberia. Then crews of any nationality could be hired. Legrand would, however, face difficulties in changing the country of registration of its bulk carriers: the French government would have to give the company an export permit to allow it to sell its ships to a foreign company, even if the company were to be controlled by Legrand. Because of the political reasons favoring the retention of ships under a French national flag, such as prestige and loss of jobs as well as pressure from powerful French unions, the government would not give the export permit to Legrand Shipping.

Pierre Legrand, however, wondered if some alternative solution allowing the company to cut costs would be legally feasible. He also considered diversifying the company in areas outside shipping. Diversification attempts had always been unsuccessful in the past, mainly because the right managers and employees could not be found. Pierre also considered the alternative of weathering the storm. Legrand had, however, been doing this for the past four years, and there seemed to be few areas where costs could be drastically cut further. The company could not continue to survive in this manner much longer.

2.   Liner Shipping

Liner shipping at Legrand Shipping had often been a secondary activity. Now that tramping, the company's primary source of income, was experiencing serious difficulties, renewed interest was given to liners.

a.   North Atlantic to Portugal-Africa Lines. As described earlier, Legrand's major activity was coastal shipping, up to the early 1940's. In 1948, a staff member of the engineering department inspecting a German vessel felt that the ship could be of use to Legrand. It was an 1830 DWT vessel which was provided to the company by the French government as compensation for war damages. The ship was not suited for coastal tramping, but Henri Legrand felt there was good market demand for such a vessel on the French to Portugal liner trade. The ship could go to Portugal with general cargo, and return with wine and ore from Setubal. The trade became very successful.

In 1952, a special ship was redesigned, with a clean 'tween deck allowing the carriage of vehicles. It was the first among modern roll-on/roll-off ships in the world. Another liner was chartered. Trading surpassed optimistic expectations, and tonnage increased five-fold to 45,000 tonnes from 1950 to 1956. A new 2,000-ton ship was purchased to replace the chartered liner. In 1960, Legrand Shipping purchased three liners of 1,615 DWT each to use on the France to Morocco trades. It integrated forward into shipping agency operations by purchasing a small firm located in Le Havre. These agency operations were later expanded at Le Havre with the purchase of container-handling equipment, and at Rouen with the creation of an office there.

Legrand Shipping Company

In 1967, a conference was formed and cargo-pooling agreements were reached with a competing foreign shipowner who was serving Portugese ports from Northern Europe. In spite of this agreement, cost competition with other lines increased rapidly throughout the year. By 1968, the liners were no longer competitive because they were flying the high-cost French flag. Ships were sold to Vora Shipping, a Legrand-controlled subsidiary located in Curacao.* Frequently, Legrand ships from then on flew convenience flags on this route. Traffic continued to grow, but slowly, over the following five years.

The 1970's. In 1972, traffic reached 68,384 tonnes, a cumulative annual growth rate of 3.5% since 1956. A revenue-pooling agreement with competing lines from Belgium and Portugal was reached at the beginning of 1973. It allowed for the reduction in the number of ships trading. Employment was found for those Legrand liners on the trade from Antwerp to Algiers, which had reopened in early 1974, following a bilateral agreement between the governments of France and Algeria. A conference was created with two other lines, providing for the pooling of revenue. The agreement stipulated that French ships had to be used in this specific trade, together with Algerian ships which obtained half the traffic. For that purpose, a conventional 4,500 DWT liner was purchased in early 1975. The growth in the Northern France to Algeria trade did not compensate, however, for the reduction in traffic which occurred in the liner trade to Portugal and Morocco. Because of the political events occurring in Portugal, this route had become less than profitable.

The trade to Morocco was also in the red because of strong competition from other lines. Liner trading to Morocco and Portugal was reduced to one ship in 1976. The pooling agreements were not renewed in 1977. By 1978, losses were accumulating on the Moroccan and Portugese trades, and service by Legrand Shipping was reduced to a minimum. The liner trade to Algeria from Northern France was affected by long waits at Algerian harbors because of intense port congestion. The conventional ships often had to wait 20 to 25 days to get in, while Ro-Ro ships hardly waited at all. Thus the 4,500 DWT Legrand

----

* In 1968, the French government had not yet placed restrictions on selling French-flag vessels to owners who could change to lower-cost flags.

liner was sold in mid-1978, and the company withdrew from the Northern France to Algeria trade in 1979.

b. **Mediterranean Lines**. Legrand Shipping's major strength had never been the transportation of general cargo. Prior to World War II, Legrand tramps would occasionally take on some heavy unit loads, however, such as railroad cars and locomotives. Because of the war, an office was set up in Marseilles in 1940. The local manager got to know a Marseilles shipowner and reached an agreement with him jointly to serve Algeria, then a French colony, with a 3,200 DWT converted coal carrier. The trade became rapidly successful, and the modified coal carrier, with its new 'tween deck, could no longer provide adequate capacity.

A ship was given to Legrand Shipping by the French government as compensation for war damages. This ship was modified to carry general cargo and wine in internal tanks. A third ship, a 1,100 DWT liner, was put on the trade in 1950. It was specially adapted to the transportation of fresh fruit and vegetables.

A year later, the company designed a ship specifically for the trade. It could carry high density bulk cargoes, wine, and heavy unit loads; had a large deck and 'tween deck area; and a high cruising speed, compared to traditional liners at that time. The company continued in the 1950's to design and have built sophisticated ships to satisfy a trade with a seemingly endless appetite.

However, in 1962, Algeria's independence from France caused a sharp decline in transportation demand. The company had to find new uses for its ships: it started a line from Italy to Portugal, and from Italy to Algeria. Two liners which were no longer cost-competitive were sold to Greek interests.

The 1970's. An Italian subsidiary, Lenare, was created in 1970. By 1971, Legrand's Marseilles office was managing eleven liners, six under Italian flag, four under French flag, and a Greek vessel under a time-charter agreement. The fleet was being constantly renewed as new traffic to oil-producing companies of the Mediterranean basin opened up. A 4,100 DWT lift-on/lift-off and roll-on/roll-off ship was designed. Nicknamed the "factory carrier", this ship had a 40-foot drawbridge which could allow horizontal handling of unit loads exceeding 600 tonnes and vertical handling of unit loads reaching 180 tonnes, up to 130 feet in length. This ship also had the ability to carry bulk cargoes and wine.

Additional roll-on/roll-off ships were designed and built in 1973 and 1974. By 1974, the fleet's average age was three years in the Mediterranean area. Some ships of older design were sold and not replaced, since the company believed that new, specialized but flexible ships contributed the best niche available for the liner trade in the Mediterranean at that time.

In 1976, the company owned seven liners, ranging in size from 4,550 DWT to 984 DWT. Average speed was 14 knots, and all but one were equipped with roll-on/roll-off cargo handling. Ships were chartered in an on-the-spot market when conditions warranted it.

The major problem faced by Legrand liners was port congestion, although it was felt that because of their roll-on/roll-off capabilities waiting time was on average much lower than that for conventional liners. Also, port congestion problems were often alleviated in Algeria when port authorities pushed over the wharf into the sea slow-moving inbound shipments. The principal problems faced by Legrand were to obtain a larger share of the revenue pool of the conference operating between France and Algeria, because of the high efficiency of Legrand liners, and also to obtain faster payments for freight from their Middle Eastern customers. The company also had to face increasingly strong inroads from foreign competitors, especially Soviet bloc countries.

As Pierre Legrand stared at the stained glass window, he thought to himself, "If only freight rates were to go up a little..."

Exhibit 13.1

BALANCE SHEETS (IN 000'S OF FF)

ASSETS

ASSETS	1977	1976
Fixed assets, net of depreciation	148,032	108,584
Real estate and buildings	1,904	2,272
Ships	141,461	78,481
Vehicles	87	103
Office equipment	586	575
Other transport equipment	2,140	1,587
Improvements	601	615
Misc. fixed assets	3	23,701
Goodwill	1,250	1,250
Other assets	26,403	24,064
LT loans and account receivables	7,065	4,951
Investments	19,338	19,113
Current Assets	42,549	42,085
Accounts receivable customers	2,336	1,586
Accounts receivable other	34,742	28,341
Cash	5,471	12,158
Loss for year	------	4,358
Total	216,984	179,091

LIABILITIES

LIABILITIES	1977	1970
Capital and reserves	53,044	58,346
Capital	18,870	18,870
L.T. capital gains	632	522
Reevaluation reserves	1,757	7,156
Investment reserves	220	220
Merging gains	30,572	30,572
Miscellaneous		
Subsidies for investment	5,032	9,992
Subsidies	5,032	1,597
Tax subsidy		8,395
Reserves for losses	3,752	1,607
Long Term Debt	105,860	70,373
Short Term Debt	48,929	38,773
Supplies payables	1,883	2,419
Misc. payables	23,349	14,851
Profit for year	367	------
Total	216,984	179,091

DETAILED INCOME STATEMENTS (IN 000'S OF FF)

	1977		1976	
	Expenses	Income	Expenses	Income
Gross income, shipping		191,539		175,903
Other income		2,504		853
Financial income		2,862		1,382
Personnel expense	52,077		45,822	
Taxes	1,187		1,000	
Harbour costs, fuel, maintenance, insurance, charters	121,235		112,310	
Transport costs and trip expenses	1,283		1,046	
Management expenses	3,538		3,672	
Financial expenses	9,586		6,053	
Payments to co-owners of ships	3,307		3,912	
Expenses chargeable to third parties		3,942		4,138
Expenses covered by reserves				15
Total	192,813	200,847	173,815	182,291
Gross income from operations		8,034		8,476

Exhibit 13.2 Continued

	1977 Expenses	1977 Income	1976 Expenses	1976 Income
Gross income from operations		8,034		8,476
Depreciation	18,473		15,054	
Reserves	4,064		250	
Loss and gains from previous years	1,856	1,370	1,510	1,147
Capital gains and loss from sale of capital goods		12,745	4	147
Exceptional losses and gains	59	1,160	2,350	991
Exceptional reserves	1,691		81	7
Investment subsidies		2,407		2,650
Taxes	289			
Carry forward of reserves		1,425		1,479
Misc. gains and losses	19	27		
Total	26,450	26,817	19,255	14,897
Net income	367 (gain)		4,358 (loss)	

Legrand Shipping Company

Exhibit 13.3

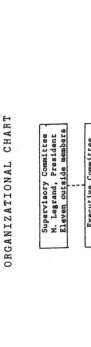
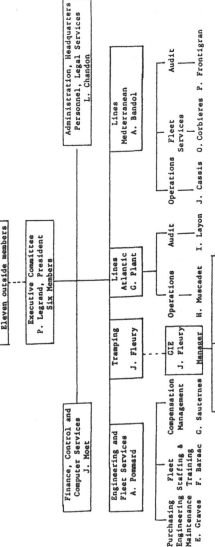

ORGANIZATIONAL CHART

Supervisory Committee
M. Legrand, President
Eleven outside members

Executive Committee
P. Legrand, President
Six Members

Finance, Control and
Computer Services
J. Moet

Administration, Headquarters
Personnel, Legal Services
L. Chandon

Engineering and
Fleet Services
A. Pommard

Purchasing   Fleet
Engineering Staffing &   Compensation
Maintenance Training   Management
E. Graves   F. Barsac   G. Sauternes

Tramping
J. Fleury

GIE
J. Fleury
Manager

Operations Chartering Control & Audit
B. Boileau D. Chinon   C. Sancerre

Lines
Atlantic
G. Plant

Operations Audit
H. Muscadet I. Layon

Lines
Mediterranean
A. Bandol

Operations Fleet   Audit
Services
J. Cassis O. Corbieres P. Frontigran

Exhibit 13.4

PARTICULARS OF TRAMP VESSELS

Name	Delivered From Yard	Length Overall (feet)	Breadth (feet)	Cubic Grain (Cubic Feet)	Summer Deadweight Tons (Metric Tonnes)	Summer Draft (feet)
JANICE	1977	608'2"	91'2"	1,714,988	38,931	37.5
EUNICE	1977	608'2"	91'2"	1,714,988	38,931	37.5
VERONIQUE	1977	606'9"	91'2"	1,672,008	38,962	37.4
ANNE-MARIE	1977	616'9"	91'2"	1,672,008	38,962	37.4
DONNA-MARIE	1967	644'11"	75'	1,502,360	31,135	35.4
MONIQUE	1968	644'11"	75'	1,502,360	31,065	35.4
BRIDGETTE	1974	573'2"	75'	1,266,179	27,243	36.0
DANIELLE	1974	573'2"	75'	1,266.179	27,243	36.0
JEANNE	1974	599'10"	73'6"	1,266.989	26,637	34.6
FRANCOIS	1974	599'10"	73'6"	1,266,989	26,637	34.6
JULIETTE	1971	591'6"	75'	1,274,437	25,650	33.4
MARIA-LOUISE	1965	618'9"	75'	1,110,228	24,452	32.1
					375,848	

* This exhibit shows the total tramp fleet of GIE, a joint venture of Legrand and another partner. Legrand contributed about half the tonnage involved.

Legrand Shipping Company

Exhibit 13.5

PARTICULARS OF LINER VESSELS

Name	Delivered From Yard	Type	Deadweight (Metric Tonnes)	Service Speed (Knots)
SETE	1972	Ro/Ro & Lo/Lo	4,100	14
GENES	1975	Ro/Ro & Lo/Lo	1,700	14
TUNIS	1973	Ro/Ro & Lo/Lo	1,400	14
SFAX	1977	Ro/Ro	1,650	14
ALGER	1977	Ro/Ro	1,650	14
DERNA	1977	Ro/Ro	2,500	15.5

270

Exhibit 13.6

PERFORMANCE SUMMARY, 1968–1978 (MILLIONS OF FRENCH FRANCS)($1 = 4.8 FF)

	1968	1969	1970	1971	1972	1973	1974	1975	1976	1977	1978(est.)
Consolidated sales	64.7	67.1	83.8	94.7	85.7	104.4	147.5	172.0	175.9	193.4	155.0
Net earnings after taxes	1.0	1.2	1.4	.99	1.0	1.7	2.0	1.7	(4.4)	.4	(17.5)
Number of employees	608	525	516	536	464	430	451	510	572	570	550
Salaries paid	13.3	12.5	12.6	14.3	12.9	13.0	16.4	21.1	26.2	29.4	32.0
Employee benefits	5.1	4.9	4.8	6.2	8.0	9.3	10.7	15.6	19.6	23.3	26.0

Legrand Shipping Company

Exhibit 13.7

SHIPS OWNED AND DEADWEIGHT TONNAGE

Year	Number of ships owned	Total DWT	Average unit DWT	Average age	Number of Liners
1949	16	79,961	4,998	-	-
1959	16	86,685	5,418	-	8
1969	15	144,396	9,626	7.9 years	3
1974	13	184,706	14,208	5.7 years	4
1978	12	193,142	16,095	5.5 years	6

Part III

THE SHIP-PORT INTERFACE

Each ship must deal with port facilities to handle
its cargo. When planning the construction of a new
vessel, a ship owner must also determine that the
appropriate port facilities are available to allow
efficient operation of his vessels. Typically, the
more specialized the ship, the more specialized the
port facility must be. The traditional break-bulk
cargo vessels were self-supporting, with cargo-
handling gear on board. Almost any general cargo port
facility could service such a vessel.

Fully cellular containerships required the
construction of specialized container terminals, with
gantry cranes and marshalling areas. Roll-on/roll-
off vessels required ramps (either on the ship or on
shore) with sufficient parking space in the terminal.

Offshore terminals for large tankers presented
some special problems. To be located outside of the
U.S. territorial sea (i.e., the "three mile limit"),
new legislation was necessary. The Deepwater Port
Act established the legal viability of these
facilities and set up a regulatory framework for
handling applicants. Congress felt that deepwater
ports would be limited in terms of desirable
locations and made it clear in the legislation that
oil companies building an offshore terminal would not
be able to monopolize such facilities to the
detriment of their competitors. Although it is
possible to construct a fixed tanker terminal
offshore, almost all such offshore terminals built
worldwide have been the floating single-point mooring
(SPM) variety.

Alternatives to constructing deepwater ports
are: 1) using smaller vessels to dock at existing
ports, 2) utilizing larger vessels that transship
their cargo at other deepwater land-based locations
(e.g., islands) for transfer to smaller ships, and 3)

273

a lightering (or lightening) operation, such as the one used by Venture Oil in Part II, where larger tankers unload into smaller vessels at sea.

If an oil company wants to invest in a deepwater terminal, a significant investment is needed. By joining a consortium, the investment for each company is greatly reduced, although control is proportionately decreased. A company must also take the time and money to follow all the procedures required by law to obtain the necessary permits.

FORMAT OF PART III

Chapter 14 deals with the issues faced by SEADOCK and LOOP, the first two consortia formed to apply for permits to build offshore terminals in the U.S. Key factors to deal with included regulatory constraints that had the potential for greatly restricting the economic benefits to the applicants.

In Chapter 15, the reader returns to Venture Oil (Chapter 11); the company is now considering the replacement of its lightening operations with an offshore terminal. Venture Oil must compare the benefits of this fixed capital investment with other alternatives available to it.

In conclusion, each shipping company generally has more than one way of meeting its port needs. However, to obtain the maximum efficiency from its vessels, a shipping firm must see that the appropriate port facilities and operations are available for proper cargo handling as an essential part of the origin-to-destination movement of the cargo.

Chapter 14

SEADOCK AND LOOP

In December 1975, SEADOCK, Inc. (a consortium of
eight oil companies and one chemical company) and
LOOP, Inc. (a consortium of six companies) applied
under the guidelines of the Deepwater Port Act of
1974 to the Department of Transportation (DOT) for a
license for each to own, construct, and operate a
deepwater crude oil terminal in the Gulf of Mexico.
These were the only two organizations to apply for
licenses.

One year later, SEADOCK and LOOP were issued the
licenses. The two corporations were given eight
months to accept or decline the licenses.

BACKGROUND

In the late 1960's and early 1970's, energy
consumption in the United States rose at rates
exceeding 4% per annum, an increase over the average
annual 3.4% reported for the period 1950-1972. Even
though U.S. energy consumption increased, U.S.
petroleum production leveled off in the early 1970's.
Consequently, crude oil imports were filling the gap,
as shown in Exhibit 14.1.

Originally, oil imports came from Latin America;
however, oil production and known reserves were
increasing in the Middle East (see Exhibit 14.2).
Trade routes between producers and consumers
dramatically increased in length. The closing of the
Suez Canal in 1967 increased the trip from the Gulf
of Mexico to the Persian Gulf by 30%. The longer
trade routes and, hence, higher transportation costs,
increased the demand for the cost-efficient
supertankers. Exhibit 14.3 shows the existing tanker
fleet and vessels on order as of November 30, 1973.

Supertankers provided tremendous savings in tanker construction and operating costs. The economies of scale were due to the fact that the amount of hull steel, machinery weights, accommodations space for crew, and other factors did not increase proportionately with increases in the size of the vessel. Exhibit 14.4 shows the savings per DWT in purchasing a larger vessel. Almost all operating costs expressed per DWT decrease significantly with increases in vessel size. The only exception is insurance, which ranges between 10% and 18% of total annual costs according to size.

Consequently, the overall costs of transporting oil are reduced as reflected by the lower required freight rate (RFR). Exhibit 14.4 shows the RFR per ton of cargo delivered. RFR is the minimum rate which covers all the owner's costs, including the return on his investment capital. The exhibit assumes a 10% return and uses oil prices prevailing before the oil embargo of October 1973.

Unfortunately, draft limitations at U.S. ports prohibited the berthing of these new supertankers, as shown in Exhibit 14.5. However, the U.S. was not the only country with the draft problem. The worldwide solution was offshore oil terminals. The most popular type of offshore oil terminal is the single-point mooring system (SPM) which is described in Exhibit 14.6. By 1974, over 100 SPM's had been put into operation around the world.

Interest in deepwater ports (DWP's) for the U.S. initiated a study directed by the Council of Economic Advisors to quantify the possible benefits for a single "superport" on the East Coast and the Gulf Coast. The study was completed in early 1973. It analyzed costs for U.S. and foreign-flag tankers with and without double bottoms, and in addition, considered a variety of potential governmental policies. Exhibit 14.7 shows the best and worst cases. Even in the worst case, where tankers serving U.S. DWP's are required to have double bottoms while tankers serving foreign ports are not, the offshore port proved to be a profitable venture.

A study was also done in 1974 that strongly suggested that new crude supplies in the form of imports would be needed on the East and Gulf coasts to satisfy the projected demand in 1985 of 23 million barrels per day (MM. BD). In the analysis, oil from the Outer Continental Shelf (OCS) and imports were found to supply 10.75 MM. BD of the 23 MM.BD required in 1985. Nearly all the 10.75 MM. BD imports or OCS supply expected would be needed on the

East and Gulf coasts. This led to estimating the number of tankers that would be required to deliver the petroleum.

Calculations showed that 1,015-100,000 DWT tankers or 404-250,000 DWT tankers would be required to carry the forecasted import level of 10.75 MM. BD. This circumstance would obviously constitute considerable traffic and thus demonstrated another aspect for the need of DWP oil terminals. Exhibit 14.8 displays these results.

Though economics showed the benefits of a DWP, the environmentalists took a different viewpoint. The environmentalists were very concerned about the increased potential of catastrophic oil spills due to increased supertanker traffic. The environmentalists did not want DWP's constructed in U.S. waters until all direct and related effects brought about by DWP construction could be established and projected with great certainty. This environmental concern would definitely be reflected in governmental licensing of DWP's.

Thus, from the economic viewpoint, the U.S. seemed to be the perfect candidate for deepwater port terminals; but guidelines and jurisdictional control of DWP's had first to be established.

SEADOCK and LOOP were organized in 1972; however, construction could not begin because of jurisdictional problems. There was some confusion as to the jurisdiction of the U.S. Federal Government outside the three-mile U.S. Territorial Sea as well as the appropriate role of specific federal agencies. Unfortunately, there were myriad government organizations that held some kind of jurisdiction in port planning and development. It was apparent that new legislation was necessary to handle licensing and to settle jurisdictional problems. A single agency had to be appointed in order to assure expeditious handling of applications and licenses. Because of the unorganized division in Congress of powers concerning port planning, discussion dragged on for two years.

PASSAGE OF DWP ACT OF 1974

On January 4, 1975, President Ford signed the Deepwater Port Act of 1974. This act only applied to offshore oil terminals beyond the territorial waters, which would include any feasible DWP in the Gulf of Mexico. The Act sets the guidelines for licensing, while designed to protect the national interest, the environment, and competition. The key provisions of the bill are:

1. **Licensing Agency**: The DOT was selected to be the single agency in charge of licensing the construction and operation of the DWP's. The DOT is obligated to consult and cooperate with all other interested federal agencies and departments of any affected coastal state.

2. **Adjacent State Veto**: Adjacent coastal states were given the right to veto any proposed deepwater port. The definition of an adjacent coastal state included:

   a. A state that is directly connected to the port by pipelines
   b. A state located within 15 miles of the proposed ports
   c. A state threatened with a possible oil spill from the port.

3. **Procedures**: The procedure involved included application, environmental impact statement, hearings, and final action by all federal agencies. A decision on the issuance of a license had to be made within eleven months. When more than one application was issued for the same location, the license was issued according to the following priority:

   a. A state application
   b. An application by an independent terminal company
   c. Any other application.

4. **Environmental Review**: The Secretary of Transportation, Administrator of the Environmental Protection Agency (EPA), and Administrator of the National Oceanic and Atmospheric Administration (NOAA) were to establish environmental concerns associated with deepwater ports which would be used to evaluate applications.

5. **Antitrust Review**: The Department of Justice must give the Secretary an opinion as to whether issuance of a license would adversely affect competition, restrain trade, further monopolization, or otherwise create or maintain a situation in contravention of the antitrust laws.

6. **Common Carrier Status**: Existing statutes
    regulating the transportation of oil and natural
    gas in interstate commerce were made
    specifically applicable to a deepwater port.

7. **Navigational Safety**: The DOT (through the
    Coast Guard) is authorized to prescribe, by
    regulation, procedures to ensure navigational
    safety around or near the port. The DOT is also
    to designate a safety zone around a port within
    which no uses incompatible with such a port are
    permitted.

8. **Liability**: Strict liability for pollution
    damage caused by a discharge from the port
    itself or from a vessel within the safety zone
    was prescribed. The bill allocates liability
    among:

    a. The licensee, up to $50 million.
    b. The owner and operator of a vessel, up to
        $20 million.
    c. A deepwater port liability fund for all
        proven damages not compensated for by the
        licensee or the owner or operator. The
        fund is created by a two cents a barrel
        charge on oil until the fund reaches $100
        million.

APPLICATIONS FOR SEADOCK/LOOP

SEADOCK, a Texas corporation, and LOOP, a Delaware
corporation, were both organized in 1972 for the sole
purpose of developing their respective deepwater
ports. A total of 13 companies participated in
SEADOCK from time to time, while 16 participated in
LOOP. The following companies, each having an equal
percentage of ownership, were involved at the time of
application:

SEADOCK	LOOP
Cities Service Company	Ashland Oil, Inc.
Continental Pipeline Company	Marathon Oil Co.
Crown Seadock Pipeline	Murphy Oil Corporation
Corporation	Shell Oil Company
Dow Chemical Company	Texaco, Inc.
Exxon Pipeline Company	Union Oil of California
Gulf Oil Corporation	
Mobil Oil Corporation	
Phillips Investment Co.	
Shell Oil Company	

SEADOCK had an estimated throughput capacity of 2.5 MM. BD and a capital cost of $658 million. There were provisions for possible expansion to 4 MM. BD at an estimated additional cost of $206 million.

LOOP had an estimated throughput capacity of 3.4 MM. BD and a capital cost of $738 million. Construction was to be completed in stages, with the first stage having an estimated capacity of 1.4 MM. BD and costing $348 million. Once the offshore platform was in place, expansion would be carried out by adding SPM's, laying pipeline parallel to the first pipeline, and expanding pumping capacity of storage facilities.

SEADOCK would be located 26 miles offshore of Freeport, Texas, in 100 feet of water. Exhibit 14.9 presents a diagram of the facility. It would consist of one pumping platform, one quarters platform, and four single-point moorings. The moorings would be connected to large-diameter (52-inch), buried pipelines, from the offshore terminal complex to the storage facility approximately 31 miles away. The onshore terminal and transfer facility would provide approximately 22 million barrels of storage capacity.

A vessel would moor to one of the SPM's and would connect a floating hose to its onboard manifold. The vessel pumps the crude through the floating hose to the offshore platform, where large capacity pumps provide power to move the crude through the buried pipeline to the booster station, which assists them in moving the oil into storage.

Phase II, if undertaken, would involve the addition of two SPM's and their connecting pipelines, an additional pumping platform, a third 52-inch pipeline, and about 10 MM. BD additional tankage at the onshore terminal.

The arrival and departure of approximately three ships of 225,000 DWT every two days would be required to meet the proposed throughput. SEADOCK considered a berth utilization factor of 60% reasonable for a facility of its configuration and operation.

LOOP would be located 18 miles offshore of Grande Isle, Louisiana, in 110 feet of water. Three construction phases were planned covering a 13-year period. Phase I, to be completed in 1980, would consist of three SPM's, each connected by a 56-inch pipeline to a pumping platform, a control platform, one 48-inch pipeline to shore, a booster station about three miles inland, and a 48-inch buried line to the storage terminal. Phase II would add one SPM, another line from the platform to the storage terminal, and possibly a booster station at the inland terminal. Phase III, planned for completion in 1989, would add two more SPM's, a third 48-inch line to the storage terminal, and possibly a second line to the onshore terminal.

Tanker routes and pipeline newtorks for SEADOCK and LOOP are shown in Exhibits 14.10 and 14.11.

CHANGING ECONOMIC CLIMATE

The decision to build DWP's was made before the effects of the October 1973 OPEC oil embargo were realized. Since then, the oil companies have had to revise their forecasts in light of the changes in crude oil price, production, and consumption.

The average OPEC crude oil price increased 333% from $3.99/BBL to $11.28/BBL between 1973 and 1974, although the price did remain below $12/BBL through 1976. However, Exhibit 14.12 shows that net imports were still increasing. The exhibit also shows that consumption of petroleum had decreased in 1974 and 1975, but increased in 1976 while U.S. production of crude oil was still decreasing.

Another major effect of the oil embargo was the decrease in tanker freight rates. Increasing worldwide demand culminated in the embargo. After the marked increases in freight rates, increased supply of tankers surpassed increases in tanker demand, which had dropped because of a cut in production and raised oil prices. Consequently, tanker rates were forced downwards. Exhibit 14.13 shows the dramatic decrease in WORLDSCALE rates after the embargo and the continued depression.

In 1974 and 1975, the depressed rates were below the total costs for tankers and did not cover all variable costs. Tanker owners were forced to take charters at prices that reflected their out-of-pocket costs. The owners faced the dilemma of whether to take a charter that just covered the cost of a voyage, whether to "lay up" the ship and wait, or whether to scrap or sell. Many ships were being laid up or scrapped. "Slow steaming" became common practice on those ships that did continue operating.

Two principal alternatives to direct receipt of VLCC's that were already in practice were transshipment and lightering at sea. Transshipment facilities to serve U.S. ports were in operation in the Canadian Maritime, the Bahamas, Bonaire, and Aruba. Crude was offloaded from VLCC's at these ports into temporary onshore storage (or directly over the jetty), from which it was then reloaded into smaller tankers that could directly enter conventional U.S. ports. Approximately 60-80% of the transportation savings attributed to direct shipment by VLCC can be realized by transshipment. However, the transshipment terminals were not U.S.-controlled, and the problem of traffic at or near principal receiving ports had not been solved.

Lightering involves the direct transfer of a portion of cargo from a deep-draft tanker to a shallower-draft vessel, so the latter (or both vessels) can then enter shallow-draft ports. With lightering, even a greater percentage of savings can be obtained than with transshipment. As a result of the reduced tanker rates, and the delay in DWP's, the practice of lightering was increasing. A VLCC would normally require five or six lighterings and would tally approximately 12 days of demurrage. Although traffic problems may be mitigated by this procedure, ship-to-ship transfer operations pose a greater threat of potential oil spills, particularly if carried out in the open sea.

GOVERNMENT APPROVAL OF SEADOCK/LOOP

Finally, on December 17, 1976, SEADOCK and LOOP received federal approval and were issued licenses. These were the first DWP licenses ever issued and contained many restrictions and conditions. Several of these conditions that concerned oil companies are shown in Exhibit 14.14.

Now after receiving approval four years after SEADOCK and LOOP were organized, the two corporations each had to decide: go or no go?

Exhibit 14.1

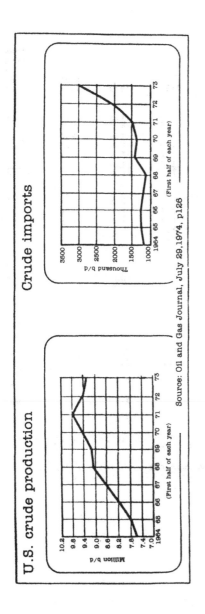

U.S. CRUDE PRODUCTION AND IMPORTS 1964-1974

U.S. crude production

Crude imports

Source: Oil and Gas Journal, July 29, 1974, p126

Exhibit 14.2

WORLD PETROLEUM PRODUCTION AND RESERVES
(IN MM. BD)

Area	1971	1972	1973	Sept. 1973	Reserves Jan. 1, 1974 (in billions of barrels)
Middle East					
Abu Dhabi	0.9	1.0	1.3	1.4	21.5
Iran	4.5	4.9	6.0	5.9	60.0
Iraq	1.7	1.5	1.9	2.0	31.5
Kuwait	2.9	2.8	2.9	3.2	64.0
Saudi Arabia	4.5	5.7	7.4	8.3	132.0
Other		1.2	1.9		41.2
Total Middle East		17.6	21.4		350.2
Africa					
Algeria	0.8	1.1	1.0	1.1	7.6
Libya	2.8	2.2	2.1	2.3	25.5
Nigeria	1.5	1.8	2.0	2.0	20.0
Other		0.6	0.6		14.2
Total Africa		5.6	5.8		67.3
Asia-Pacific					
Indonesia	0.9	1.0	1.3		10.5
Other			0.9		5.1
Total Asia-Pacific			2.2		15.6
Europe			0.4		16.0
Western Hemisphere					
U.S.	9.5	9.5	9.2		34.7
Canada	1.4	1.5	1.8		9.4
Venezuela	3.6	3.2	3.4		14.0
Other		1.3	1.8		17.7
Total Western Hemisphere		15.7	16.1		75.8
Communist nations			9.3		103.0
Total World			55.2		627.9*

*World Petroleum reserves of 627.9 billion barrels has an energy equivalent of 3,640 quads.

Source: Exploring Energy Choices, Preliminary Report of the Energy Policy Project of the Ford Foundation, 1974.

Exhibit 14.3

ANALYSIS OF TANKER FLEET BY AGE AND DWT
TO 30 NOVEMBER 1973

DWT	Pre-1946 NR	DWT	1946/50 NR	DWT	1951/55 NR	DWT	1956/60 NR	DWT	1961/65 NR	DWT	1966/70 NR	DWT	1971/73 NR	DWT
10/ 19,999	94	1,504.8	39	599.1	271	4,588.2	205	3,527.8	44	682.4	56	880.4	37	520.3
20/ 29,999	3	70.9	28	792.0	121	2,965.9	208	4,731.7	93	2,173.3	94	2,194.6	70	1,826.1
30/ 49,999			2	61.9	72	2,514.1	385	14,696.9	159	6,523.7	49	1,994.1	44	1,521.7
50/ 69,999							43	2,268.3	254	14,562.3	43	2,707.7	7	410.6
70/124,999							16	1,432.7	137	11,621.7	236	21,586.0	35	3,391.5
125/174,999									1	137.1	37	5,418.7	26	3,579.1
175/224,999											111	23,103.2	50	11,265.3
225/299,999											32	7,707.9	161	40,368.1
300,000 +											6	1,960.5	6	2,302.0
TOTAL	97	1,575.7	69	1,453.0	464	10,068.2	857	26,657.4	688	35,700.5	664	67,553.1	436	65,184.7
% OF OVERALL TOTAL	0.4		0.4		2.4		6.5		8.7		16.4		15.9	

DWT	TOTAL EXISTING NR	DWT	%	TOTAL ON ORDER NR	DWT	%	OVERALL TOTAL NR	DWT	%
10/ 19,999	746	12,303.0	4.9	39	589.5	0.3	785	12,892.5	3.1
20/ 29,999	617	14,754.5	7.1	66	1,619.2	0.8	683	16,373.7	4.0
30/ 49,999	711	27,312.4	13.1	145	4,925.8	2.4	856	32,238.2	7.9
50/ 69,999	347	19,948.9	9.6	25	1,472.1	0.7	372	21,421.0	5.2
70/124,999	424	38,031.9	18.3	203	19,822.9	9.8	627	57,854.8	14.1
125/174,999	64	9,134.9	4.4	145	20,330.2	10.1	209	29,465.1	7.2
175/224,999	161	34,368.5	16.5	15	3,059.7	1.5	176	37,482.2	9.1
225/299,999	193	48,076.0	23.1	330	84,644.0	41.8	523	132,720.0	32.3
300,000 +	12	4,262.5	2.0	180	65,874.2	32.6	192	70,136.7	17.1
TOTAL	3,275	208,192.6	100.0	1,148	202,337.6	100.0	4,423	410,530.2	100.0
% OF OVERALL TOTAL	50.7			49.3			100.0		

Note: Does not include special fleet for LPG, solvents, etc.
Rebuilt tonnage has been included in year of rebuild.

Exhibit 14.4

ECONOMICS OF TANKER CONSTRUCTION
AND OPERATION BY SIZE

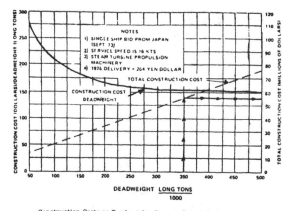

Construction Costs vs Deadweight. Source: Joseph D. Porricelli and
Virgil F. Keith, "Tankers and the U.S. Energy Situation: An Economic
and Environmental Analysis." *Marine Technology*, Vol.11, No.4
(October 1974), copyrighted by the Society of Naval Architects and
Marine Engineers and included herein by permission of the
aforementioned society.

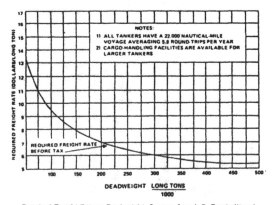

Required Freight Rate vs Deadweight. Source: Joseph D. Porricelli and
Virgil F. Keith, "Tankers and the U.S. Energy Situation: An Economic
and Environmental Analysis." *Marine Technology*, Vol.11, No.4
(October 1974), copyrighted by the Society of Naval Architects and
Marine Engineers and included herein by permission of the
aforementioned society.

Exhibit 14.5

PORT CAPABILITIES AND TANKER DRAFT

Port and Harbor Capabilities

Port of Harbor Area	Max. Draft Vessel Using Area (feet) 1969	1970	Controlling Depth (feet)	Aver. Tidal Variation (feet)	Approx. Max. Dredgible Depth (feet)
Portland, Me	51	51	45	9.0	60
Boston	41	42	40	9.0	40-60
New York (Ambrose)	45	44	45	4.5	60(Narrows)
(Kill Van Kull)	40	40	35	5.0	38
Delaware Bay to Philadelphia	46	46	40	4.1 to 5.9	41
Philadelphia, Pa	40	41	40	6.0	41
Baltimore, Md	40	40	42	1.2	60
Hampton Roads, Va	44	47	45	2.5	60
Jacksonville, Fl	35	35	40	2.5	44
Port Everglades, Fl	38	39	40	2.5	42
Tampa, Fl	35	35	34	2.0	>40
Mobile, Al	40	40	40	1.5	45
Pascagoula, Ms	38	39	38	1.6	50
New Orleans, La	40	39	40	1.0	45
Baton Rouge, La	40	40	40	1.0	40
Beaumont, Tx	37	39	40	1.0	47
Galveston, Tx	39	40	36	2.0	52
Houston Ship Channel	40	40	40	1.0	45
Corpus Christi, Tx	40	39	45	1.0	50
Los Angeles, Ca	52	45	51	5.4	>80
Long Beach, Ca	46	51	52	5.5	>80
San Francisco Bay Entrance, Ca	50	51	50	5.7	>100 50 (Interior)
Columbia River	38	38	42	2.0	48
Entrance Puget Sound	39	39	100-500	1.1	>100

Source: Waterborne Commerce of the U.S. Corps of Engineers, U.S. Army.

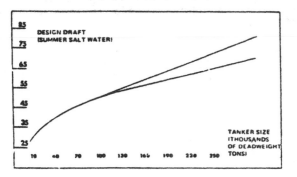

Design Draft of Supertankers and Deadweight Tonnage.
Source: *Technology Review*. Volume 75, No.5 (March/April.1973), p.57

Exhibit 14.6

SINGLE-POINT MOORING SYSTEMS

A single-point mooring (SPM) system is the link
between the hoses that are connected to the vessel
and the pipeline to shore. SPM's are either fixed
towers or floating bouys, as shown in Figures 14.1
and 14.2. The figures show the two most common
types, CALM and SALM. SEADOCK planned on using the
SALM system, and LOOP planned on using the CALM. The
main advantage of these SPM systems is that the
moored tankers are free to weathervane into the
prevailing weather. Though ships could remain moored
in seas greater than 20 feet, usually berthing
operations were limited to six-foot to eight-foot
seas--since a mooring launch is usually greater than
12 feet--because of the dynamic motion of the hose.
      In the CALM type, the mono-mooring buoy is a
cylindrical steel hull ranging in size from 33 to 55
feet in diameter which serves as a stationary
floating platform. The SALM differs from the CALM in
that the mooring buoy is anchored to a base on the
sea floor by means of an anchor chain which is
attached some 60 feet or more below the ocean surface
to a fluid swivel housing at the top of the anchor
leg. An advantage of this type over the CALM is that
hose wear is reduced at the connection of the hose to
the buoy since the connection is below the surface.
The mooring buoy is approximately 16 feet in diameter
and 25 feet high.

Exhibit 14.6 Continued

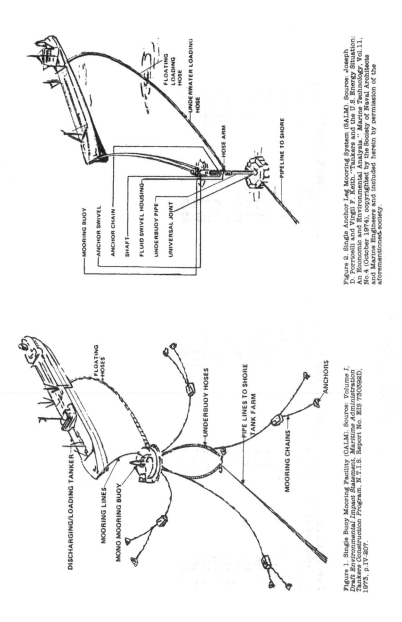

Figure 2. Single Anchor Leg Mooring System (SALM). Source: Joseph D. Porricelli and Virgil F. Keith. "Tankers and the U.S. Energy Situation: An Economic and Environmental Analysis." *Marine Technology*, Vol. 11, No. 4 (October 1974), copyrighted by the Society of Naval Architects and Marine Engineers and included herein by permission of the aforementioned society.

Figure 1. Single Buoy Mooring Facility (CALM). Source: *Volume I, Draft Environmental Impact Statement, Maritime Administration Tankers Construction Program, N.T.I.S. Report No. EIS 7503923D, 1975*, p.IV-207.

Exhibit 14.7

SAVINGS RESULTING FROM
A GULF COAST DEEPWATER PORT

Throughput (Millionbarrels per day)	Worst Case*		Best Case**	
	(Cents per barrel)	(Millions of dollars per year)	(Cents per barrel)	(Millions of dollars per year)
0.600⁻	-14.2	-31.10	-4.7	-10.29
1.400⁻	-0.4	-2.04	2.7	13.80
1.805	-3.6	-23.72	3.8	25.04
2.400⁻	0.1	0.88	8.4	73.58
3.248	4.0	47.42	11.50	136.33
4.175	4.6	70.10	12.0	182.87
6.782	7.7	190.61	14.9	368.84
10.700	10.0	386.90	17.1	661.60
10.900	10.1	401.83	17.2	684.30
14.700	11.1	595.57	18.2	976.52

Exhibit 14.7 Continued

SAVINGS RESULTING FROM AN EAST COAST DEEPWATER PORT

Throughput (Million barrels per day)	Worst Case* (Cents per barrel)	Worst Case* (Millions of dollars per year)	Best Case** (Cents per barrel)	Best Case** (Millions of dollars per year)
0.600	-4.0	-8.76	3.3	7.23
0.800	-1.6	-4.67	5.7	16.64
1.000	-0.2	-0.73	7.2	26.28
1.135	0.4	1.66	7.8	32.31
1.200	1.0	4.38	8.4	36.79
1.572	3.2	18.36	10.5	60.25
2.000	5.3	38.69	12.7	92.71
2.500	6.6	60.23	14.0	127.75
3.200	7.4	86.43	14.8	172.86
5.106	8.1	150.96	15.5	288.87
6.600	9.1	219.22	16.5	397.49

*In this case, tankers serving U.S. deepwater ports are required to have double bottoms while tankers serving foreign ports are not.

**In this case, for the most part, tankers serving both United States and foreign ports are required to have double bottoms.

¯Tug-barge distribution of crude oil assumed.

Source: Congressional testimony of William A. Johnson, Energy Advisor to the Deputy Secretary of the Treasury. Deepwater Port Act of 1973, Joint Hearings Before the Special Joint Subcommittee on Deepwater Ports Legislation of the Committees on Commerce, Interior, and Insular Affairs; and Public Works, United States Senate, Ninety-Third Congress, July 23, 1973, pp. 181-182.

Exhibit 14.8
ESTIMATED IMPORTS FOR 1985

Locating New Refinery Capacity by Aggregate Analysis and PAD Transfer

PAD	1973 Existing Ref. Capacity MBD	1985 Projected Ref. Capacity MBD	1985 Projected Demand MBD	1985 PAD Transfer (Export or Import) MBD
I	1.809	7.391	9.200	0
II	3.537	.340	6.210	(2.334)
III	5.522	0	3.910	1.611
IV	0.432	0.750	0.460	.722
V	2.200	1.019	3.220	0
Total	13,500	9,500	23,000	0

Cargo-Carrying Capacity for Tankers on Selected Routes

Route	Voyages/Year	60,000	Cargo Capacity Tanker (In Tons) 100,000	250,000
Persian Gulf to PAD V and return	5.2	58,200	97,600	245,600
Persian Gulf to PAD I and return	5.0	57,800	97,200	244,700
Persian Gulf to PAD III and return	4.9	57,800	97,000	244,500
Mediterranean to PAD I and return	12.0	58,700	98,300	246,800

Total Number of Either 100,000- or 250,000-DWT Tankers Required to Carry a Forecasted Import Level of 10.75 MBD

Size Tankers Used	Number of Tankers Required[a]
100,000	1015
250,000	404

[a]Number of tankers rounded to the nearest integer.

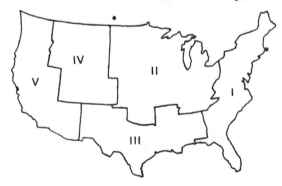

The Five Petroleum Administration for Defense (PAD) Districts.

Exhibit 14.9

SEADOCK PORT

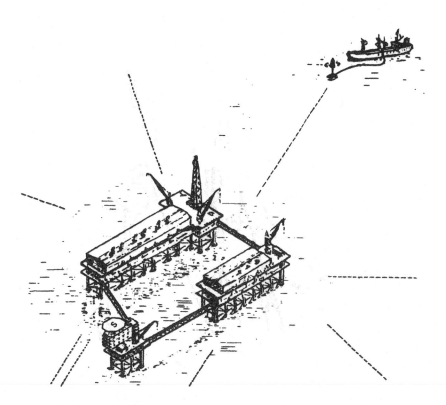

Source: SEADOCK

Exhibit 14.10

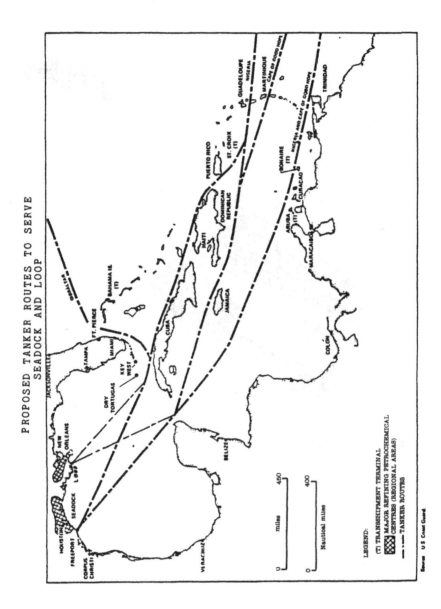

PROPOSED TANKER ROUTES TO SERVE
SEADOCK AND LOOP

Exhibit 14.11

AREAS SUPPLIED BY SEADOCK AND LOOP
DEEPWATER PORTS

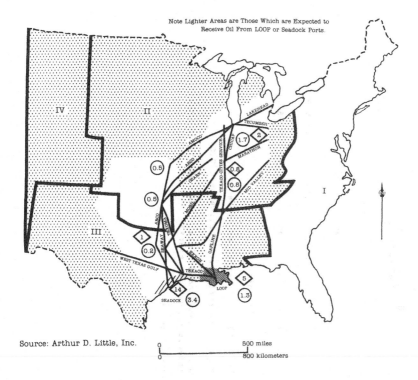

Note Lighter Areas are Those Which are Expected to
Receive Oil From LOOP or Seadock Ports.

Source: Arthur D. Little, Inc.

LEGEND:

  Seadock Regional Areas

  LOOP Regional Areas

Existing Crude Pipelines

◯ MMBD of Existing Refinery
Capacity

◇ Billions of Pounds per Year
of Existing Ethylene Capacity
I-IV are PAD Districts

SEADOCK and LOOP

Exhibit 14.12

U.S. OIL USAGE
1973-1976

	'73	'74	'75	'76
U.S. Net Imports of Crude Oil*	1251.45	1343.45	1583.27	2040.48
U.S. Consumption of Petroleum**	6334.55	6082.73	5951.09	6395.45
U.S. Production of Crude Oil	3544.18	3377.27	3223.45	3138.55

Units: Million barrels per year.

Assumed 5.5 million BTU's per barrel of crude oil.

Geographic coverage: The fifty United States and D.C.

*Includes crude oil, lease condensate, and imports of crude oil for the strategic petroleum reserve.

**Includes lease condensate.

Exhibit 14.13

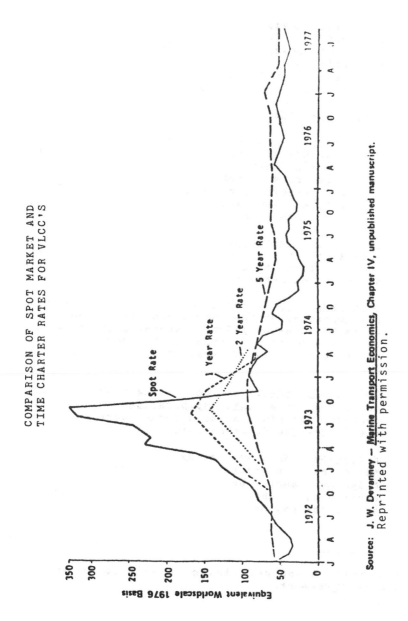

COMPARISON OF SPOT MARKET AND
TIME CHARTER RATES FOR VLCC'S

Spot Rate

1 Year Rate

2 Year Rate

5 Year Rate

Equivalent Worldscale 1976 Basis

Source: J. W. Devanney — Marine Transport Economics, Chapter IV, unpublished manuscript.
Reprinted with permission.

Exhibit 14.14

KEY REGULATORY PROVISIONS OF LOOP/SEADOCK LICENSES

1. Oil Spill Liability: Each company would be required to sign a Guaranty Agreement imposing joint and several* liability among all owners. Not only does the corporation have "unlimited" oil spill liability, but the owners could also be accountable.

2. Expansion: The port would have to expand if:

    a. Ordered by the Secretary of Transportation.
    b. Shareholder or group of shareholders holding more than half the shares of outstanding stock request expansion.
    c. Any stockholders request expansion and are willing and able to bear and finance all associated costs.

3. Ownership Adjustments: After five years of operation and thereafter at intervals of not greater than three years, any owner has the option of adjustment of stock ownership.

4. Open ownership: For a period of not less than six months after the issuance of the license and at each expansion point, ownership shares would be available to any person or business entity on the same terms as one available to the existing owners.

5. Connecting Lines: All connecting pipelines must be owned by a single corporation which shall operate the pipeline as a common carrier under the Interstate Commerce Act.

6. Proration: When delivering oil to the pipeline, historical shipments cannot be used as a guide. Shipment must be accepted regardless of ownership, quantity, source, destination, specification, or properties.

----

* "Several" means pertaining to each party of the Guaranty Agreement.

Exhibit 14.14 Continued

7. Operations Manual: All operation procedures are
    to be included in a Port Operations Manual which
    is to be approved by the Commandant of the U.S.
    Coast Guard.

Chapter 15

VENTURE OIL:
FEASIBILITY ANALYSIS OF AN OFFSHORE TERMINAL

In November 1980, Will MacKay was reviewing an
interoffice memorandum which suggested a joint
venture to construct a deepwater port 12 miles off
Freeport, Texas (Exhibit 15.1). MacKay was Vice
President-Marine of Venture Oil. He had considered
potential investments in deepwater ports for several
years. The decision that lay before him was whether
to commit to a 30% interest in this latest proposal,
the Lone Star Offshore Terminal (LSOT).

BACKGROUND

The Deepwater Port Act of 1974 allowed for the
construction of offshore oil terminals outside the
three-mile U.S. Territorial Sea. Applications were
filed for LOOP (Louisiana Offshore Oil Port) and
SEADOCK in 1975 (see Exhibit 15.2 for facility
descriptions). Both were issued licenses in August
1976; however, only LOOP was built. SEADOCK fell
through after Exxon, Mobil, and Gulf pulled out of
the partnership because they were not willing to
accept the heavy restrictions and conditions included
in the license. Some of the conditions are
highlighted in Exhibit 15.3. The other six partners,
including Venture Oil, could neither absorb the 53%
interest left by the three departing companies or
find new partners. After SEADOCK failed, the Texas
Deepwater Port Authority (TDPA) was created by the
Texas legislature. The TDPA was to be the same
physical facility as SEADOCK, except it would have a
different financial and ownership structure. The
TDPA, set up as an agency of the State of Texas,
would be supported by the sale of revenue bonds.
However, the TDPA was unable to secure the throughput
commitments it needed to finance the revenue bonds.

300

Although Will MacKay was disappointed that SEADOCK had failed, Venture Oil's lightening program, which began in August 1976, had proved to be an efficient program.

Lightering* became more attractive as single voyage rates declined, thus reducing the cost of demurrage. Exhibit 15.4 shows single voyage rates for VLCC's and MR's through 1980. Exhibit 15.5 gives the demurrage costs for the different vessel sizes and rates for the Es-Sider to Houston voyage.

The proposed LSOT was a scaled-down version of SEADOCK. The facility was to be located approximately 12 miles offshore in 69 feet of water and would include only one single-point mooring (SPM).

The SPM would be connected to the operational platform by a 56-inch subsea pipeline, and the platform would be connected by a pipeline to an offshore receiving terminal at Freeport. The deep-draft vessel's own pumps would supply the horsepower requirements for discharging the crude. Possible flow rates would be between 73,000 and 117,000 barrels per hour, depending on the type of crude oil. LSOT would have a capacity of handling 0.5 million barrels per day (MM. BD).

VLCC's up to 350,00 DWT and a maximum of 1200 feet long would be serviced. VLCC's greater than 200,000 DWT would still have to lighter, but there would be only two lighterings compared to the usual six.

The crude oil would be discharged onshore at a terminal in Freeport which has 4 million barrels of storage. A pipeline from the terminal would send crude up a 30-inch line to Cushing, Oklahoma, where lines would distribute the crude throughout the Mid-West.

The small scale of LSOT has many advantages over the unsuccessful SEADOCK. Some of these advantages are:

1. The investment is much smaller ($150 million versus $658 million).

----

* The terms "lightering" and "lightening" are used interchangeably, although some people refer to lightering to mean complete unloading of a large vessel into smaller vessels, and lightening to mean partial unloading into one or more smaller ships, where the large vessel subsequently proceeds to a dock for final unloading.

2. The throughput is more in line with the
   drop in imports (0.5 MM. BD vs. 2.5 MM.
   BD).
3. The discharge, after mooring, at the SPM is
   directly to existing tankage at Freeport,
   and therefore less new storage would have
   to be provided.
4. The partial lightening for Lake Charles
   cargoes would obviate the need for an
   expensive pipeline connection to Lake
   Charles.
5. Some delivery flexibility (i.e., to third
   parties) would be retained, since the
   lightening operation would not be
   completely abandoned.

The project's cost was estimated at $150 million
to be shared with three other oil and chemical
companies. These firms also had lightening
operations similar to that of Venture Oil's.

REGULATIONS

Mr. MacKay knew that Venture Oil could easily afford
a 30% share of the project (see Exhibits 15.6 and
15.7 for financial data). However, the LSOT still
had to apply to the Secretary of Transportation for a
license to construct and operate the facility, as
required by the Deepwater Port Act of 1974. Thus the
license could include all the government restrictions
that caused Exxon, Mobil, and Gulf to drop out of the
SEADOCK proposal. However, Mr. MacKay felt that the
Department of Transportation's perspective had
changed and that all or most of these restrictions
might be eliminated or modified.

OTHER OPPORTUNITIES

While MacKay was still arriving at a decision,
Venture Oil was approached by another oil company
interested in joining the project. This would
obviously spread the capital investment and risk, but
the other company would only join if the SPM was
moved from 69 feet of water to 90 feet of water.
This deeper water depth would be necessary to handle
the company's tankers in a fully loaded condition.
Mr. MacKay now had to decide how to proceed.

Exhibit 15.1

INTEROFFICE COMMUNICATION

To: W.C. MacKay

From: K.A. Burke

Date: November 25, 1980

Subject: FREEPORT MONOBUOY ECONOMICS

A study of the savings to the Marine Department resulting from the use of a monobuoy to be built offshore Freeport has been completed. The basic assumption used is that savings will be realized by deleting tonnage from the fleet. The monobuoy would carry all Venture Oil cargoes for Freeport, eliminating the need for Freeport-sized lightering vessels (55,000 DWT). Also, the monobuoy would decrease the discharge times for most vessels, allowing those ships less voyage times and therefore more voyages per year. This results in the carriage of the same cargo volumes with less tonnage. No depreciation or tax calculations have been made here.
Import volume forecasts were developed (Attachment 1) for the years 1984 through 2003. All crude is imported from either Libya or the Persian Gulf. The estimates assume that Venture Oil's refineries will be operating at full capacity and that marketing will sell everything produced.
Ship operation and demurrage costs, where necessary, were calculated for the vessels over the 20-year period (Attachments 2 through 5). Initial figures for these calculations were obtained from several sources and escalated for the 20-year period. Capital costs were based on new building costs from our standard voyage files, escalated to 1984 using GNP deflators. New vessel costs in 1984 are estimated to be $112.7 million for a VLCC, $39.6 million for a 55,000 DWT vessel, and $43.5 million for a 70,000 DWT vessel.* It is assumed that vessels for the fleet are either built for delivery in 1984 or purchased or chartered in that year in a balanced

---

* The cost of a used VLCC, in 1984, was estimated at $30 million.

market. The capital costs are annualized for 20
years at 15% interest (which includes a pre-tax
profit incentive).

Fuel prices were escalated using the GNP
deflators plus a projected real cost increase of
petroleum products. Operating costs are from the
standard cost file, escalated with the GNP deflators.
This same escalation table was used on the port
charges for Ras Tanura and Es-Sider, which were
obtained from the Operations Department. Current
tolls for a Suez Canal transit were escalated at 10%
annually.

There are four sizes of ships for which costs
and requirements have been calculated. A VLCC is
assumed to carry 2 million barrels (270,000 tons at
7.4 average BBL/ton). An LR2 would lift 800,000
barrels (110,000 DWT). The lightening vessels are of
two sizes, according to the optimum sizes of vessels
for the two discharge ports. Cargo for Lake Charles
would be lightened by 70,000 DWT LR1's, with a
carrying capacity of 60,000 tons. Freeport volumes
would arrive there in 55,000 DWT MR's, carrying
40,000 tons.

CARGO OPERATIONS

Fully laden VLCC's will arrive in the U.S. Gulf of
Mexico from Libya and the Persian Gulf. (Because of
inadequate storage facilities and scheduling
problems, it is assumed that the VLCC's will not
carry full cargoes destined solely for Freeport.)
The ships would normally be fully lightened by both
sizes of the shuttle vessels in an average 15 days.
With the monobuoy, the VLCC's will be lightened of
their Lake Charles cargo by LR1's, then proceed to
the monobuoy, where they will discharge the Freeport
cargo (see Attachment 8). Lightening is especially
important since a fully loaded VLCC's draft exceeds
the draft limitations at the monobuoy.

There is a definite time savings experienced by
the VLCC's when discharging at the monobuoy as
compared with full lightening. As mentioned above,
the average lightening operation will take 15 days
for a complete discharge of a VLCC, involving six
lighterings. However, with a monobuoy present, only
two lighterings over a three-day period will be
necessary for the Lake Charles cargo. Shifting from
the lightening position to the monobuoy and the
discharge at the monobuoy would cover 1.5 days.
Total time for the entire discharge period would be

about six days, which includes an added 40% to cover weather delays and other unknown parameters. This nine-day difference in discharge time allows for shorter total voyage days, and thus more voyages per ship when a monobuoy is used.

LR2's will originate from Es-Sider with cargoes exclusively for Lake Charles. Since light-loaded LR2's can enter Lake Charles, they would be partially lightened by LR1's, then proceed directly into Lake Charles for complete discharge. The presence of the monobuoy would have no effect on this operation.

VESSEL SAVINGS

In this scenario, full VLCC's will originate from Es-Sider during the 1984-1988 years and from Ras Tanura for all 20 years. LR2's will be used between 1986-2003 carrying Libyan crude.

Use of the monobuoy to discharge the VLCC's results in the use of one less VLCC in each year than with full lightening. There will be no savings of LR2's because they will be carrying cargoes destined exclusively for Lake Charles, which will not be affected by a monobuoy at Freeport. The monobuoy will eliminate the need for the Freeport-sized MR's. This would mean two less 55,000 DWT vessels in 1984-1985, three less in 1986-1988, and two less for the remaining years.

There are no savings in LR1's because they will be used to lighten the Lake Charles cargoes from the VLCC's and LR2's. In 1985, the situation reverses and there will be one more LR1 required with the monobuoy than without. The reason for this is that with or without the monobuoy, the tonnage requirement for lifting the Lake Charles cargo exceeds the capacity of two LR1's. When the MR's are present in the fleet, they would be able to carry the excess cargo that the LR1's could not carry into Lake Charles. However, there are no MR's in the fleet when a monobuoy is used. Therefore, an extra LR1 is needed to pick up the slack in tonnage left by the elimination of the smaller vessels.

Total savings (Attachment 7) for this case were computed on the basis of the number of ships saved each year multiplied by the annual total costs (capital, operating, voyage costs) for each size of ship.

KAB/ms

Exhibit 15.1 Continued
Attachment 1

GULF COAST CRUDE OIL IMPORTS
(THOUSAND BD)

	1984	1985	1986	1987	1988	1989-2003
FREEPORT						
Libyan crude	76.2	38.1				
Persian Gulf Crude	____	30.0	90.0	90.0	90.0	90.0
Subtotal	76.2	68.1	90.0	90.0	90.0	90.0
LAKE CHARLES						
Libyan Crude	54.2	70.0	48.4*	52.3*	41.1*	28.5*
Persian Gulf Crude	72.1	72.5	75.7	79.2	82.5	85.6
Subtotal	126.3	142.5	124.1	131.5	123.6	114.1
TOTAL	202.5	210.6	214.1	221.5	213.6	204.1

*For Conservative Freeport Monobuoy economics, LR-2 movement of these
 volumes should be considered.

Exhibit 15.1 Continued
Attachment 2

ANNUAL COSTS
VLCC PG TRADE W/O SPM
FREEPORT SPM
(IN $000)

YEAR	FUEL	PORT CHARGES	TOLLS*	VOYAGE COSTS	OPERATING	CAPITAL	TOTAL ANNUAL COSTS
1984	11348	182	1528	13058	4084	18005	35147
1985	12801	196	1681	14678	4402	"	37085
1986	14170	211	1849	16230	4741	"	38976
1987	15672	227	2034	17933	5101	"	41039
1988	17318	244	2237	19799	5484	"	43288
1989	19067	262	2461	21790	5873	"	45668
1990	20935	280	2707	23922	6273	"	48200
1991	23008	299	2978	26285	6700	"	50996
1992	25286	319	3275	28880	7168	"	54053
1993	27789	342	3603	31734	7663	"	57402
1994	30540	365	3963	34868	8192	"	61065
1995	33564	390	4360	38314	8757	"	65076
1996	36887	417	4796	42100	9361	"	69466
1997	40538	446	5275	46259	10007	"	74271
1998	44552	477	5803	50832	10697	"	79534
1999	48962	510	6383	55855	11435	"	85295
2000	59137	582	7723	67442	13068	"	80510
2001	59137	582	7723	67442	13068	"	80510
2002	64991	623	8496	74110	13969	"	106084
2003	71425	666	9345	81436	14933	"	114374

*Ballasted VLCCs would return to the Persian Gulf via the Suez Canal.
Toll charges escalated at 10%.

Exhibit 15.1 Continued
Attachment 3

ANNUAL COSTS
VLCC LIBYA TRADE W/O SPM
FREEPORT SPM
(IN $000)

YEAR	FUEL	PORT CHARGES	TOTAL VOYAGE COSTS	OPERATING	CAPITAL	TOTAL ANNUAL COSTS
1984	10683	481	11164	4084	18005	33253
1985	12050	519	12569	4402	"	34976
1986	13340	559	13898	4741	"	36644
1987	14754	601	15355	5101	"	38461
1988	16303	646	16949	5484	"	40436
1989	17950	692	18642	5873	"	42520
1990	19709	739	20448	6273	"	44726
1991	21660	790	22450	6706	"	47161
1992	23804	844	24648	7168	"	49821
1993	26161	903	27064	7663	"	52732
1994	28751	965	29716	8192	"	55913
1995	31597	1031	32628	8757	"	59390
1996	34725	1103	35828	9361	"	63194
1997	38163	1179	39342	10007	"	67354
1998	41941	1260	43201	10697	"	71903
1999	46093	1347	47440	11435	"	76880
2000	50656	1440	52096	12224	"	76880
2001	55671	1539	57210	13068	"	82325
2002	61183	1645	62828	13969	"	94802
2003	67240	1759	68999	14933	"	101937

Exhibit 15.1 Continued
Attachment 4

ANNUAL COSTS
55,000 DWT LIGHTENING VESSEL
(IN $000)

YEAR	CAPITAL	OPERATING	VOYAGE	TOTAL ANNUAL
1984	6326	3714	4121	14161
1985	"	4004	4607	14937
1986	"	4312	5074	15712
1987	"	4640	5582	16548
1988	"	4988	6130	17444
1989	"	5342	6715	18383
1990	"	5705	7338	19369
1991	"	6100	8028	20454
1992	"	6519	8784	21629
1993	"	6969	9607	22902
1994	"	7450	10509	24285
1995	"	7964	11490	25780
1996	"	8514	12574	27414
1997	"	9101	13763	29190
1998	"	9729	15056	31111
1999	"	10401	16492	33219
2000	"	11118	18034	35478
2001	"	11885	19754	37965
2002	"	12705	21630	40661
2003	"	13582	23674	43582

Venture Oil: Offshore Terminal Analysis

Exhibit 15.1 Continued
Attachment 5

ANNUAL COSTS
70,000 DWT LIGHTENING VESSEL
(IN $000)

YEAR	CAPITAL	OPERATING	VOYAGE	TOTAL ANNUAL
1984	6958	3795	5119	15872
1985	"	4091	5722	16771
1986	"	4406	6301	17665
1987	"	4741	6931	18630
1988	"	5096	7610	19664
1989	"	5458	8336	20751
1990	"	5829	9108	21895
1991	"	6232	9963	23153
1992	"	6662	10900	24520
1993	"	7121	11919	25998
1994	"	7613	13036	27607
1995	"	8138	14252	29348
1996	"	8699	15596	31253
1997	"	9300	17069	33327
1998	"	9941	18672	35571
1999	"	10627	20451	38036
2000	"	11361	22360	40679
2001	"	12145	24490	43593
2002	"	12983	26814	46755
2003	"	13878	29346	50182

Exhibit 15.1 Continued
Attachment 6

FLEET COMPOSITION
NUMBER OF VESSELS

		1984	1985	1986	1987	1988	1989-2003
w/o Monobuoy	VLCC's	7	8	9	9	9	8
	LR2's	0	0	1	1	1	2
	70m DWT	2	2	2	2	2	2
	55m DWT	2	2	3	3	3	2
w/Monobuoy	VLCC's	6	7	8	8	8	7
	LR2's	0	0	1	1	1	2
	70m DWT	2	3	2	2	2	2
	55m DWT	0	0	0	0	0	0
Vsls. Saved	VLCC's	1	1	1	1	1	1
	LR2's	0	0	0	0	0	0
	70m DWT	0	(1)	0	0	0	0
	55m DWT	2	2	3	3	3	3

Venture Oil used the following descriptions for vessel size
categories:

General Purpose (GP): 16,500 to 24, 999 DWT

Medium Range (MR): 25,000 to 44,999 DWT

Large Range 1 (LR1): 45,000 to 79,999 DWT

Large Range 2 (LR2): 80,000 to 159,999 DWT

Very Large Crude Carrier (VLCC): 160,000 DWT and
above

Exhibit 15.1 Continued
Attachment 7

ANNUAL SAVINGS: MARINE
(IN $000)

Year	VLCC Savings	Monobuoy vs. Full Lightening		Total
		55m DWT Savings	70m DWT Savings	
1984	34200	28322	-0-	62,522
1985	36031	29874	(16771)	49,134
1986	37810	47136	-0-	84,946
1987	39750	49644	"	89,394
1988	41863	52332	"	94,195
1989	44094	36766	"	80,860
1990	45453	38738	"	85,201
1991	49079	40908	"	89,987
1992	51937	43258	"	95,195
1993	55067	45804	"	100,871
1994	58489	48570	"	107,059
1995	62233	51560	"	113,793
1996	66320	54828	"	121,148
1997	70813	58380	"	129,193
1998	75719	62222	"	137,941
1999	81088	66438	"	147,526
2000	86965	70956	"	157,921
2001	84397	75930	"	160,327
2002	100443	81322	"	181,756
2003	108156	87164	"	195,320

Exhibit 15.1 Continued
Attachment 8

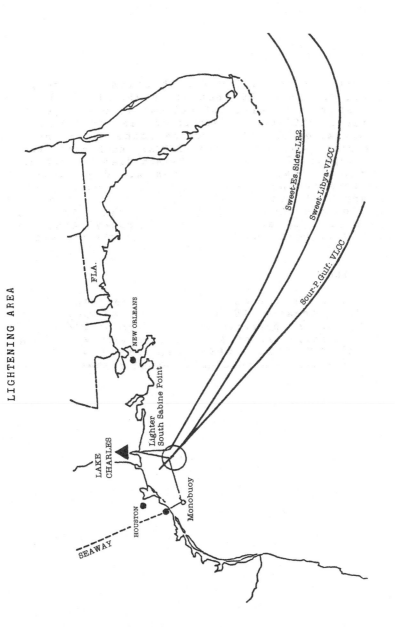

Venture Oil: Offshore Terminal Analysis

Exhibit 15.2

CHARACTERISTICS OF SEADOCK AND LOOP

SEADOCK, INC.

SEADOCK was to be located 26 miles off Freeport, Texas, in about 100 feet of water. It would have been able to receive 500,000 DWT ultra-large crude carriers (ULCC's). It was to consist of one pumping platform, one platform for personnel quarters, and four single-point moorings (SPM's), each connected to the pumping platform by a 52-inch diameter submarine pipeline. Two 52-inch lines would connect the platform to the onshore terminal, about 4.5 miles inland. It had a projected capital cost of $658 million and throughput of 2.5 MM. BD. SEADOCK was financed completely by nine corporations, each holding an equal number of shares in the consortium.

LOOP, INC.

LOOP is a similar complex with three single-point moorings located 18 miles south of Grand Isle, Louisiana, in approximately 110 feet of water. LOOP had a capital cost of $738 million with a throughput of 3.4 MM. BD. LOOP was financed by six corporations, each holding an equal number of shares.

Exhibit 15.3

KEY REGULATORY PROVISIONS OF LOOP/SEADOCK LICENSES

1. <u>Oil Spill Liability</u>: Each company would be required to sign a Guaranty Agreement imposing joint and several* liability among all owners. Not only does the corporation have "unlimited" oil spill liability, but the owners could also be accountable.

2. <u>Expansion</u>: The port would have to expand if:

   a. Ordered by the Secretary of Transportation.
   b. Shareholder or group of shareholders holding more than half the shares of outstanding stock request expansion.
   c. Any stockholders request expansion and are willing and able to bear and finance all associated costs.

3. <u>Ownership Adjustments</u>: After five years of operation and thereafter at intervals of not greater than three years, any owner has the option of adjustment of stock ownership.

4. <u>Open ownership</u>: For a period of not less than six months after the issuance of the license and at each expansion point, ownership shares would be available to any person or business entity on the same terms as one available to the existing owners.

5. <u>Connecting Lines</u>: All connecting pipelines must be owned by a <u>single corporation</u> which shall operate the pipeline as a common carrier under the Interstate Commerce Act.

6. <u>Proration</u>: When delivering oil to the pipeline, historical shipments cannot be used as a guide. Shipment must be accepted regardless of ownership, quantity, source, destination, specification, or properties.

----

* "Several" means pertaining to each party of the Guaranty Agreement.

Exhibit 15.3 Continued

7. Operations Manual: All operation procedures are
    to be included in a Port Operations Manual which
    is to be approved by the Commandant of the U.S.
    Coast Guard.

Exhibit 15.4

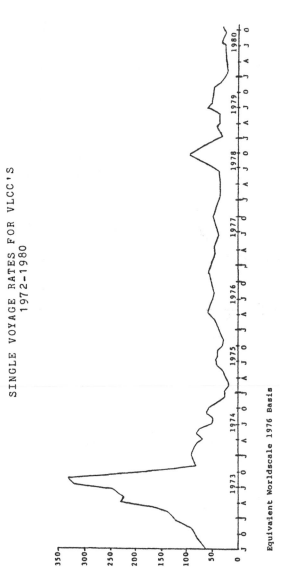

SINGLE VOYAGE RATES FOR VLCC'S
1972-1980

Equivalent Worldscale 1976 Basis

Exhibit 15.4 Continued

WORLDSCALE FOR 40-69,999 DWT (MR'S)
CARIBBEAN TO U.S. EASTERN SEABOARD

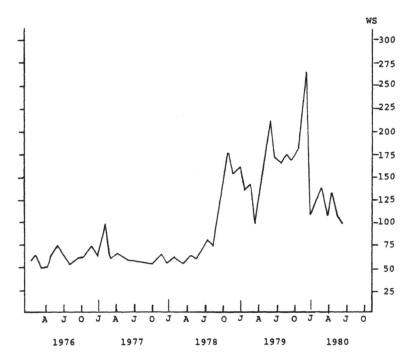

Exhibit 15.5

DEMURRAGE COSTS

Year	Demurrage Costs at WS 100 ($/day)				WS 100 for Houston ($/ton of oil)
	MR	LR1	LR2	VLCC	Es-Sider Voyage
1/1/71	6,660	8,580	14,760	38,280	N/A
1/1/72	6,840	8,880	15,480	37,440	5.76
1/1/73	6,840	8,880	15,480	37,440	5.61
1/1/74	6,950	9,025	15,700	38,550	5.84
1/1/75	8,175	10,950	19,850	50,950	8.23
1/1/76	8,600	11,550	19,175	54,875	8.90
1/1/77	8,675	11,700	21,625	55,800	8.97
1/1/78	8,875	12,025	22,375	58,000	9.25
1/1/79	8,875	12,025	22,375	58,000	9.35
1/1/80	12,150	17,500	32,950	83,950	10.91
7/1/80	13,400	19,550	37,700	98,600	14.53

Exhibit 15.6

FINANCIAL DATA
TEN-YEAR REVIEW 1970–1979

(millions of $, except per-share amts.)

	1979	1978	1977	1976	1975	1974	1973	1972	1971	1970
REVENUES BY PRODUCT										
Refined petroleum	7,138.0	5,116.9	4,470.7	4,030.4	3,766.8	3,479.3	2,355.9	1,911.1	1,593.6	1,375.9
Crude oil	2,663.4	2,203.0	2,190.3	1,979.1	1,889.7	2,218.7	1,020.5	838.0	744.9	677.9
Natural gas	549.0	448.0	392.7	336.6	221.3	158.8	132.2	105.5	94.8	78.4
Coal	1,322.9	961.6	1,105.5	1,152.3	1,026.3	747.0	473.7	421.0	320.9	312.3
Chemicals	792.0	601.9	441.9	319.9	293.3	376.8	221.0	200.0	200.3	178.0
Other sales and services	386.1	351.1	339.2	385.1	302.2	298.3	267.6	173.3	146.4	138.1
Other operating revenues	31.0	60.5	32.2	41.3	57.0	19.6	8.7	12.7	17.3	16.0
Nonoperating revenues	200.5	103.8	79.1	107.6	108.1	45.2	11.4	34.0	3.5	35.5
Total from continuing operations	13,082.9	9,871.8	9,051.8	8,352.3	7,666.1	7,343.7	4,491.0	3,695.6	3,121.7	2,812.6
COSTS, EXPENSES, AND TAXES										
Purchases of crude oil	3,419.0	2,763.5	2,826.4	2,630.2	2,441.6	2,751.0	1,291.8	868.3	726.9	641.9
Other costs and operating expenses	4,416.8	3,310.7	2,775.5	2,403.3	2,383.5	2,091.2	1,166.6	1,129.7	985.2	875.4
Selling, general, and admin. expenses	624.8	486.9	466.4	430.4	374.1	324.2	278.5	227.3	219.2	201.2
Exploration expenses	237.8	233.9	213.4	180.6	174.8	145.4	103.0	81.3	89.0	72.6
Depreciation, depletion and amortization	398.3	343.3	340.3	318.8	297.6	243.1	238.9	181.1	161.4	148.3
Loss on long-term nat. gas sales contract					29.6					
Interest and debt expense	167.0	147.1	117.9	120.5	119.3	104.6	82.1	68.3	67.4	61.7
U.S. federal income taxes	244.2	146.9	174.7	194.3	137.5	86.2	40.6	33.8		22.4
U.S. state income taxes	8.1	4.9	6.4	7.0	4.4	4.4		3.2	3.0	
Foreign income taxes	1,407.8	794.4	742.2	623.7	517.9	493.6	250.3	205.5	175.1	120.8
U.S. excise taxes	203.4	232.3	239.9	246.4	246.5	238.2	256.3	234.6	211.1	200.5
Other taxes	1,089.4	915.0	723.5	635.3	618.5	530.1	539.2	472.8	359.7	304.1
Minority interest in subsidiaries' net income	50.9	41.6	44.6	38.6	34.1	29.6	20.2	14.9	11.7	9.8
Total from continuing operations	12,267.5	9,420.5	8,671.2	7,896.1	7,339.7	7,041.4	4,270.9	3,519.8	3,011.1	2,669.1
INCOME										
Income from continuing operations	815.4	451.3	380.6	456.2	326.4	302.3	220.1	175.8	110.6	153.5
Income from discontinued plant foods and related operations									4.4	1.5
Income before extraordinary items	815.4	451.3	380.6	456.2	326.4	302.3	220.1	175.8	115.0	155.0
Extraordinary items									(19.4)	
Net Income	815.4	451.3	380.6	456.2	326.4	302.3	220.1	175.8	95.6	155.0
AFTER-TAX FOREIGN CURRENCY ADJUSTMENTS										
Long-term debt	(6.8)	(14.2)	(9.0)	(1.5)	12.5	(15.1)	(16.0)	6.7	(13.6)	
Other	2.7	(17.5)	(13.1)	5.0	3.4	(12.5)	(4.0)	3.6	(8.8)	
Total	(4.1)	(31.7)	(22.1)	3.5	15.9	(27.6)	(20.0)	10.3	(22.4)	
PER COMMON SHARE DATA										
Income before extraordinary items	7.58	4.20	3.55	4.34	3.20	2.98	2.18	1.75	1.14	1.43
Net income	7.58	4.20	3.55	4.34	3.20	2.98	2.18	1.75	.94	1.43
Dividends	1.70	1.43	1.35	1.15	1.00	.85	.76	.75	.75	.75
Book value	35.06	29.20	26.43	24.22	20.52	18.31	16.17	14.72	13.61	13.41
Market price – high	49.25	32.13	38.00	40.88	37.50	29.25	27.63	20.13	19.88	16.13
– low	28.00	24.50	27.50	29.75	20.25	14.50	13.38	12.50	12.25	9.33

Exhibit 15.6 Continued

(millions of $, except as indicated)

	1979	1978	1977	1976	1975	1974	1973	1972	1971	1970
RATES OF RETURN (%)										
Ret. on stockholders' average equity	23.5	15.1	13.9	19.3	16.3	17.1	13.9	12.0	8.2	11.3
Ret. on av. borrowed and invested capital	17.9	12.0	11.1	14.0	12.0	12.3	10.4	8.9	6.7	8.3
BALANCE SHEET DATA										
Net working capital:										
Cash and marketable securities	1,068.8	695.4	748.5	1,054.7	530.6	547.9	287.4	196.0	143.6	175.7
Other	(135.9)	210.1	171.9	(74.8)	37.9	73.2	181.2	127.4	263.1	198.7
Investments and advances	217.3	179.4	160.6	128.2	2,114.8	106.1	103.7	103.0	97.1	88.0
Net property, plant, and equipment:										
Owned	5,120.3	4,090.2	3,488.6	3,064.7	2,796.9	2,433.4	2,117.2	2,079.1	1,879.5	1,839.5
Leased	227.9	233.2	262.4	357.9	322.6	303.9	323.7	227.1	202.9	197.7
Total assets	9,311.2	7,445.2	6,625.2	6,409.4	5,519.8	4,949.4	4,009.5	3,491.4	3,255.0	3,198.9
Long-term debt	1,367.4	1,219.6	1,066.1	1,041.4	901.4	892.5	700.5	702.0	711.0	675.6
Long-term capital lease obligations	254.3	268.9	283.0	377.9	342.9	319.0	337.6	246.1	219.1	197.2
Minority interest in subsidiaries	284.8	257.7	222.5	191.0	165.9	143.8	123.8	112.2	114.2	111.1
Deferred credits and other liabilities	1,130.3	811.7	626.0	531.7	466.6	368.4	311.9	263.1	234.2	249.8
Stockholders' equity	3,783.1	3,147.8	2,849.6	2,609.3	2,112.5	1,880.2	1,659.6	1,513.8	1,404.3	1,383.5
CHANGES IN FINANCIAL POSITION										
Funds available:										
Funds from operations	1,520.9	1,013.5	890.1	872.4	745.1	654.6	567.6	408.9	356.6	360.4
Sales of fixed assets and investments	98.1	158.8	95.4	137.6	126.0	83.2	56.8	67.2	132.7	38.3
Addition to long-term debt	233.3	310.0	88.1	214.1	105.8	230.4	51.7	65.6	76.2	88.4
Addition to capital lease obligations	1.0		2.5	59.3	47.5	9.6	107.1	43.6	35.5	42.5
Issuance of equity securities				148.7						
Other sources (net)	67.3		48.3	13.1		38.4	11.4	8.2	11.8	4.0
Total	1,920.6	1,476.3	1,124.4	1,445.2	1,024.4	1,016.2	794.6	593.5	612.8	533.6
Funds applied:										
Capital expenditures	1,561.6	1,107.2	834.6	775.3	796.4	667.6	372.7	457.8	387.4	365.3
Investments and advances	21.9	5.4	15.5	2.9	3.5	3.2	4.8	11.5	20.0	11.6
Addition to assets under capital leases	2.1	171.4	2.6	19.0	44.5	9.7	99.1	40.0	23.4	29.0
Reduction of long-term debt	92.4	14.0	74.8	77.9	82.1	58.6	71.1	67.1	53.3	69.7
Reduction of capital lease obligations	15.7	14.0	97.4	24.3	23.6	28.2	15.6	16.6	13.6	12.4
Dividends on Common Stock	182.9	153.0	144.7	120.3	101.6	85.9	76.5	74.9	74.8	78.1
Dividends on Preferred Stock				.6	.8		1.2	1.5	1.5	1.6
Dividends to minority interests	16.3	13.6	13.8	13.5	12.0	9.6	7.8	7.4	6.5	5.8
Other applications (net)		25.9			12.6					
Total	1,893.2	1,491.1	1,183.9	1,033.8	1,077.1	863.7	649.4	676.8	580.5	573.5
Increase (decrease) in working capital	27.4	(14.8)	(59.5)	411.4	(52.7)	152.5	145.2	(83.3)	32.3	(39.9)
STOCKHOLDER AND EMPLOYEE DATA										
Shares outstanding (thousands):										
Common—weighted-average for year	107,580	107,396	107,183	104,920	101,608	101,011	100,333	99,906	99,774	103,798
—at year-end	107,673	107,423	107,354	107,021	101,938	101,242	100,810	100,045	99,878	99,593
Preferred—at year-end	137	191	211	278	370	442	483	681	723	783
Number of stockholders at year-end:										
Common	71,532	70,588	70,125	66,681	64,813	69,192	71,361	79,329	84,712	84,898
Preferred	1,547	2,056	2,274	2,815	3,274	3,650	3,919	4,181	4,727	5,070
Number of employees at year-end	40,502	42,780	43,141	43,899	44,028	41,174	39,796	38,092	40,509	38,443

Venture Oil: Offshore Terminal Analysis

Exhibit 15.7

ESTMATED COSTS OF THE LSOT

Capital Cost = $150 million

Yearly Operating Costs:

1984	-	$ 5,111,000
1985	-	5,621,000
1986	-	6,183,000
1987	-	6,801,000
1988	-	7,482,000
1989	-	8,230,000
1990	-	9,053,000
1991	-	9,958,000
1992	-	10,954,000
1993	-	12,049,000
1994	-	13,254,000
1995	-	14,579,000
1996	-	16,037,000
1997	-	17,641,000
1998	-	19,405,000
1999	-	21,346,000
2000	-	23,480,000
2001	-	25,828,000
2002	-	28,411,000
2003	-	31,252,000

Note: Estimated life is on the order of 20 years.

Made in the USA
Middletown, DE
16 October 2021

50410574R00186